W9-BVJ-491

Building a Healthy Family

by Bill Flatt, Ed.D.

CHRISTIAN COMMUNICATIONS

P.O. Box 150
Nashville, TN 37202

Copyright © 1993 by Gospel Advocate Company

IT IS ILLEGAL AND UNETHICAL TO DUPLICATE COPYRIGHTED MATERIAL.

The material in this book represents a considerable investment of effort, skill, time and finances from both the author and the publisher. If this material is photocopied and circulated to avoid buying a book for each student or reader, the author is defrauded of duly earned royalties, and the publisher does not sell enough copies to support the publication.

All rights reserved. No part of this publication may be reproduced, stored in a retrieval system, or transmitted in any form or by any means — electronic, mechanical, photocopying, recording, or any other — except for brief quotations in printed reviews, without the prior written permission of the publisher.

Scripture quotations include the Holy Bible: New International Version, copyright 1973, 1978, 1984 by the International Bible Society. Used by permission of Zondervan Bible Publishers.

Published by Christian Communications
A division of Gospel Adovocate Company
P.O. Box 150, Nashville, TN 37202

ISBN 0-89225-421-1

10 9 8 7 6 5 4 3 2 1

OVERTON MEMORIAL LIBRARY
HERITAGE CHRISTIAN UNIVERSITY
P.O. Box HCU
Florence, Alabama 35630

Dedication

to my family

MY GRANDPARENTS: Henry Franklin Flatt, Delia Flatt, Hiram Way, and Ollie Fox Way.

MY PARENTS: Benton Madison Flatt, and Cleo Ann Way Flatt.

MY BROTHERS AND SISTERS: Rosa Lee Fox, Leamon Anderson Flatt, Donald Franklin Flatt, Dowel Edward Flatt, Kenneth Ray Flatt, Linda Faye Anderson, and Wanda Gail Crabtree.

MY LOVING WIFE: Irma Louise Dyer Flatt
Married April 5, 1955.

OUR CHILDREN: Stephen Carl and his wife Linda, Timothy Donald and his wife Pam, and Daniel Lewis, and his wife Lea Ann.

OUR GRANDCHILDREN: David Madison Flatt, and Kevin McFarlin Flatt

With love, respect, and appreciation

Foreword

Dr. Bill Flatt is one of the great men of today. He is a Christian gentleman, one who is eminently prepared, both by academics and by experience for the writing of this enlightening and much-needed book.

He and I have been closely associated in the work at Harding University Graduate School of Religion for almost **thirty** years. I have found him to be a true friend, an able teacher, and an effective author. Bill has a heart of gold and is constant in his devotion to the church, his family, his friends, and his work. The good he is doing cannot be measured, and his influence through his teaching, preaching, counseling, and writing will continue to live indefinitely.

I am deeply grateful to be called a friend of Dr. Bill Flatt.

W. B. West, Jr., Th.D.
Dean Emeritus
Harding University Graduate School
of Religion
Memphis, Tennessee

6

Foreword

Greetings!

Thanks for reading this book. I have put a lot of myself into it because I thought that would help you identify with me as a person and as a family man.

I have quoted from the American Standard, the New International, and the King James Versions of the Bible. My personal practice is to read from several translations.

I have tried to show sensitivity to current gender issues by using his/her at times and plural forms of pronouns at times. A few times I have exemplified various points with men or women as examples when the points being made are applicable to both sexes. Often, I've reverted to the traditional he or him to refer to both sexes. No offense is intended.

I disguise my illustrations by changing names and other facts to protect confidentiality. Often they are composite profiles from numerous clients. For example, my illustration of a couple who did not spend much time together could fit hundreds of couples I have counseled. I discuss it in terms of one couple to enhance reader interest.

I thank my friend and colleague, Dr. Allen Black, and our son, Tim, for their feedback on this manuscript. Both read it carefully and gave valuable suggestions. Thanks also to my friend and colleague, Dr. Phillip McMillion for his comments on chapter one.

I also appreciate the encouragement of my special friend, Dr. W. B. West. He's priceless! He has been a close confidant of mine for years. No one has been of more encouragement to me in my professional development over the years than has he. Thanks, my friend. I appreciate you!

I also thank my beautiful wife, Louise, for typing this manuscript and for her valuable comments! She typed the original copy, and Deborah Dabbs, former missionary and one of our students at Harding University Graduate School of Religion, typed the final copy on her personal computer. Thanks also to Debbie!

As you will notice, especially if you are a scholar, I use a rather informal style of writing in this book which includes some broken sentences. I've been asked to do that by stylistic advisors. And such a style sort of fits the book: I see myself as a psychologist and marriage and family therapist who is sitting and talking with you. That's informal. Throughout the book I have kept my clients and future clients in mind. I try to be sensitive to their feelings and their thoughts. I then interact with them.

Thanks again. And may God bless you as you read.

CONTENTS

| | Page |
| INTRODUCTION .... | 11 |

1.	A Good Foundation....................................	19
2.	Commitment..	39
3.	Emotional Maturity	59
4.	Spiritual Development	71
5.	Love and Affection....................................	85
6.	A Healthy Family Structure......................	103
7.	Effective Parenting	121
8.	Effective Communication..........................	141
9.	Growth and Change	159
10.	Anger and Conflict Management Skills......	183
11.	Ability to Cope With Crises	199
12.	A Healthy Sense of Humor	223
13.	Healthy Self-Esteem	253
14.	Continuing Efforts to Prevent Divorce......	273
15.	Other Healthy Traits................................	289

—Realistic Expectations

—Quality Time With Each Other

—Work and Responsibility

—Self-Discipline

—A Willingness to Ask for Help

| REFERENCES... | 301 |
| APPENDICES .... | 305 |

Introduction

Building Better Homes. How to build a healthy family. What comes to your mind as you read those words?

Once when I used this theme for a week-end meeting at a church, some called the church office and asked what advice I was going to give on building houses.

No. That's not what that seminar on this book is all about. But, this idea can serve as a useful metaphor for us.

Picture a vacant spot of ground on which to build a house. Visualize piles of lumber, brick, sheet rock, roofing, and other materials. Continue your vision by adding bags of nails, hammers, and other tools. Then watch the various carpenters and other skilled workers as they lift, hammer and saw. Watch as the house is built one step at a time! Good material is used. A great deal of skill is required. Much effort is exerted.

The analogy seems a good one for building a home, a healthy family, a family that functions well from one stage to another throughout life. Good people are essential for building better homes. Extensive efforts and proper tools are required. And sometimes expert assistance is needed as well.

So, that gets us off to a good start. Stay with me as we proceed.

It was back in the early 1970's that my brothers, Leamon, Don, and Dowell, first suggested that I speak on the home during one of our campaigns for Christ in Murfreesboro, Tennessee. I was reluctant because I never wanted to put myself forward as a model son, husband, or father. I know at least some of my limitations and mistakes. But, I finally agreed. The topic was Ingredients of a Christian Home. The six ingredients I suggested were love, loyalty, conversion to Christ, obedience, work, and encouragement. I concluded with a story of Admiral Byrd's exploration of the South Pole. One day he wandered away from his hut and got lost. There were no trees, no markers to guide him in finding his way back "home." To keep from getting hopelessly lost, he stuck his walking stick down in the ice, tied his red handkerchief to its top, and looked

11

for his hut while circling the stick, in ever-widening circles until he could barely see it. He then would return to the stick, move it, and begin circling it again. On his third circling attempt, he found his hut. I concluded by saying that our home becomes our center from which we radiate out into the world. It is the place where we are loved, guided, and accepted.

As I write this now, it all seems a bit idealistic. So many families don't get along well. So many marriages are unpleasant experiences and many end in divorce. As a counseling psychologist and marriage and family therapist, I am aware of child abuse and spouse beatings. Usually the wife is the one beaten. Most of the time I have a few victims of incest as clients. Some are as young as two; others are as old as 70, and the pain is still there. I have treated several perpetrators of incest. The experience is so ugly that most of them suppress much if not all of the experiences from their conscious memory. Victims often do the same.

No family is perfect, and many are miserable. While talking to my father and my uncle J. D. Flatt recently, I learned a great deal that I didn't know about my roots. Evidence that they and our son, Danny, have collected show that the Flatts in America came from England and some still live there today. The same is true of the Way, Fox, and Birdwell families, all connected with my family tree. As you would guess, not everything I discovered was beautiful. There was a divorce among the early pioneers of the Flatt family in America. There are divorces in our extended family today. You are not looking at the Waltons in this book. I had a good family but not a perfect one.

Some of our relatives spent time in prison for murder and moonshining. One of my ancestors, a preacher, married four times. Generations later they still talk about it.

Why am I telling you all of this? Because I don't want you to think that my family is so perfect that you can't identify with it.

We have had our share of hardship and pain. My paternal grandparents reared 13 children on a 40-acre hillside farm in Jackson County, Tennessee, a county where our roots go back for generations: Billy Way (Bill) Flatt, Benton Madison Flatt, Henry Franklin Flatt, Benjamin Bartlett Flatt, John Madison

Flatt, and at least to Isaac Columbus Flatt, who is buried in the Ike Flatt Cemetery down below the Antioch Church of Christ on Flynn's Creek in Jackson County. If you trace our roots back through a few more Henrys and Williams, you finally get back to a William Flatt who came to New Jersey from England in 1694.

My maternal grandparents, who lived next door to us, in the same county in Middle Tennessee, lost four children before they were ten years old. Their little boy Jesse, just below Moma, was dragged to his death by a mule when he was nine years old. Mom watched him bleed to death in her father's arms. That experience made such an impression on her that she mentioned it again not long before she died.

Ma Way suffered for years with severe depression. I can still remember hearing her loud cry when I was a boy. They did not know what to do to help her. I would be working in a field just below their house, and I could hear her loud cry. I can still feel her pain!

Mom had rheumatic arthritis just after she gave birth to my brother, Don. This terrible disease bent her back severely so that she was not much taller than four feet when she died at age 74.

All of this made a lasting impression on our family. Mom was depressed herself for several of her last twenty-five years of life. It was something that she seemed to be ashamed of—like she was doing something wrong.

Yet, she lived a good life. She was a good wife to our father for 54 years and a great mother to her eight children. Though often sad, she persevered. She cooked, she washed clothes, she cleaned house, she canned vegetables and fruit. She helped our Dad rear eight children on a 40-acre farm, which Dad bought from Uncle Dock Flatt for $770 when I was four years old. Dad still lives in that old home place, located in the Union Hill Community of Jackson County, Tennessee.

I can remember well the day we moved there. I was already going to school at age four. Can you believe, I was in pre-primer? Dad had told us before we left home to walk to our two-room school that morning that we were going to move into our own house that day and for us to stop there as we came

13

from school that afternoon. And, you guessed it. Rose, Leamon, and I forgot and were walking past our new home when Daddy called to us from his new front yard, "You're home now." He was so proud of his new farm. He owned it himself. He didn't have it paid for, but it was his.

Dad told me recently that he could still remember the day that he made his last payment on his note for the farm to Mr. Whitson. He said it was one of the happiest days of his life.

There had been a tragedy in Uncle Dock's family. It happened in our back yard not long before we moved there.

Uncle Dock had a problem with alcohol, moonshine that some farmers in our county often made. While drinking one day, he shot and killed his son, Lee, age 20.

Uncle Dock spent several years in jail. His wife divorced him, and his family was permanently impaired as you might guess from all of this disaster.

Our family, like all others, is far from perfect. We have had our joys and pains like everyone else.

Gary Collins recently wrote a helpful article in the *Christian Counseling Today* journal on "What Makes a Healthy Family?" In this article he uses three labels to designate different types of families which exist in America today: The traditional family (1940-1960), the individualistic family (1961-1987), and the diversified family (1988-1990's).

In the traditional family, there was conformity to social norms, clear roles with male authority, and commitment to permanence in marriage. Family tradition, loyalty, solidarity, and partnership were major family values.

The individualistic family was characterized by individualism, commitment to careers, striving for personal peace and affluence, and commitment to self. Personal fulfillment, individuality, romantic love, and freedom to do your own thing were major values. Narcissism!

The diversified family is divided into two sub-groups: The pluralistic family and the new realistic family. The pluralistic family is open to non-traditional family forms, is flexible, diversified ethically and willing to make changes. Major values include tolerance, openness to change, and respect for individuals.

Characteristics of the new realistic family included realism, firm religious beliefs that are not rigid, belief in marital stability and the importance of child rearing. Major values include commitment, child development, and respect for individuals.

By studying these recent family eras, I can see some principles we need to stress. Personally I value the Judaeo-Christian ethic, so I have the most problem with some pluralistic families: homosexual marriages and heterosexual partners living together without marriage. I value the traditional family, but I can see that we often twist family roles to fit our personality quirks and thus damage individuals within the family. That fact, however, does not negate the value of a two-parent, "traditional" family. I see the value of full-time homemakers, but I do not condemn career mothers. I wish they could stay home with the children until they go to school, but sometimes they can't! The Bible does not authorize sex outside of marriage; but after sex happens and women get pregnant, I am glad to see single mothers bring their children to church and live by Christian principles. Blended families have special problems, but many of them are very Christian and very healthy. Not all family forms are of equal value for childrearing. Two parents who love each other form the basis for an ideal family structure. And this is not meant to put down other legitimate forms such as widowhood or a single-again, divorced mother. Sometimes these matters are out of her control.

What I would emphasize as a Christian is for you to apply biblical teachings to yourself and to your family. The result might not look exactly like any of the recent family types. Some families called traditional are good, some bad. If biblical principles are applied to individualistic families, I believe they would be less individualistic, perhaps less committed to careers (though careers are important), find real peace that passes understanding, strive less for affluence, and be less concerned about self, more concerned about others. Such changes would bring personal fulfillment, preserve some individuality, enhance togetherness, and empower romantic love in marriage. Not bad. Healthy!

Some non-traditional family forms are wrong, such as homosexual partners and heterosexual partners living together without marriage. Diversified ethics may only mean that equally good people often have different opinions; yet it often means that every idea is equally ethical, a view that is absurd! Flexibility is a healthy sign, indicates a willingness to grow and make needed changes. All of us need to learn to be tolerant yet firm in our convictions. When we disagree, we do not have to be disagreeable. Healthy people express their views without being obnoxious or projecting omnipotence. Show respect to others.

The new realistic family need not go against Christian ethics. In fact, its characteristics and values can be consistent with Christian ethics. Realism. Marital stability. Flexibility. Childrearing. Commitment, respect for individuals. All sound good to me. Families can be different and yet be Christian.

So, if you are a Christian, examine your family form to determine if it violates Christian ethics. Then apply Christian principles in your family to make it better family in every way. It's tricky, but possible.

What I want to emphasize is that I am aware of different types of families. Some are traditional, some non-traditional, some one career, some two careers. In some, the wife works as needed, but the husband basically supports the family. In some, the wife does virtually all of the house work while in others this work is shared. I have had a few clients in marital therapy who have a sort of reverse arrangement: The wife works outside the home, and the husband keeps house. I am aware of the prevalence of divorce and blended families. I know about unhappy homes. What I'm saying is that I don't want you to think that I am just dealing with ideals. What I am going to say about building better families can be adapted to use profitably in all kinds of families. **All healthy families seem to have some things in common**. I'm going to concentrate on **those ingredients**. I believe what I have learned in helping to build our home can be very helpful to you. I hope I don't come across as being proud or a know-it-all. I have learned some valuable lessons from my family of origin, my community of origin, my immediate family, my education, my colleagues, and my professional activities that I believe are valuable. Read on. I'll share them with you.

Best wishes as you continue. I care about you and your family. Working together, we can start where you are and build a better home.

Remember as we proceed that **nobody's family can say they are free from trouble**. A healthy family is not a trouble-free family. **A healthy family** is a family that **learns to grow through difficulties**. And perhaps we can all do that.

One

A Good Foundation

Principle Number 1:
A healthy home is built on a good foundation

The story came out in the daily paper in Memphis a few years ago. A certain man was sitting in his den when his fireplace suddenly sank about 10 feet into the ground. He was shocked, couldn't believe his eyes. The house was almost new. Well-built. What in the world was happening?

What happened was that the house was built on ground that had been "filled in." It was a low, sort of swampy area originally. The developers had hauled in a lot of dirt and built up the ground. But, it was not solid. It began to sink. In fact, many houses in the neighborhood sank! Their houses were cracked and torn, many beyond repair.

They tried to sue their builders but were unsuccessful. They weren't to blame. They had the same experience with their bankers and the government. Nobody was responsible, and they were left paying payments on houses that were destroyed.

Why did all this happen? Their houses were built on shifting, unsettled ground. Bad foundations. The houses looked good: built of brick, concrete, iron, and wood. Yet, they crumbled. They were built upon shifting sand.

I'm sure this sad story has happened many times in marriage. Much pain is experienced. It all seems so unfair and tragic. It all looked good and seemed right, but it wasn't. A house or a family is no better than its FOUNDATION.

Building better homes. How to build a healthy family. It all starts with a good foundation.

Good foundations can be different. We have lived in four different houses in Memphis. Three were built on concrete slabs, one on a traditional foundation. Different, but all four were solid and stable.

All good foundations for building better families are not the same, but they have many similarities. They are all solid, firm.

I know what you may be thinking at this point: My family foundation was not good, so it's hopeless for us! Not so. Just more difficult. Bear with me.

Right now, I want to talk to unmarried people. Look at what you are building on as you start to build a home. Foundations are crucial.

I'm talking about persons, families of origin, beliefs, expectations, rituals, religion, traditions, similarities and differences. Add **character** and underline it. What kind of person are you marrying? They will affect you tremendously and may be a parent to your children. They will affect relationship patterns in your marriage and family.

Murray Bowan, a well-known family therapist, contributed greatly to our own understanding of emotional health. He developed a scale to measure emotional health: a zero to 100 scale that is discussed in *Family Evaluation* which he co-authored with Michael Kerr. A zero represented a complete lack of emotional health; a hundred, complete emotional health and maturity. The zero side also represents a complete lack of differentiation between emotions and intellect and between the individual and his or her family of origin. Such a person cannot distinguish between thoughts and emotions and is not differentiated at all from his or her family of origin. They are sort of like a big family ego mass. The individual has not become separated as a person from the family. He or she is but a part of the family. No autonomy. No individuality. No sense of personhood. Not a good candidate for leaving father and mother (Genesis 2:24). He said that none of us reaches the 100 side of the scale. Most people operate at perhaps the 40 to 60 range. The 100 side of the scale represents complete differentiation. Emotional maturity. Clear thinking. Logic. Integration of personality. Autonomy. Individuality. Ability to relate. Ability to appreciate roots, yet able to leave as well to form other relationships such as in marriage.

Another point that Bowen makes is that most of us do not grow or decline emotionally more than five points from our parents' level of emotional maturity. If our parents averaged a 45 in emotional maturity, we will usually fall in the range between 40 and 50. Not too optimistic but perhaps true. So—don't marry an emotional infant and expect to make an emotional giant out of him or her. You probably can't pull it off.

As you can see, Bowen sees individuals in relationship to families. He would never try to understand an individual without looking at them in context of their parents, siblings, and grandparents. Intergenerational building.

By now, you are probably reacting negatively to what I am saying. That's okay. I want to challenge you. "I don't have to be like my parents and grandparents," you say. "It's not set in concrete. I know of people who are completely different from their parents." Perhaps so, yet they are influenced greatly by them. And, you can't understand them without viewing them in context, as a part of their family system. Remember the word "intergenerational." That's the key word here. Each generation builds upon the shoulders of previous generations. They are influenced by their heritage even if they cut off emotionally from them. In such a case, they often expend much of their energy maintaining the cut-off, preoccupied with keeping a safe distance. Children of alcoholics, for example, who stay sober because they're determined never to be like their parents, nevertheless must be seen in family context to be understood. You learn that having alcoholic parents keeps them away from alcohol.

A student of mine told me a few years ago that he had inherited a gene from his dad that might cause him to get a terrible disease and die young. His struggle was to decide whether or not to have children and perhaps pass this tendency on to them.

I just returned from golfing nine holes, the third time I have gone this year and almost my record high for a year. My golfing partner told me that he had been divorced twice and that he had gotten custody of a child by his second wife who had falsely accused him of incest. He said, "I married a woman who was just not cut out to be a mother. She was really messed up." I counsel with many couples who seem to be married to the wrong person: personality differences, different wave lengths, and constant irritation of each other. They just don't seem to match at all!

I have seen such couples really work to improve their marriage, yet it is much more difficult for them than for many other better-matched couples. Their marriages are built on shaky foundations. They have to work harder to make their continuing in marriage possible.

If all of this is true, then the foundation of a marriage needs to be strong. It becomes an important question **before** marriage. Picking the right mate is probably the most important task in building better homes. So, let's talk about that for a while.

Picking a mate is a part of America's way of romantic marriage. Dating and growing together are a part of our relationship-centered marriages.

In some cultures, parents do the picking. One of our Korean students at the university where I teach drove from Memphis to New York, picked up his bride-to-be, whom he had never met before, and married her. His aunt arranged the pairing. I asked the student if he just picked her up and then went and married her. He replied, "Oh no. We get acquainted for a few days first. Then marry."

Another such student told me that their parents usually selected a bride for them and made arrangements with the prospective bride's parents for the wedding. He then added, "Most time, son see pretty girl. Point to her and tell father, 'Get her for me.' Father agree. **Then** go see other father."

In such traditional cultures of the past, a bridal price was sometimes paid to compensate the family for their daughter's labor. A dowry was sometimes provided by the family of the bride in agricultural societies to enhance the attractiveness of the bride. With a good dowry, she would likely be more in demand.

In modern Western society, **romantic love** and **compatibility** are deciding factors for marriage. Both the **heart** and the **head** get involved to some extent in the process. There needs to be a balance between passion (infatuation), commitment (covenant, love), and intimacy (companionship, friendship). A triangle that is off-balanced in any direction does not provide a good foundation for marriage.

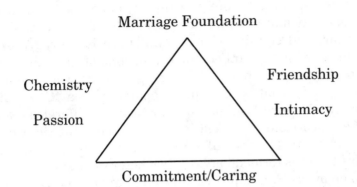

We can gain significant insight about mate selection by studying various approaches to mate selection. One such theory is that **like marries like**. Important factors in this theory are race, ethnicity, religion, education, occupation, emotional maturity level, and geographical proximity. The couple begin with similar backgrounds and proceed through similar interests to compatible personality traits in an effort to find someone to meet their needs.

Another theory of mate selection is that **opposites attract**. In this theory, individuals try, perhaps subconsciously, to complete their personality deficiency by finding another who **has** what they **don't have**. Put them together and the Gestalt (configuration) is complete. Common examples are dominant-submissive couples, father-daughter couples, mother-son couples, and nurturing person-person who needs to be nurtured couples. These are drawn together into what seems to be a perfect match, but trouble often follows. After a while together, one of them becomes unhappy.

Then, there is the **stimulus-value-role** theory of mate selection which says that you find the best mate you can find, given what you have to offer. In this theory, **stimulus** refers to such positive attributes as physical attractiveness, social skills, competence, and status. **Value** refers to compatibility of standards and beliefs. **Role** refers to the expectations you believe the potential partner will fulfill.

Another mate selection theory is called the **dyadic-formation theory** which proceeds along six steps: perception of similarities, establishment of rapport, openness with each other, role anticipations and marriage, role adjustments to fit each other, and couple orientation. There is a progressive involvement with each other, the establishment of boundaries, commitment to each other, and an emerging identity as a couple.

Then there is what is sometimes thought of as a **"Christian perspective"** which has both similarities and differences with the other theories and valued by many throughout the world. The "Christian theory" of mate selection begins with a **covenant** that is formed between two heterosexual people who wish to be married, and proceeds through **grace** shown toward each other. They learn to appreciate and accept each other, develop feelings of security when together, and learn to forgive each other. They do not use their power to inflict harm but instead to **empower** each other to be all that they can be. They serve each other as Christ serves the church (Ephesians 5:21-33). This, done in love, assists each to grow into a more mature person. All of this is accompanied by intimacy: knowing, understanding, caring, being genuine when together.

Whatever approach you are influenced by in mate selection, you, your family, and your community are all involved to some extent. In America, the individual takes precedence; in traditional cultures, the family; in some African and Indian tribes, the community.

And then we must remember the **baggage** of prior experiences that everyone brings to the marriage: their families of origin experiences, and their individual differences in personality. Previously married persons bring additional baggage from their previous marriages. Let me give you an example or two. Sue married "an older man" when she was 16. He beat and abused her. They divorced months later. She began to date again at age 18. Most of her dates "had their hands all over me," she reports. She then went out with Jim who was different. Jim was polite, respectful, a good conversationalist, and "didn't try anything." He didn't give her a goodnight kiss until the fifth date. She fell for Jim, but it turned out later that he was gay. Their marriage has been very inadequate and frustrating to Sue. She thought it was her fault—"something must be wrong with me"—for years. Then she found out the truth and has debated about divorcing him for some 20 years since then. Experiences can **blind** our eyes to truth.

Roy and Nell were both in their second marriage. Roy's first wife had "cleaned me out financially" when they divorced. "She just wanted my money," he asserted. Nell's first husband "was always looking for another woman." Want to guess what the main problems were in their marriage? Roy's problem was that "she watches me like a hawk." Nell's was that "he is too stingy with his money. He got me to put my house, car and bank account into both of our names, and told me he would do likewise. Then, after I did, he wouldn't. And I'm bitter about it. I feel like he doesn't trust me. How can we build a marriage on a lack of trust?" Baggage gets in the way of a good relationship.

I hope you'll allow me to use the Bible since I've been influenced so much by it. I believe it is inspired by God and a very helpful guide in building better families. There is some sort of Christian quotation on the headstones of all of my ancestors back to Isaac Columbus Flatt. My mother's tombstone has a quotation on it from the twenty-third Psalm: "The Lord is my Shepherd. I shall not want," a quotation she made while in a coma just before she died and evidently the last words she ever said.

With this in mind, I'd like to discuss an ancient biblical text involving Abraham as he "picked a wife" for his son of promise, Isaac (Genesis 24). What an unusual story! Our customs are different from theirs, but perhaps we can learn something from the principles discussed in this story.

Abraham wants Isaac to marry a woman from his extended family, for him to live in Canaan (the promised land), and not in Mesopotamia, the land of his forefathers.

The emphasis here is upon **God's** activity in choosing the right woman for Isaac. Abraham's religion was heavily involved in the total process. In Genesis 24, God will guide Abraham's servant in his search for a wife for Isaac. The servant prays to God for guidance and praises God for his subsequent success. The servant requires a sign from God and receives it. He is guided to Rebekah who is courteous, helpful, beautiful, and Abraham's brother Nahor's granddaughter. The servant gave her a nose-ring and two gold bracelets and related his mission.

Rebekah leaves with Abraham's servant. Laban and Bethuel agreed that the Lord "was at work" in this matter. The servant gives Rebekah additional gifts and pays Laban and Milcah, her brother and mother, the bridal price, a customary practice among the Hurrians. As was their custom, they sought the bride's permission before the family made their final decision. Rebekah agreed. Then, before she and Abraham's servant left, Laban and Rebekah's mother (and perhaps father also) invoke a two-fold bridal blessing on her: that she may have many descendants and that her descendants might possess the gate (city) of those who hate them.

Isaac and Rebekah met and married, and Isaac took her to his departed mother Sarah's tent as a symbol of their marriage. She never got to see her family of origin again, but she and Isaac evidently had a good marriage.

All of this ancient story seems strange to us. We don't do it that way now, and I for one rejoice that we don't. I'm glad, for example, that I knew Louise before we got married. Her beauty and gentle nature attracted me to her. Yet, I think there are some helpful guidelines in this ancient story of Isaac and Rebekah for picking a mate. If so, what are they?

1. **Consider God's will** in picking a mate. I'll admit that I don't always know what God's will is. Sometimes I wish he would just speak to me as he did to ancient fathers. Some things could be clarified that way. Yet, he does what he chooses, and we sometimes struggle to discover what is the right thing to do. Yet, the truth is that they sought God's guidance, and so should we. Solomon says that we are to acknowledge God in all of our ways, and he will guide us (Proverbs 3:6).

The Bible does give some **general directions** for our search. We are told it is possible to commit adultery by marrying the wrong person (Matthew 5:32, 19:1-9). Christians are encouraged to marry Christians (II Corinthians 6:14-18, I Corinthians 7:39). Rebekah was of the same religion as Isaac. Both worshipped Jehovah God, not the gods of the Canaanites. This was important to Abraham and Isaac, though in their case it had much to do with their heritage and special mission with God. Their descendants were instructed later on in a similar manner. They were not to make marriages with the people of the land (Deuteronomy 17:1-4). The reason for the prohibition was that such spouses would turn their children away from following God to serve other gods. In one instance, they were instructed to put away their foreign wives (Ezra 10:19, 44; Nehemiah 13:23-27). Though Christians are not exactly parallel with them as far as lineage is concerned, we are told to "Come out from among them, and be separate" (II Corinthians 4:14-18).

I don't believe that marriages between Christians and non-Christians are invalid, I just think they are more difficult. Much research on marriages as well as logic and experience support this claim. In such marriages, religion, the lack of religion, or conflicts in religion often become divisive. Religion in my own family has been a unifying factor. It's something we share, one of the deep glues that holds us together and guides us in our lives.

2. Pick an **industrious** person. **Rachael** was willing to work. She was busy drawing water for her family and for visitors when Abraham's servant first saw her. Our work today is usually different but no less necessary. The apostle Paul said that if any would not work, he should not eat (II Thessalonias 3:10). Seems harsh perhaps, but it indicates the importance of work.

We don't notice how important work is until we see some family member who refuses to work at all. I have seen this many times in families I have counseled. In one such family, the wife wouldn't work. She would not cook, sweep, make beds or do anything. And she no longer worked outside the home as did the husband. I realize that the husband should help with homemaking if the wife works outside the home and that many husbands don't do so. But this case was not like that. The husband worked hard to bring home the bacon and provide well for his family. The wife sat and did nothing. He came home from work, cooked, swept, and washed clothes. He took them out to eat most of the time, which got old to him.

I know you're saying, there must be another story behind all of this, and there is. He wouldn't help her at home when she worked outside the home and raised their children. They divorced about six years after her sit-down strike.

Marry someone who is willing to work, to be industrious. Teach your children to work. They need to learn. Everyone in a family must contribute in some way to the family's welfare.

3. Pick a person who is **attractive** to you. Although I'm not sure how much Rachael's looks had to do with her selection as Isaac's wife, she is described as being very attractive, "very fair to look upon" (Genesis 24:16).

I realize that attraction is a vague idea. What is attractive to one is sometimes repulsive to another. Some men like overweight women. Most don't, not at least in our culture. A ring in the nose is attractive in some cultures but not in ours. However you define attraction for yourself, you should be attracted to the person you marry. It helps bring you together. And with our romantic-compatibility marriages, some attraction is highly desirable for most couples. Otherwise, they may tire of each other rapidly.

I did pre-marital counseling once with Susie Doe (I disguise all of my illustrations of clients to protect confidentiality). She was unsure of her decision to marry her fiance. She liked him. They got along well. Enjoyed being with each other. But she did not feel comfortable with him when others were around. When I asked her to explain, she said that she felt bad about saying it: that he was **ugly**. I realize that he might have been handsome to someone else and that he can't help how he looks, yet that he was ugly to her was significant to me because it affected her social activities and her feelings. She was ashamed of him!

Since she had already told me that she wanted to have seven children after they got married, I asked, "What if they all look like him?" We both laughed, but she decided to call off the engagement. I felt good about her decision. Both of them deserved something better.

4. Pick a person who is **not a bed hopper**. Rebekah is described as a virgin (Genesis 24:16). Virginity before marriage, though not practiced by many today, was a custom then as in early America. Christianity still teaches that sex outside of marriage is wrong. Of course, biblical teachings about virginity apply to both sexes.

I would not say that people who have sex before marriage will not have good marriages. I know of many who have. I

would say that bed hopping, going from one sexual partner to the next and much sex separated from love, is not good preparation for marriage. I have seen such practices cause lots of marital problems.

Joe and Jean were such a couple. Joe was extremely promiscuous before marriage. Jean was not. Joe thought of love-making as exciting sex, period. Sex was what lovemaking was all about. And he knew many sexual techniques which other women had thrilled him with before, many of which Jean did not like. Joe was disappointed, and Jean wanted much more than just sex. She wanted affection, sweet talk and long periods of lovemaking that involved "the communion of two souls in a deep sort of intimacy." Joe didn't know what she was talking about. His pre-marital sexual activities helped cause their marital problems. They almost divorced before they began to learn how to meet each other's expectations for love and sex.

I'd like to point out here that research does not indicate that living together before marriage improves marriage or lessens the chance of divorce. In fact, just the opposite is true. Living together before marriage is a somewhat negative factor in marital happiness and the probabilities of divorce.

5. Pick a person who is **hospitable.** Following polite customs of her day, Rebekah gave water to strangers and their animals. She then invited them to spend the night at her family's place (Genesis 24:18-25). Today, Christians are taught to practice hospitality. In doing so, some have entertained angels unawares (Hebrews 13:2). Entertaining people in your home extends family influence and helps develop personality and social interaction skills in children.

6. Pick a person who is **able to give and receive love**. Rebekah seemed to be such a person. Gift-giving was a custom connected with engagement and Rebekah followed the custom. She graciously accepted the ring for her nose and the bracelets for her arms. We need to learn how to accept and to give tokens of our love and affection. This is in line with what William Glasser, M.D. says in his book *Reality Therapy* about a healthy person. A healthy person is one who can give and receive love. And a healthy person is one involved in something worthwhile.

I have seen it over and over again in counseling. Some can give love but not accept it. They back off when affection is offered. They misinterpret warmth as manipulation. Others receive love but do not give it. They are takers, and takers starve their spouses emotionally and leave them vulnerable for an affair. Emotionally mature people can give and take love. Emotionally immature people do not make good spouses.

7. Pick a person who **has a good family**. I know this is a tough one for many to accept because there are exceptions to the rule. People from unhealthy homes sometimes emerge healthy. The child of an alcoholic may hate alcohol. The child of an emotionally unhealthy family may be emotionally healthy. The child of a sinner may become a saint. But most of us would agree that these are exceptions rather than rules. Such occurrences are not usually so. We tend to be a chip off the old block. The proverb is often true: "As is a mother, so is her daughter" (Proverbs 16:44). Someone said it this way: If you want to know what your wife will be like in 25 years, look at her mother. This reminds me of Bowen and other intergenerational family therapists who say that one must be understood in the context of several generations.

Laban was devious and greedy, yet his and Rebekah's family had some desirable characteristics. They were of the right lineage to fulfill God's promise to Abraham (Genesis 12-22). You could argue that Isaac and Rebekah succeeded in marriage in spite of her family. Yet the identity of her family was important to Abraham. Laban, though devious, fed Abraham's camels and provided water to wash their feet. Rebekah's entire family were gracious hosts. They were not all bad.

Our concerns about family are not a matter of special lineage as was the case with Isaac and Rebekah; yet because in a sense we do marry a family, we have legitimate concerns about our spouse's family of origin. Remember Bowen's point. We marry a person who has been and will continue to be influenced by a family. We should take a long look at that family. Look at the father. Observe interaction patterns. Ask yourself, "Do I want to be married to someone like that 25 years from now?" If not, proceed with caution.

8. Pick a person who **can make decisions**. When asked an important question, Rebekah knew her mind and made a significant decision. "Will you go with this man?" they asked.

"Yes, I will go," she replied (Genesis 24:57-58). We need to know our own minds before we can be good marital partners.

I have counseled with probably as many as 500 troubled couples, perhaps more. Many of these couples have told me that they never did get along with each other, not even before they married. Often they say they wanted to call off the wedding but to do so would have been embarrassing. It had gone too far: invitations had been mailed, presents accepted, and the wedding garments purchased. What else is there to do but marry? So, they got married and regretted it from that day forward.

You can be sure that the way we **act before marriage** is a **good preview** of things to come. How we make decisions, how we handle conflict, and how we communicate are good examples of things to come.

Notice especially how your fiance acts when "they don't get what they want, when things don't go their way." Do they yell? Scream? Slap? Hit the wall with their fist? Drive fast? Curse? Clam up? If so, they will do it even more after marriage. Count on it! Rely on your head at least a bit and not solely on your heart. And do this before you fall in love or you may lose your ability to think much. When passion kicks in, the mid-brain and emotions take over while thinking, the upper brain and the frontal lobe kick out of gear. Remember, it's better not to marry than to marry the wrong person. It's better to be embarrassed than to be miserable for years!

9. Pick a person who has her **family's blessing**. Rebekah's family gave their blessing to Rebekah and Isaac (Genesis 24:60). You may not agree that this is necessary. Perhaps you know of exceptions to the rule, but the rule is still valid. Going against the wishes of parents is not the best way to begin a marriage. It complicates family of origin issues that can cause many difficulties later.

10. Pick a person who will make a **good parent**. Rebekah's family blessed her by saying: "Our sister, be thou the mother of thousands of ten thousands, and let thy seed possess the gate of those who hate them" (Genesis 24:60 ASV). As we date before marriage, we need to keep in mind that this person may someday be the parent of our children. Even if you don't plan to have children, sometimes you do. Birth control methods are

not foolproof. We should marry someone who would appear to be good parent material: a mature person, a good role model, a person who cares for others and is unselfish.

11. Pick a person whom you **love**. Isaac took Rebekah to his mother's tent. She became his wife, he loved her, and she comforted him after his mother's death (Genesis 24:67). We should marry someone who would be glad to live with us with all this implies: love, sex, companionship. If love is not there—unselfish caring, friendship, companionship, sex, passion—your prospects for a good marriage are slim. Don't marry. Keep looking.

If you are already married and are out of love, keep trying. Love can be rekindled. I've seen it done many times. Hang on to whatever aspect of love that you still have—caring, passion, or friendship—begin there, and build on that. Remember it's easy to convince yourself that you are out of love when things aren't going right in a marriage. Keep trying!

12. Be a good pick yourself! Isaac was a good pick for Rebekah. Laban and Bethuel thought the marriage "proceeded from the Lord" (Genesis 24:50). I wish we could have that kind of assurance. We don't, so we have to take our time and do our best. Get to know how they act in various situations over a significant period of time. Spend time together when you may not look or act your best. Study together. Do laundry together.

Isaac had certain **positive features**. He cooperated with his father and divine guidance in picking his mate. He was from a good family. Who has not been impressed by Abraham and Sarah? Their faith moved mountains. He and his father provided a gold nose-ring and two gold bracelets for Rebekah, a beautiful custom which they observed. He had prospered well and could support a wife (Genesis 24:35). He gave gifts to Rebekah and her family including the bridal price (Genesis 24:53). He went out to meet Rebekah upon her arrival astride a camel (what a picture!). He loved her (Genesis 24:67). A good husband for a good wife. A good foundation on which to build.

I hope these guidelines from ancient days will help you start your marriage on a solid foundation. I'll admit that I am being a bit idealistic but perhaps still helpful. If you don't build your home on a good foundation, chances are it will shift upon the unstable sand, break and fall.

Perhaps most important is for you to be a good pick for someone who is looking for a good mate. Try to be the kind of person **you** would want to **pick** and start building your home on a solid foundation.

If you are already married, as many of you are, try to be the kind of person your mate will enjoy. Be easy to live with, fun. Be helpful. If you are not married, and do not wish to ever marry, that's your choice. Just try to be the kind of person others will enjoy being around. Then, maybe we can all get along better.

QUESTIONS FOR COUPLES TO READ
AND DISCUSS BEFORE MARRIAGE

1. Why do you want to get married?

2. What was your family of origin like? How do you want your family to be like them? How different? What will make it hard for you to leave your family of origin? How often will you visit them? They you? What would you call overinvolvement of your inlaws? Underinvolvement? What sorts of things would you talk over with them?

3. What traditions do you wish to establish in your new home? Do you plan to have family devotionals? Prayer before meals?

4. What are your goals in life? How important is God and religion to you? How will your religion affect your life and your marriage? How involved do you plan to be in your religious group?

5. What were your dating experiences like?

6. What do you understand marriage to be like? How much time do you spend together? How close do you get? How much do you share with one another? How can you be an individual and married at the same time?

7. How important is sex in your relationship? Are you well informed about the physiology of sex? Do you feel guilty about sex? How will you handle differences in sexual mood, appetite, and desire after marriage?

8. Have you ever had any frightening experiences? Child sexual abuse? Incest? Rape?

9. Do you have homosexual tendencies? Experiences?

10. What do you plan to change about your mate? How?

11. How do you communicate? Do you talk about your feelings? How does your mate communicate when angry? When disappointed?

12. What are your roles and responsibilities? How many hours per week does each of you plan to work? How are decisions made? How would you like to see leadership function in your home? Do you sometimes give in to each other? Will both of you work outside the home? What will be done with the money? Who does what at home?

13. Have you worked out a budget? What items do you consider necessary, desirable, or extra? Can you afford to get married? Who will administer the funds—write the checks? How will decisions on budget matters be made? How far in debt should you go? For what reasons?

14. What expectations do you have for your marriage? Do you expect your spouse to make you happy, to meet your needs?

15. What is your greatest concern as you approach marriage?

16. How many children do you plan to have? Do you want boys or girls? What are some dangers in having a preference? Have you discussed birth control methods? The pill? Diaphragm?

17. How were you disciplined as a child? Will you use this method with your children? If not, how will you discipline them? How do you feel about spanking children? Describe someone with children who are well-behaved. What type of discipline do they use? Would you be comfortable using it?

18. Do you ever "rub each other the wrong way"? When? How? How often? How do you handle it?

19. Why do you think your marriage will work? How do you complement each other?

20. Are you committed to each other for life? How serious are the wedding vows?
21. Do you use drugs or alcohol?
22. What leisure activities do you share? What activities do you wish to do alone?
23. What friends do you wish to keep? How will you cultivate new friends?
24. Where will you live? How will you decide when it is appropriate to move to a new location?
25. What are your wedding plans? Date? Ceremony? Participants?
26. What do you plan to do on your honeymoon? What expectations do you have?
27. Are you willing to do pre-marital counseling?
28. Would you like to see a counselor for preventive therapy after you have been married a few months?

SPECIAL QUESTIONS FOR UNMARRIED COUPLES WHEN THE WOMAN IS ALREADY PREGNANT

1. How would you describe your relationship?
2. What options do you have?
   a. Suicide. Remember that God has given you life, and he wants you to use it for a good purpose. Suicide is no real answer. It just adds to the problems.
   b. Abortion. Remember that life begins at creation, is given by God, and is created for fulfillment. How will abortion affect your spiritual life? Your life in general?
   c. Single parenthood. What is your financial situation? Are you aware of Federal programs that might help? Maternity homes? Temporary foster homes? How will this affect your educational and career plans? What do you want? Will you blame the child in the future for your problems? Can you give to the child willingly

and not as a martyr? Can you provide the necessary support and nurture for the child? How do your parents feel about it?

d. Adoption. Agape and other such agencies may help. What is best for the child? Would you get any satisfaction from knowing that your child has a good home and that his/her parents experience great joy in being his/her parents? Have you considered a temporary foster home arrangement?

e. Married parenthood. Would you marry each other if she were not pregnant? Is having a baby a sufficient reason to get married? Can you afford to get married? Will you resent the baby later on for "messing up your plans"? Do you want to live with this person for the rest of your life? Are you ready for many changes that will come in your life because of marriage and parenthood? Would you have to live with parents? How do you feel about it?

3. Have you visualized how each decision might affect your life?

4. Do you understand that God loves you, accepts you, and is willing to forgive you?

5. Have you worked through any feelings you have of loneliness, anger, anxiety, fear, depression, rejection, and guilt?

6. Have you secured proper medical care for the baby?

7. Did you get pregnant in order to get married?

8. Why do you think that your decision is right?

9. Are you willing to see someone for pre-marital counseling?

10. Are you willing to go back for preventive therapy a few months after marriage?

QUESTIONS FOR PREVIOUSLY MARRIED COUPLES

1. Why did your previous marriage end?

2. What did you learn from each previous marriage that will make it hard for you to marry again?

3. What did you learn from each previous marriage that will help you if you marry again?

4. What is your view of marriage?

5. What do you fear most as you contemplate this marriage?

6. What is your understanding of such scriptures as the following on divorce and remarriage? Deuteronomy 24:1, Malachi 2:10, Matthew 5:32, 19:1-9, Mark 10:1-11, Romans 7:1-7, and I Corinthians 7.

7. What patterns do you see in your experiences together?

8. Where will you live?

9. How will you deal with step-children, ex-spouses, and ex-relatives?

10. Will step-children live with you? If so, how will parenting work? What role will the step-parent play in parenting?

11. Do you have a pre-marital financial and property agreement? Do you need one?

12. Do you pay alimony and/or child support? If so, how do both of you feel about it?

13. What part does God and the church play in your life?

14. What roles will each of you have in your marriage?

15. Have you worked through the grief of your former marriage? Are you still hurt, angry, guilty, ashamed, disappointed, depressed? Are you ready to marry again?

16. Will you compare your new spouse to your former spouse? How?

17. If you remarry, how will it affect your life? Will you be accepted by your friends? Church?

18. Why do you think that this marriage will work?

19. What are your wedding plans?
20. Are you willing to see someone for pre-marital counseling?
21. Would you like to go back for preventive therapy after you have been married a few months?

Two

Commitment

Principle Number 2:
Healthy Couples Keep Their Vows

A friend of mine and his wife, very dedicated Christians, were about to celebrate 30 years of marriage together. "We have a good marriage **now**," he said, "although we had a lot of rough times the first few years. But we had a commitment to each other. That's the way we were raised."

This couple was unique, very different in many ways as far as personality is concerned. Yet, they worked it out.

Why? Commitment. They knew they had to work it out. They were raised that way.

I know that it takes much more than commitment to build better homes, to develop healthy families. I know that some committed couples stay together and help make each other miserable. In fact, some people seem to thrive on that mission. Yet, I have counseled with many couples who express sentiments similar to those of the couple mentioned above. They stayed together because of commitment when all else seemed to be gone from their marriage, and built a healthy marriage. If commitment is this important in marriage, I want to emphasize it as I talk with you concerning **your** home.

The Bible teaches that a man is to leave his father and his mother and **cleave** to his wife. They become one flesh (Genesis 2:24). Commitment. A permanent relationship but one that is sometimes hard to maintain.

Helen Doe was only 22, married for two months. She wanted a divorce. She thought she loved Raymond, her husband, but knows now that she doesn't love him. The one thing she knows is that "I won't live with a man I don't love." When I asked her for reasons to stay together she could not think of any. The marriage vows and her Christian faith she said did not affect her decision to divorce in any way. Yet, just two months before, she had said, "I believe that marriage is for life. I will never divorce no matter what. It's against my religion. I'm taking him for better or for worse."

Should commitment be a **glue** that holds us together over the rough spots of marriage? Do our marriage vows have any meaning? Until death do us part. **This** person and **this person only** for as long as we both shall live.

I know that vows are changing, but most of the couples I counsel repeated these traditional marriage vows to each other. What are the implications of such vows?

THE BIBLE AND MARITAL COMMITMENT

Most people of Western culture have been influenced by what the Bible teaches about commitment in marriage. What it says has been our yardstick in theory although we sometimes fall short of what it says in practice.

Then perhaps a good starting point for us is with biblical teachings on commitment. What does the Bible say about commitment in marriage?

1. Marriage is for life. A man is to **cleave** to his wife (Genesis 2:24) as though glued together. You are no longer two but one flesh. "Therefore what God has joined together let not man put asunder (Matthew 19:6 ASV). Remember that phrase? If you were married in church, the minister probably used it to end your marriage ceremony. It usually comes right after the pronouncement of husband and wife and right before "You may kiss your bride," the most enjoyable part of the marriage ceremony! Jesus said that Moses **tolerated** divorce because of the people's hardness of heart, but from the beginning "it was not that way. I tell you that everyone who divorces his wife, except for marital unfaithfulness, and marries another woman commits adultery" (Matthew 19:9 NIV). Vows are serious business!

Several hundred years before Jesus was born, a prophet named Malachi made a similar statement. God, he said, did not like spiritual adultery. It upset him when his people worshipped other gods. Likewise, he hates divorce (Malachi 2:13-16). True, the emphasis was against a husband's treacherous dealings with his wife. But, the general statement, "God hates divorce," seems to be broader than just a certain kind of divorce. He seems to be very displeased with **all** divorce. Scriptures sometimes say that God **allows** divorce, but it never says that **he is pleased with divorce**.

The apostle Paul is in agreement with Malachi and Jesus. In Paul's Corinthian letter (I Corinthians 7:10-15), he urged married couples who were separated to reconcile. He also encourage a Christian married to a non-Christian to remain married if the spouse was willing to do so. The non-Christian might leave, but "don't you leave," he says.

Moses, Malachi, Jesus, and Paul are all saying that marriage is for life. An **exception** was given by Moses and Jesus, but the rule was **marital permanence**. What does all of this mean?

2. Rash vows should not be made. Did you ever make a rash vow, then regret it? "I'll never let my kids act that way. I'll teach them how to behave!" Many parents live to eat such words. "I'd never let my kids marry the child of a divorced parent. It runs in families, you know." Many divorced parents have told me that they had made such statements to their children **only** to regret it after **their** divorce. Ora was a very ultra-conservative Christian. She believed there were very few Christians, mostly those who went to the lectureship at her church's school of preaching. Then, her children grew up, got married to mates from various denominations, and she took her words back. In fact, she began to say that what you believe or do doesn't matter. "It's all of grace." We should be careful about what we say.

Vows are like that. They should not be made rashly. Solomon said that it is a snare to make vows rashly (Proverbs 20:25). The best illustration of an unwise, rash vow was spoken hundreds of years before Christ by a judge named Jepthah (Judges 11:25-31). In his vow to Jehovah, he promised that if God would deliver the children of Ammon into his hand, then he would offer "Whatsoever cometh from the doors of my house to meet me, when I return in peace from the children of Ammon, it shall be Jehovah's, and I will offer it up for a burnt offering" (ASV). A rash vow indeed! Do you know who came out first to meet him upon his return home? His only daughter! He kept his vow and offered her up as a burnt offering to God although God did not want such offerings. A rash vow! A foolish vow! Better left unsaid!

True, Jepthah was in a double bind. "Wrong" either way he went. Wrong if he killed his daughter for sure, and "wrong" if he went against his vows!

I've seen several marriages that seemed like this. Bert was a dangerous wifebeater. He had tried counseling for a while and "it didn't do any good." His wife had been reduced to "a non-person." Her personality had been almost completely destroyed. She didn't believe in divorce and couldn't stay married. She thought she was wrong if she divorced, and she knew she was wrong if she stayed married. I know that some of you will say "let them separate but not divorce," but even such a solution is still not a good solution. Either way you go seems bad.

I personally think Jepthah was wrong in killing his daughter. I believe "the lesser of two evils" would have been to break his rash vow. I guess you could say that such a move would be the right thing to do in his situation.

The reason I mentioned Jepthah's vow was to show how seriously our spiritual forefathers, the Jewish people, took their vows. They took them very seriously! And so should we.

3. We should be very careful in picking a mate for life. This is true for many reasons.

Our **mate may influence us** a great deal. Eve ate of the forbidden fruit and gave some to her husband, and he ate of it as well (Genesis 3:6). Israel was instructed to not marry with the people of the land because they will "turn away thy son from following me that they may serve other gods." Such actions would bring God's anger against them and destroy them (Deuteronomy 7:1-4).

Of course, the influence from mates can be good as well as evil. I'm sure that Job's influence on his wife was mostly positive. He suffered greatly: lost his 10 children, his property, and his friends, yet he maintained his integrity. "Blessed be the name of the Lord" (Job 1:21), he said. I remember a woman named Imogene who was a faithful Christian and a mother of four small children. One Sunday morning there was a 12-inch snow on the ground in their beautiful Tennessee hills, and she couldn't get their car out to go to church with her children. So, she got all of them dressed and started out the door on foot. Her husband, no doubt concerned for their safety, discouraged their going by saying "You'll be the only ones there. Very few people are going to heaven anyway." As she and the children began their two-mile walk into town, she replied, "I want to be one of them." As I look back on that incident that happened in 1960, I doubt if she should have taken those children out in that kind of weather (who knows for sure?). Yet her simple, trusting, faith still influences me as I'm sure it did her husband and children.

We live up close with our spouses. They see our weaknesses and vulnerabilities. The good side of this is that they often see us as we are, and this information is reflected back to us and can be used to help us grow. The bad side is that they often pull us down. So, because of the tremendous influence of our spouse on us, we should try to marry a wholesome, healthy person whose influence on us will be good. And perhaps more important, we should resolve to be a **good** influence on our spouse and children. The consequences of our influence are great. They reach even beyond the grave. The Hebrew writer says that Abel "being dead, yet speaketh" (Hebrews 11:4). His example of faith still is a part of that great cloud of witnesses that we look to for encouragement to faithfully run the race set before us (Hebrews 12:1-4).

Our **mates may be difficult** to live with. Solomon had some 300 wives, so he should know! He says that the contentions of a wife are a continual dripping (Proverbs 19:3). An Arab proverb says: Three things make a house intolerable: *tak* (the leaking of the rain), *nak* (a wife's nagging), and *bak* (bugs). Though Solomon says more about a wife who is hard to live with than a difficult husband (with 300 wives, perhaps we'll excuse him), yet he gives instructions to contentious men as well: "As coals are to hot embers, and wood to fire, so is a contentious man to inflame strife" (Proverbs 26:21 ASV). Mates are sometimes hard to live with.

Yet, they may be **a joy** to live with. From experience I know that this is true. Louise, my lovely wife of 38 good years, is **easy** to get along with. She is gentle and kind when I don't **deserve** such treatment.

Moses instructed married men not to go to battle or take other governmental assignments for the first year of their marriage that they might "be free at home one year, and shall cheer his wife whom he hath taken" (Deuteronomy 24:5). He was to be cheerful! He was to spend time with his wife and exert a cheerful influence on her. I wonder if Moses knew that the first year of marriage is the period when most are likely to have critical adjustment problems. **Today** more couples get divorced the first three years than at any other time. And the first year is critical. Many things to work through.

If a man had "betrothed a wife, and hath not taken her, let him go and return unto his house, lest he die in battle, and another man take her" (Deuteronomy 20:7). Solomon adds to these thoughts that a man should "rejoice in the wife of thy youth. As a loving hind (deer) and a pleasant doe, Let her breasts satisfy thee at all times; And be thou ravished always with her love" (Proverbs 5:18-19). Spouses need to be loyal to each other, and a pleasant and wholesome influence.

A spouse can **help us see our blind spots**, our **rough undeveloped parts**, and by love, acceptance, gentleness, and encouragement help us to grow and become more mature. Selection of the right mate for us is a key starting point for this whole process.

Also, for such long-range growth to occur, we must see marriage as **permanent**. We marry not until **love** do us part (though many want this), but until **death** do us part. When someone takes a long, close look at us, they say "change!" **Change here** a little, **change there** a lot. Though we don't like it, such instructions given in gentle love, can be a blessing, a growth experience for us. Love does not bear fruit without labor which can transform our soul. It's like climbing a high mountain. Unless we are willing to accept the long struggle upward, we will miss the new horizon to be seen from the top of the mountain. **Permanence** in marriage can bring happiness, closeness, and dignity, in sickness and in health, not merely the attainment of selfish desires. In a marriage, we find ourselves absorbed in a **greater purpose**, and we rise above the passing struggles of the moment. The idea of until death do us part, is much more than a burden to be borne. It is **a rope** that ties us and helps us climb to the mountain top; it is **the bones** that hold the body together through stresses and strains. Marital bonds are evidence of love, not bondage as in slavery. As we accept God's will for ourselves and our home, his grace is there to provide mercy and help in time of need (Hebrews 4:16).

This attitude is in contrast to that of one married man who on his golden wedding anniversary cried as the huge anniversary cake was cut. A friend asked, "Why are you crying? This should be one of the happiest days of your life!" The man replied, "Yes, I know, but we had a shotgun wedding. My father-in-law told me he would send me to jail for 50 years if I didn't marry his daughter; and I was just thinking that if I had gone to jail, **today**, I would be a **free man**." Surely marriage is not like that for most of us. In a strange, paradoxical way, marital bonds help us to grow, to love, to be a real friend. to really know what intimacy is all about, to be free to grow and be all that we can be.

I just realized that I am being idealistic again. This is not the whole story, you're right. Nobody's marriage is like this! True! Yet, I share these lofty ideals because I have experienced them myself and have seen other people experience them. My parents had 54 years together before my mother died in 1984. My in-laws, Paskell and Flora Dyer, had 51 such years before she died. I have been very close with lots of couples who had good marriages, who were easy and wholesome to live with. And, I have counseled with hundreds of couples who were just the opposite. They would not let their mates get by with saying one word that they did not like. It's like "walking on eggshells" many of them tell me. Or "living with him is like being with a time bomb. You don't know when it is going to explode." Many such people do not work it out. It may be that they don't know how to say what they need to say in the right way, or it may be that they refuse to accept any sort of constructive criticism or disagreements. I don't always know. I just know that their conversations often go in circles. Nothing is accomplished. I also know that many of them separate and divorce, run from themselves and from their problems. Now they can go back to seeing themselves through their own eyes and start all over again. One of my clients, Jerry Ferrell, recently went through his fourth divorce at age 35. When I mentioned to him that we often repeat dysfunctional patterns, he said, "You mean I have made the same mistakes four times?" I asked, "Did you?" He replied, "Yes. My **temper** is **still** a problem." Each marriage revealed this problem that **he** had, but he ran from its solution. And, until he learns to deal with his anger in more constructive ways, he will probably relive these same patterns with slight variations in many other relationships in the future, in other marriages or in close relationships at work, in extended family, or with friends. You see, it's always somebody else's fault! Why should **we** change?

We should keep our marriage vows made "before God and these witnesses," until death do us part. Living in the early Christian church, Ambrose in *De Abraham* admonishes married people not to seek a divorce because they had their own wife and were not allowed to marry another while she was still living, even though the law might allow it. He who divorces his wife rends his own flesh and divides his own body, he continued. A woman who commits fornication does not cleave to her husband; she is neither one flesh or one spirit with him, but she divides and separates herself by such fornication, he argued. He continued by saying that marriage involves the will, the contract, subjection, love, security, closeness, mutuality, loyalty, and the uniting of minds and hearts. It is a spiritual bond, a work of God, permanent. A lot of those words turn us off today. But I wonder if we can have what we want in marriage without them.

John and Carrie thought **they** could. They were a young liberated couple. Both were attractive. They were raised "in the church" but had decided to have an open marriage. "We won't get jealous. We agreed that both of us could sleep with others if we wished. It will make our marriage better," they reasoned.

Here is the rest of the story. He came home early from a trip one day and knocked on the door. No answer. Yet, her car plus another one was in the driveway. He knocked harder and harder. Finally, just as he kicked the door in, she was there to get hit in the face with it as it slammed open. Her face was split open. He ran the partially dressed man out of his bedroom. Not as liberated as he thought he was! You see, the same bond that ties us to our wife, ties her to us, and that's special. It allows us to be more intimate. She's mine. I can afford to let her know me, to get close. Even the best sex, according to Masters and Johnson in *The Pleasure Principle,* is with someone you are intimate with, vulnerable and close. Then, it's more than sex. It's love. Such people don't just have sex, they make love. It's okay to "just have sex" at times with your mate, but most of the time in an intimate marriage, sex is more than "just sex," it's love. It's communication on a deep level. It's like **becoming one** in a deep, meaningful sense. Caring. Loving. Sharing. Giving pleasure. Receiving pleasure. Ecstatic experiences! "Let her breasts satisfy you at all times. Be ecstatic in the arms of the wife or husband of your youth" (Proverbs 5:18-19).

Jerome, in the fourth century A.D., made an appeal for unity in marriage based upon the idea that God took only one rib from Adam and made only **one woman** for him. The **two,** not three or four, became one flesh.

Incidentally, God made **Eve** for Adam, not **Steve.** He wanted them to multiply. Biology implies heterosexual marriage, not homosexual!

It seems to me that the state should take a strong interest in preserving heterosexual marriages and not homosexual ones. Children need a father and a mother in the home. Research continues to emerge that reveals this. Current trends represent a threat to the well-being of children. Homosexuals "marry." They are pushing for government approval of this "civil right."

Our whole culture is working against the well-being of children. Parents get addicted to drugs. Fathers abandon children. Boyfriends and husbands abuse mothers and children, parents marry and divorce casually, many live together without marriage, and parents neglect their parenting responsibilities. No love. No discipline. No guidance. No protection. Irresponsibility. Little commitment to family! We too often give up on mutuality in favor of individuality and self-centeredness. "I've gotta be me," we sing. But, who takes care of others?

Research and common sense tell us clearly that some environments are better than others for children. Parenting behavior has far-reaching social consequences. Society has a stake in how we build our homes.

I would like to see our government make and promote policies that help us build healthy families. Such policies would encourage heterosexual marriage, require parents to support their children financially, and promote two-parent families. Such families were strongly endorsed in a 1991 bipartisan National Commission on Children report on family. Most advocates of welfare reform now agree that marriage provides the strongest foundation for families and the best route out of poverty for women and children. All of this requires commitment, commitment not only to God and mate but also to children. Commitment to God and family.

Sounds almost like our grandson David's Tiger Cub scout pledge. Not bad either.

Such a solid foundation for the home has long been a tradition in Judaeo-Christian cultures. Vows are sacred. They cement our commitment and are to be kept. Moses wrote, "When a man makes a vow to the Lord or takes an oath to obligate himself by a pledge, he must not break his word but must do everything he said" (Numbers 30:2 NIV). Again in Deuteronomy 23:21-23, Moses wrote that we are not to be slack in keeping our vows because "God will require it of you." We are to do what we say we will do. Solomon said that it is better not to vow than to vow and break it. When you do this, he said, you are letting your mouth cause you to sin. Isaiah promised to keep this vows (Isaiah 19:21). The psalmist of Psalm 22:25-26 promised the same. Later in the belly of a big fish, Jonah promised to "pay what I vowed" (Jonah 2:9). Paul, a great follower of Jesus, shaved his head to keep a vow (Acts 18:18). Several football coaches have also done that to keep a vow they made before the big game.

Broken vows **displease God**. Abraham and Sarah were in Egypt when it happened. To save Abraham's life they agreed to say that they were siblings instead of marital partners. This led to Sarah's being taken into Pharoah's palace as his wife and to God's punishment of Pharoah and his nation (Genesis 12:10-20). The same sort of experience was shared by their son, Isaac and his wife Rebekah. Abimelech in Gerar was the king involved in their triangle (Genesis 26:1-11). Although Rebekah was never actually taken by another man as wife or lover, their deception made it a possibility which agitated Abimelech. Such an action would have "brought guilt upon us," he said. So he gave orders not to molest Isaac and Rebekah.

Marriage is designed to be lived for life. It influences us greatly. It provides the best underpinning for building healthy families.

I know all of this sounds idealistic to many of you. It's hard to reach. But a person's reach often exceeds his grasp, and his reach for ideals pulls him upward; and in this case toward a better home. My point is that it is okay to have ups and downs and problems in marriage. It's normal. Commitment makes the difference in that you weather the storms and keep your eye on the final destination.

SOME IMPLICATIONS OF COMMITMENT IN MARRIAGE

What does all this mean in our marriages? So, we're committed. Then what? What difference does it make?

Jerry Doe was one of my students. He came into my office one day a few years ago while I was working on a lecture on Commitment in Marriage to be delivered at Ohio Valley College within a few weeks. Though very busy, I stopped to talk with Jerry. When he learned of my lecture he made some valid practical comments about commitment in **his** marriage. Much trouble, three children. Many thoughts of divorce. He wanted to get away. Didn't love her anymore. Then he remembered Psalm 15:1-4, and it "forced" him to turn around and face the problems in his marriage with the resolve to "keep my word and to do things better." So, he said, "I began being more a doer of the word than a hearer of the word. I put out effort, quit fault-finding. I resolved to tell her I loved her; not because I felt it, but because she needed to hear it." He justified his "lie" by saying to himself that he was loving her with "all the love I could come up with at that point." The more he began to tell her her "good points," the more they became stronger. It was nurturing and healing to her. "Her love to me just turned around," he reported. "My vow," he continued, "had not only been to my wife but to God as well. Even when I was on the ropes, I remembered my vow to God, and I just determined to make the marriage work. It was a point of honor." It was because he hurt so much that Psalm 15 meant so much to him. He had to keep his vows even when it hurt. "Such a man," the Psalmist said, "will be blessed." When he determined to keep his vow, he decided to make the marriage work. The more he worked on his marriage, the better it became. "Criticism," he said, "becomes either a stone that crushes you or a stepping-stone to greater heights. I was obedient to the Lord, and the Lord was able to do exceedingly, abundantly above what I thought he could do. I never imagined that I could ever love my wife again. When **I** did better, **she** did better. Now, I look at her, and I can't believe that I ever wanted to divorce the best thing that ever happened to me. I learned to minister to her needs, and that made our marriage much better."

I'll admit that doing what we should does not always make marriage better. We can't control the other person. It takes two to tango or to make a marriage what it needs to be. At a certain point in marital dysfunctions, good actions often bring bad responses. "I don't want his flowers or presents **now**. Why didn't he do that five years ago?" a distraught wife asks. At that point, the husband is in a double-bind. Wrong if he does, and wrong if he doesn't! If you catch yourself at this point, please allow **something** he does to be right. Otherwise you are hopelessly stuck!

Matt called me over the phone just before their scheduled appointment for marital therapy. Like many in that situation, he had some instructions on what I should tell his wife. "Tell her," he said, "that she has no scriptural right to divorce me. I have **never** committed adultery." He admitted having beaten her several times. And, one time when she was pregnant, he hit her in the stomach, and she lost the baby. Yet, he had fulfilled the law of marriage: he had not committed adultery.

I complimented him for his fidelity to this part of biblical teaching but then asked him what else the Bible says about marriage. What about love, honor, and protection? What if our commitment covered all of these weighty matters of the law? A faithful husband he should have been, but he should not have left undone the other weighty matters of "the law." Like many of us, he picked the scripture he liked, the one that was to his advantage, while he ignored others that are also important such as Ephesians 5:21-33 on unselfish love, submission, and respect.

Absalom, king David's son, technically kept his vow unto the Lord even as he began to rebel against his father, "God's anointed one." Even during the ceremony in which he was keeping his vow unto the Lord, he was planning insurrection against his father. He sent for Ahithophel, David's counselor, and increased his conspiracy against his father. To me, his show of piety had a hollow ring. Even as he carried out his vow to God, he deprived his father of most of his supporters. David, the loving father, told his son to "go in peace" as Absalom went away to prepare for battle against him. By the time David's men knew what was happening, they were powerless to intervene. His worship was ostensible. He was playing a game! Having lost many of his better warriors, David had to flee from the king's palace and from the city. There is more to service than worship, even sincere worship, and there is more to marriage than not committing adultery, as important as that is! Keeping our vows in marriage means more than not committing adultery. Integrity, caring, friendship, intimacy, being emotionally present for our mates is also "in the vows." Love, respect, and honor are strong words with many positive behavioral implications. They won't allow us to pick our scriptures in a narrow, self-centered way. We are to live by **every** word that proceeds out of the mouth of God (Matthew 4:1-11).

Commitment means dedication, a loving perspective, surrender of vain pride, giving up some individuality for the sake of togetherness, and adaptability. As we die to self-centeredness, we emerge in marriage with a new identity. We become one flesh. Still two in a sense, but yet one, two sides of one coin. Each becomes a part of the answer to the other's needs. Marriage becomes a spiritual experience. In marriage we meet with each other and before God and "these witnesses." The marriage ceremony is not an empty ritual. It has much practical meaning.

1. In a Christian wedding ceremony, we are saying that we intend to do God's will as we understand it. Why? Because we believe that he owns us, that we were bought with a price, and that we are to therefore glorify **him** (I Corinthians 6:13-20). To Christians, this means that we are to put God first in our homes (Matthew 6:33). His will becomes our directive for marriage as well as for the rest of our lives. All of this obligation to God is implied by God's presence in the marriage ceremony. We then try to live with a sense of being in God's presence all of the time. This affects how we worship, how we serve each other (Ephesians 5:21), and how we build a meaningful, loving, respectful relationship in our marriage. When we give ourself to God and to our family, we grow toward **greater maturity**. Doing God's will becomes our **script**. Doing God's will becomes more important than whether we are **in** or **out** of love in marriage.

Looking at marriage this way, we may continue in a bad marriage and give it our best because we believe it is God's will to do so, even when we are out of love. You see, if being in love, if being always happy with our mate, were our main objectives, divorce would seem reasonable when we feel out of love. **But**, if our vows and God's will become primary, marital love is eclipsed by a higher priority: "Until death do us part." You see, God owns us: Not love, not pleasure, not career, not personal growth, not fulfillment. We all **want** these characteristics in our marriage and they are desirable, but they are not as foundational as is God's will that says "I hate divorce." It's like he is saying: "Work it out, you can work it out."

Zinzedorf, a mystic, said that the marriage bed is as pure as the sacrament, yet no more enjoyable than wine in the church sacrament. I think he was right about the purity of sex in marriage but wrong to rule out pleasure in marital sex. Pleasure is not always sinful! And aren't we glad for that!

What I am trying to emphasize is that the norm for staying married in our culture is all wrong. This norm goes something like this: **If** two people fall in love, they should marry; **unless** they fall in love, they should **not** marry; if they cease to love each other, they should divorce.

What if our norm for marriage and love went something like this: We should love the person we marry with all that this implies; if we do not love the person, we should not marry him or her; if we fall out of love, we should keep our vows even when it hurts. Think better thoughts. Practice the Golden Rule. Act better. Be more loving, more unselfish. Show more concern. Serve. Demonstrate respect for each other. This would provide a basis for the rekindling of love and for a better home. It's not easy, but it's beautiful. And, remember, if you try and it still doesn't work, you have done well, and I hope you will feel good because of it. Do what is right, and you'll feel better. Not always, but usually. It will not always work, but it can't be wrong to do what you know is right.

2. Another implication of commitment in marriage is marital **sex**. The covenant we make in marriage implies that two become one flesh (Genesis 2:24; I Corinthians 7:1-5). The marriage bed is **pure** (Hebrews 13:4). Sex is enjoyable for most. Sex was created by God. He created sex organs, sex glands, and the possibility of sexual feelings. Sex is for pleasure and "to prevent fornication" as well as for procreation (Proverbs 5:15-19; I Corinthians 7:1-5).

Stella was twenty-eight when she came to me for counseling. Her diagnosis was hysteria. She married at age 24, lived together with her husband for eight months but never had sexual intercourse. I felt sorry for both of them. She literally **ran** around the bedroom to get away from him. "If I had known you were like that," she said to her husband, "I would never have married you. You're a dirty man." Stella was horrified of sex. She had what seemed to be an overly religious neurotic mother who never got along with men. "They just want to get you pregnant." She told her daughters that you can't depend on any man and that sexual intercourse is painful. "A man's penis," she said, "is as big as a baseball bat." Wow! Stella remembers these messages from age four. She was uptight around men. She thought that sex was dirty. Her husband divorced her. How tragic!

3. **Sexual loyalty** to one's mate is also implied by commitment. We are committed to each other. When I said "I do" to Louise, I said "I don't" to all others.

Solomon warned against the other woman, the woman that flatters with her words, that forsakes her husband and forgets the covenant of her God. Her way inclines unto death. "None that go unto her return again, Neither do they attain unto the paths of life" (Proverbs 2:16-20).

Most people I counsel with have not had affairs. Many have, and it presents a difficult crisis in their marriage. I encourage them to patch it up, to look at factors leading up to the affair, to take individual responsibility for what they have contributed to the affair, and to make constructive changes. Yes, both of them need to examine themselves. The affair is not justified by the mate's actions but is often a response to them. He wanted sex, she had a headache and turned her back to him. He hurt and called her a cold fish; she got colder. He got hurt and angry and began talking to a female "relative" or to someone at work. They became emotionally close, almost like they were married. Then the last step toward sex was a small one indeed. This is a typical scenario. I've seen it 100 times! Sometimes it's the wife who has the affair. The husband is aloof, "not emotionally there for me—not intimate. Not much **real** conversation." So she turns to a "relative," a close friend, or someone at work to have "her needs" met.

Jasper was a man who had been cold-shouldered many times. His wife just was not interested. "I think," she said, "that I could go the rest of my life without sex and not miss anything." Most women I counsel with are not like her. Jasper felt guilty for what he had done. Sex with a woman at work, "And she couldn't hold a candle to my wife. She's not even good looking, but she listens to every word I say. I can tell her about anything, and she is not judgmental." His words that now stick in my ears are that he **lowered his standards a little at a time**. Morality became relative to him. "It's not may fault," he reasoned. But it was! He must take responsibility for what he did, and his wife must take responsibility for what **she** did. Otherwise, both are excused, and no one changes. You see, in such a case, if no one is to blame, why should they change?

I'm not interested so much in placing blame as I am in getting you to take responsibility for what you do. To recognize that you are a part of your marital or family dysfunctional pattern. You can't control **her**, but with God's help and great discipline, you **can** control **you**. And **that** will make a difference. **You** can do something different, and your marital pattern will be affected, hopefully in a healthy direction. At least, when you do right, you'll probably feel good.

4. **Unselfish love** and giving are also implied by commitment in marriage. Marriage is a **covenant of love**! Husbands are to love their wives as Christ loved the church and gave himself up for it (Ephesians 5:25). The same is required of wives. This kind of love is unselfish, kind, not easily provoked, overlooks faults, and never fails (I Corinthians 13).

In the marriage ceremony, most of us vowed to love and honor our mate always. Even when we don't feel like it, we can show love to our mate. We care. We want their needs to be met. We want to "be there" for them. We do what is best for them. We serve. Such love is more from the upper brain where we think than from the middle brain where we feel or from the lower brain where we are moved by instinct. Our thinking does not get so muddled by our negative feelings that we lose our ability to **think**, to be **logical**. We do what is **the loving thing** to do even when it is not appreciated. The marriage ceremony implies love and giving of self to each other in marriage.

5. I may be straining to make a point, but I'll say it anyway. Commitment implies **forgiveness**. A covenant of love implies forgiveness. The prophet, Jeremiah, spoke of God as husband to his people. When they sinned, he forgave them (Jeremiah 3:13-14). In marriage, we are in a loving covenant relationship. When we "sin" against each other, we forgive each other. Jesus said, "Blessed are the merciful, for they will be shown mercy" (Matthew 5:7 NIV). I have received mercy, so I show mercy. This is a motivating verse for me. Mercy. Forgiveness. Jesus said that if we forgive others, God will forgive us; and if we don't, he won't (Matthew 7:12-14).

The prophet Hosea had an adulterous wife. At God's direction, he went and brought her back home. Our **love** as well as God's love can be **redemptive**. In doing what he did, Hosea acted contrary to the customs of his day. Such love by God toward Israel led that nation to be sorry for her spiritual adultery. He charmed her, took her to the wilderness and spoke to her heart. Following this was a new marriage and paradise regained. Such love can lead to remorse, forgiveness, and renewal in marriage. The Lord just wanted backsliding Israel to return to him and to acknowledge their iniquity (Jeremiah 3:12-13). He forgave them and his anger subsided. For a small moment, Isaiah said he forsook them, but "with great mercies I will gather you" (Isaiah 54:6-7).

I have seen forgiveness unstick many stuck marriages. They were bitter. They couldn't even talk constructively. Then, they forgave each other and proceeded with a better marriage. It's not easy, but it can happen. This is what I wish for **your** marriage and family. You can't have a good marriage unless you forgive each other for mistakes. We all goof-up at times and need forgiveness.

Let me just conclude this chapter with a few more brief remarks. I've spent a lot of time on commitment in marriage because I think it is extremely important. And I believe you can see my point.

Too many people today take marital commitment lightly. "I wasn't raised that way," they say. But you probably talked **that way** before marriage if not in your marriage ceremony. I encourage you to live up to what you said. **Marriage** is **for life**. We must **keep our vows even when it hurts**. Remember, it's easy to see many ways out of marriage when we are looking for them. We often see what we are looking for. This life-long commitment of love implies getting priorities straight in our lives, marital sex and romance, sexual loyalty to our mate, unselfish love and giving, and forgiveness.

These are excellent goals, not easy goals. But they are goals you **can reach**. As a starting point, I challenge you to go back, study, and renew your marriage vows. Then, let the implications of this commitment help you build a better home. Your marriage deserves it. Your marriage is worth saving. With God's help, you can save it. Healthy couples keep their vows.

BUILDING EXERCISES FOR YOUR MARRIAGE

1. Discuss with your mate what commitment means to you.

2. Get a copy of your marriage ceremony, if possible, and review with each other what you promised each other. Reaffirm you vows.

3. What behaviors will you change out of this study of commitment?

4. Are you easy to live with? If not, discuss how you need to change.

5. Make a list of five needs that you want your mate to meet for you. Exchange lists and discuss them. Make specific plans to implement actions to meet each other's needs as much as possible.

6. Make a list of five things you like about your mate and read them aloud to him/her.

7. How is commitment so foundational for building better families?

8. If you are not yet married, discuss with your prospective mate what commitment means to each of you. Good luck. I'm interested in helping you build a healthy home. Get personally involved with what I am saying as we move forward, and you will make a difference in your marriage. Believe me, a good marriage will greatly enrich your life and the life of your entire family. Perhaps the best thing you can do for your children is to work toward a good marriage. It's the first step toward building a healthy family.

Three

Emotional Maturity

Principle Number 3:
Healthy families have good emotional maturity

What do healthy families have in common? A solid foundation, commitment, and emotional maturity.

Emotional maturity means ability to trust, individual autonomy, good mental healthy, and the ability to relate well to others. An emotionally mature person would be able to function well as an individual and to develop a sense of belongingness in a new family. She would be able to leave father and mother and cleave to her husband and become one flesh (Genesis 2:24).

Not much is said in the literature on families about emotional maturity or mental health. Yet, in many of the families I counsel, it is a significant factor. A situation may be presented as a "simple marital or family problem" but often involves much more than that. The father just threatened to make his seven-year-old daughter leave home if she did not do what he said. The wife had been severely depressed for 10 years. The children are having continuous nightmares of losing their parents. All of this involves emotional and mental health.

I am not saying who can and who can't get married. I **am** saying that emotional maturity is a significant ingredient of a healthy family. You can't build a healthy family with unhealthy individuals. First, the unhealthy individuals would have to grow through their difficulties. Time and proper treatment

59

might help. But, unless they become emotionally mature, they will hinder the building of a healthy family.

Perhaps you are still wondering what I mean by emotional maturity. Good mental health is another way of saying it. Perhaps it would help if I gave some examples of poor mental health and of good mental health.

Murray Bowen in *Family Evaluation* developed a scale by which he approximated emotional maturity. The scale went from zero (minimum emotional maturity) to 100 (maximum emotional maturity). My guess is that those on the bottom half of his scale would have significant difficulties in marriage and as a parent. Perhaps it would help you to see some characteristics of persons along the various points on his scale.

0-25: These persons would not have emotional differentiation (separation and individuation) from their family of origin. They would still just be part of their family of origin ego mass. No sense of self, no individuality, little ability to differentiate thinking from feelings. Their emotions and thinking would be fused and would not operate independently. They live mainly in the **feelings** world. They operate on borrowed self, get their sense of self from their family of origin. They are emotionally needy. Strike out at nothing, are highly reactive to others. Narcissistic, very preoccupied with themselves. To love and be loved requires much energy, with little energy left for goal-directed activities. It is difficult for them to be comfortable. There is a high level of chronic anxiety and much emotional reaction to their environment. They do not seem to be aware of alternatives. Many criminals, schizophrenics, and incorrigible drug addicts fall within this first quartile of emotional maturity. For our purposes, it is difficult for people at this low level of mental and emotional maturity to maintain long-term marital and family relationships.

Couples from this quartile would be expected to have all kinds of marital and family problems. They would especially have problems with individual and family boundaries. They would stay in almost constant contact with their family of origin, who would in turn try to hold on to their child. Or they might disown each other. They would suffer from serious anxiety and depression and compete with their children for attention. Under stress, they would probably develop psychotic symptoms such as hallucinations, inappropriate affect (feelings), and orientation and judgment problems. I would not expect them to stay married long or to change much.

The second quartile has a better change for marital and family happiness. Yet, they often have many difficulties. I would guess that many people with serious marital and family problems would fall at this level of emotional maturity. How would they be expected to act?

26-50: Remember that what I am doing here is not an exact science. Neither Bowen's measurement nor my description of quartiles is precise. They give an approximation of how persons would be expected to act at different levels of emotional maturity. At his quartile, persons have a poorly defined sense of self; which means that they borrow self from others, a sort of pseudo-self. When something goes wrong in relationship, their pseudo-self leaves and they suffer from low self-esteem. They have some capacity to differentiate from their family of origin and between thinking and feeling but not in a mature fashion. They lack beliefs and convictions on their own and borrow from others. They merge quickly into the prevailing ideology and look to outside authorities to support their desire to create a good impression. Their self-esteem is dependent upon the approval or disapproval of others, and they are apt students of non-verbal cues that give such signals. They have low levels of basic self and high levels of pseudo-self. Beliefs and feelings are fused. They may seem to know it all and be hard to influence. Often emotionally tense, they develop neurotic symptoms of depression, anxiety, and compulsions. They are very dependent upon the situation they are in for emotional stability. If things go well, they are stable; if not, they are not. They seem to be always in search of the ideal close relationship but would probably be threatened if such a possibility presented itself. They have some capacity for working to raise their level of differentiation or emotional maturity, but they usually do not raise it more than five points from one generation to the next.

THELMA AND HERMAN

Thelma and Herman would probably fall into this quartile of emotional maturity. They were both 36 and had been married for 16 years. Thelma came for counseling. She tried to get Herman to come with her, but he would "never go to a shrink. Don't believe in them. They're not scriptural. If a person is a real Christian, he would not get depressed," he asserted.

Thelma was depressed. She cried a lot during our first session. She made a 39 on the Beck Inventory which indicated severe depression. She marked such items as these:

—I am so sad or unhappy that I can't stand it.

—I feel I have nothing to look forward to.

—I feel I am being punished.

—I blame myself for everything bad that happens.

—I would like to kill myself.

—I have greater difficulty in making decision than before.

—I wake up several hours earlier than I used to and cannot get back to sleep.

—I get tired from doing almost anything.

—I have no appetite at all anymore.

—I have lost more than 15 pounds.

Thelma also complained of anxiety and stress. Her "nerves were shot," and their marriage was "on the rocks." She was so sad that she "can't stand it," she said. She had constant headaches and stomach problems. Her negative self-talk went something like this:

—I'm not a good Christian.

—What's the use?

—I don't want to live.

—Herman cares more for everyone else than he does me.

—With Herman, I'm wrong no matter what I do.

—I can't make it without Herman.

—He's smarter than I am.

—My parents never liked me.

—People will reject me.

—I can't divorce.

Thelma was molested by a strange man at age seven and "got lost in the crowd" in her large family of origin. She described her parents as extremely stingy, which embarrassed her. Her clothes were always "hand-me-downs." She felt ashamed of their old house which was "always dirty" on the inside.

Thelma described her husband as the head of the house. "What he says goes," she said. He would continually remind her that if she were a good Christian, she would not be depressed or question anything he said.

Thelma continued to lose weight and get more depressed. Herman finally came to see me "to help her." He complained that they married young and that she was his little girl at first, "but she has changed. She is no longer subject to me. Her personality has changed. She is insecure and doesn't give herself to me like she did before."

Herman seemed to be very rigid, one who "knew it all." He was too willing to speak for God which made it very difficult for Thelma to disagree with him on anything, and she had several issues that needed attention. She seemed scared in counseling to say anything negative about her husband. She was afraid that he would abandon her, and she "couldn't stand that."

Thelma stayed in counseling until her symptoms of depression and anxiety subsided. Then, Herman convinced her to quit "wasting our money on shrinks. All they are interested in is our money anyway."

Their marriage improved some but not much. I would guess they may slip gradually back into their old dysfunctional patterns. He puts his foot down which creates tension. She absorbs the tension and translates it into depression and anxiety. She can't talk about it with her husband. Listening too much to your wife would indicate weakness to him.

As a psychologist, I thought it was next to impossible to successfully treat her depression without treating their marital dysfunctions. But, because of his reluctant participation in marital therapy, our chances with the marriage were slim. A few improvements, and then they called it off.

What I was hoping for was to see him move toward being secure enough in his Christianity to mellow some on his concept of the man's headship position in the marriage. He could have mellowed some and still retained his leadership position in the marriage. His rigidity indicated weakness as a man and not strength. I wanted to see him quit using the Bible against her and to realize that depression has a number of causes. Pronouncing it as sinful is no help. I hoped to get him to where he could listen to Thelma and talk to her as an equal. This would require growth on his part.

I wanted to see her learn to assert herself enough to find healthy solutions, if possible, to their marital problems. I wanted her to learn to value herself as being okay. Good self-esteem! I wanted her to learn to articulate her frustrations and feelings rather than just clamming up and getting depressed and anxious. There is some hope for a marriage like theirs, but they will have to work at it to have a good marriage and to keep her symptom free.

JUNE AND WILLIE JOE

June was only 14 when she came to see me. Overweight and pregnant by a black man named Willie Joe. She was from a family of four. Had two brothers and a sister. Her parents were getting divorced, and her older sister was living with "a black man." She described her father as extremely prejudiced against blacks. She reported that she began running away at night and having sex with black boys when she was 12. She said she was raped by a black man when she was 13. She had also had sex many times with white boys. Both of her brothers were in trouble with the law. Into drugs and theft.

We discussed her options. She decided to have the baby and give it up for adoption. Afterward, she became very depressed. Felt like she betrayed the baby, "never gave it a chance."

June eventually ran away from her parents and lived with a friend. She resents both of her parents. Her mother "was selfish, two-faced,a back-stabber, a betrayer, a conspirator, and an adulteress." Her father was "stupid, weak, impulsive, rigid, stubborn, selfish, hypocritical, unaffectionate, and cruel." He wanted to "play God." Her father called her a "heathen, a slut and a nigger-lover." She thought her dad was "stupid" for allowing her mother to live with him after she had affairs with various men, two of whom were black. June said they were "using" each other. She worried about her dad's hitting her two brothers "all over." She said her parents "never stick with what they say." She would have killed herself if "my boyfriend hadn't talked me out of it." June did try it once but did not succeed. Sometimes, she said, "I just want to give up."

June's dad described her as lazy, confused, undisciplined, and messy. "They don't appreciate anything I do or show any respect. They're just like their mother," he continued.

June had bad dreams frequently. In one such dream, she was in the house being followed. She kept hearing her father yell from a distance, "She's a disgrace. I can't believe she is doing what she's doing. She's awful. She's just trying to embarrass me." June woke up crying. In another dream, she was at her own funeral. Her boyfriend was there. It was awful. A strange thought kept coming to her in the dream that if she could get to her boyfriend, that he would understand that she was alive. "I was mutilated," she said. "Came apart. Could not get anybody's attention."

In another dream, her dad was not speaking to her. She went to bed. Her dad came, tied her up, and cut the baby "out of me. Held it up over my head. Said it was for my own good. He could forgive me **now**," she reported. She woke up crying. She still desperately wanted her dad's approval but did not believe she would ever get it.

June wanted to marry her boyfriend, but his family objected. Called her a slut.

As you can see, June was not ready for marriage. Had she gotten married, she would have carried too many unsolved personal issues into the marriage, and there would have been problems. She was especially shocked and hurt that Willie Joe's parents did not want him to marry a white girl. They pointed out that she was not ready for marriage and that interracial couples have many unique problems to face. They did not want that for their son.

If June married **anyone,** I would anticipate several problems. She would replace her father with her husband and continue her ambivalent ways toward him. She would try to borrow a sense of self-esteem from him. She would expect a great deal of reassurance from her husband—that he loves her, that she is okay . . . She would probably get depressed when such reassurances failed to be sufficient as they are destined to be. She would probably continue to have a tendency to sabotage her own efforts toward success.

As it was, she stayed in counseling long enough to alleviate her depression symptoms and "leave her parents to live with a friend." Such leaving, however, is not indicative of emotional maturity but is an emotional cut-off quite different in nature. Such is common with emotionally immature people, not well-differentiated as autonomous, adult people.

Just getting older would not in itself mature June. She might still drop friends fast, separate from or divorce her husband, just cut off emotionally when disappointed. Often such people have a string of emotionally cut-off relationships—brothers, sisters, parents, spouses, friends. It all proves to them that people are not dependable. Actually it may prove that she grew up with a love-deficit and that she is expecting everyone she meets to pay the love debt owed by her parents. The tragedy is that they can't pay it! She has to learn to grow through her difficulties, a difficult task indeed, and give to herself a sense of being okay. Accept herself.

The sad thing about dating in such a case is that a person like June can convince some man that **he** is the **one** she has been looking for to meet her needs. She has finally found the **one** person who can make her whole. Such is an example of an emotionally immature person and how they might relate in marriage.

51-75: Most of us probably fall either in the second or third quartile of emotional maturity. In this third quartile, people can make independent decisions with self-discipline. Their intellect can overrule their emotions. They have fairly well-defined opinions and beliefs but may hesitate to articulate them. They are more aware of the difference between feelings and intellectual principles. They may not live up to their knowledge but are freer to have a choice between being governed by feeling or intellect. They have less chronic anxiety, are less emotionally reactive. They have more solid self and less pseudo-self borrowed from others. They are more free to move back and forth between intimate emotional closeness and goal-directed activity. They handle crises well. More stress is required to produce anxiety in them.

JUDY AND BOB

My guess is that Judy and Bob would fall into this slot of emotional maturity. They came for counseling with marital problems. She was a secretary; he a college professor. She worked and put him through school. Now that he has a good career, she feels no longer needed. Her chief complaint is that he spends an awful lot of time with his graduate assistant, an attractive female. She and her husband argue daily. She screams and yells. Sometimes throws things. He keeps his cool. Her mother once had an affair. She is suspicious and jealous of Bob.

Bob says that Judy misinterprets things, "she manipulates me, pulls off from me, is possessive, very anxious about circumstances. She is also sweet and lovely but is mean." She accuses him of having an affair. Quizzes him a lot, threatens to leave. "She wants to be miserable," Bob continues. She either "mopes or yells or throws plates." Judy sometimes gives him the silent treatment and refuses to cooperate.

Bob stopped going to church. Started smoking and drinking, and spending more time with Helen, his teaching assistant. He could talk to her about anything and needed someone at this particular time. Helen was very willing to be there for him. She accepted him just as he was. They committed what I call emotional adultery before they ever had sex. They were in love. Eventually, Judy and Bob divorced and gained split-custody of their four children. He got the boys, she got the girls.

I worked with them more than a year, mostly with her. He wouldn't come, and she "was the one who was sick." Her anxiety level was high. So, we worked on relaxation and stressors while she continued to talk about Helen.

As I think about it now, I wonder what caused what. I'm not sure. He later admitted to me that there was a special relationship with Helen long before he admitted it to us, which makes me think that Judy was perhaps right more often than I thought at first. Yet, I also wonder if Judy's emotional immaturity led her to be jealous and insecure and to manipulate Bob which pushed him away and toward Helen. I don't always know. I think it usually is a combination of things. Perhaps Judy's anxiety was caused by the other woman. Maybe she could have handled the marital relationship if her husband had been devoted to her. Who knows? I just know that such marriages go well up to a point and then go bad. I believe it has something to do with personal characteristics as well as circumstances. Emotional maturity. As emotional maturity decreases, it takes less stressors to cause anxiety. As emotional maturity increases, it takes more stressors to cause anxiety.

76-100: Bowen thinks that few people operate on this level of emotional maturity. Such people are principle-oriented, goal-directed. They begin growing away from parents in infancy and become inner-directed adults; sure of their beliefs, yet not dogmatic or fixed in their thinking. They can listen without reacting and communicate without antagonizing others. They do not foster or participate in the irresponsibility of others. They are secure. Their functioning is affected little or none by either praise or criticism. They respect the identity of others, are able to assume total responsibility for themselves, and do not become **overly** responsible for others. They are able to reflect and think clearly. They are aware of their dependence on others and are free to enjoy relationships. They are able to choose between being guided by feelings or thoughts. They do not have a need for others that can impair functioning and do not use others. They are self-sustaining (in relationship to others) and tolerant. Their expectations are realistic. They are not preoccupied with their place in the hierarchy and not prone to engage in polarized debates, not ready to argue. They tolerate intense feelings and can adapt to most stressors without developing symptoms. Complete emotional maturity. A fully-developed self.

As Bowen admits, nobody reaches a score of 100. Yet, people who operate in this top quartile most of the time are able to form good relationships and are able to develop good problem-solving skills. They think. They act more than they react. They have choices. They are able to leave father and mother and cleave to their spouse. They will have problems like everyone else, but they remain intact as a relatively autonomous person through their difficulties.

I'd like to think that all of us can grow in emotional maturity. Experts such as Bowen think that such growth amounts to only about five points from one generation to another. And Bowen points out that the five points can be subtracted as well as added. We've probably all seen examples of such decline or growth. What I'm saying is this: emotional maturity of husband and wife is a significant ingredient in building better homes. That's our starting point. Without it, our building materials are suspect, and our results may be disappointing.

GROWING ASSIGNMENTS

1. Discuss with your mate whether you operate more from your mid-brain (emotions) or your upper-brain (thinking, logic). Give examples.

2. Is it possible to be too much upper-brain? Logical but no feelings. If a person is stuck in the logic gear, is he/she emotionally mature? Why? Why not?

3. How does mental illness relate to your marriage vows? Is it covered by "for better, for worse"?

4. Who is a good example to you of an emotionally mature person? How does he/she act? How would such a person deal with your problems?

5. Are you able to love your mate even though she/he is not emotionally mature?

6. What does "love never fails" mean in I Corinthians 13? How does it relate to your relationship problems?

7. What is there about your emotional immaturity that you can do something about? What cannot be changed? What can you get help with?

Four

Spiritual Development

Principle Number 4:
Healthy spiritual development will help
you build a healthy family

Not long ago I was in church one Sunday morning, and we were singing a song that moved me deeply: "Marvelous Grace of Our Loving Lord," by Julia H. Johnson and Daniel B. Towner. The particular words that spoke volumes to me were these, "Grace that is greater than all our sin."

There is a spiritual solution to our human dilemma: grace that exceeds our sin and our guilt. You need that grace.

I have heard God's message of grace all of my life, but this particular use of words in this song drove the message home to me in a new way. We all make mistakes and feel guilty. Most of us believe in God and feel accountable to him. His grace is the answer to guilt and to other basic needs.

You may be thinking that you don't have a need for God, but you do. I have found that God is a central fact of life. He's at the center of everything. God through Jesus Christ provides a context in which we love, move, and have our being. That's my perspective. That's woven into the fabric of my life.

I have seen it so many times. A mother has lost a child. A young man has terminal cancer. A couple has a son who is addicted to drugs. Right now, my father and Louise's father are in the same hospital. When they go home, they will both need someone to stay with them. The Christian religion gives all of us a philosophical context from which to work through all of

71

these difficult situations. Sometimes a spiritual solution is the only option we have. Let me encourage you to develop your spiritual life, beginning right now, as you build a better home.

I have been blessed by many Christian ancestors on both sides of my family. Not bragging. Just thankful. They weren't perfect. Just Christians. Good people. I learned a lot from them. Pa Flatt was a very practical sort of Christian. I can hear him now, "'Y,' I don't have to go through the church to help anybody. 'Y,' if my neighbor had need and I knew it, I'd just do what I could to help him."

I can remember one time when Burton Fox's house burned. It was during church one Sunday morning. All of us left church at Union Hill in Jackson County, Tennessee and went around there to see if we could help. It was too late. The house was in full flame. I'll never forget the scene. Canned food popping. Burton, his wife Cleo, and their 11 children, crying. "The only thing we have," Burton said, "are the clothes on our backs."

Well it was a sad scene indeed. Everything could not be replaced. Yet, that small Christian community and surrounding communities helped rebuild their house and reclothe them! That's where "the rubber meets the road" when it comes to religion. Pure and undefiled. We just wanted to be of help. Would have been embarrassed if anyone had bragged about what we had done.

My Ma Flatt, mother of 13 children, was quite a woman. Gentle, industrious, and never said an unkind word about anyone as far as I know. Once I was sitting on their porch and listening to a conversation about a neighbor who was, they said, a bootlegger. We talked a while, and then Ma came out of the house and said, "Yes, but he is good to his children." People need to be criticized at times I guess, but it's nice to have someone like Ma Flatt as a model. I saw Jesus in her.

I'll tell you more later about my Pa and Ma Way and my parents. They were all good Christian models for me.

GRACE, A PLACE TO STAND

Right now, back to grace, a place to stand. This idea comes from the Bible in Romans 5:1-2: "Being therefore justified by faith, we have peace with God through our Lord Jesus Christ;

through whom also we have had our access by faith into this grace wherein we stand; and we rejoice in hope of the glory of God" (ASV). The grace of God, a place to stand!

God has always been gracious to people. I believe he was especially gracious to us when he sent Jesus Christ to the world. "Grace and truth came through Jesus Christ" (John 1:17).

There is a section of Scripture in the Bible that helps us understand something of the scope of God's grace and what it does. It's found in Titus 2:11-3:7. Here we find that **grace brings salvation**. Saved through grace (Acts 15:11)! The apostle Paul preached the "gospel of the grace of God" (Acts 20:24) and that we are saved "through the washing of regeneration and renewing of the Holy Spirit" (Titus 3:5). The new birth. Grace through faith (Ephesians 2:8-9). By the grace of God, Jesus tasted death for every person (Hebrews 2:9). Paul said that we are justified freely by God's grace through the redemption that is in Jesus Christ (Romans 3:23). This grace that brings salvation has appeared to all people (Titus 2:11). Mercy. Acquittal. He paid the price. Grace, a place to stand. Knowing my own inadequacies, I'll never again minimize the importance of the grace of God in my life.

Grace also **teaches**. It teaches us the gospel of God's grace (Acts 20:24). It teaches us to deny ungodliness and worldly lusts and to live self-controlled, upright, and godly lives (Titus 2:11-12). The Cretans where Titus lived were notoriously turbulent and quarrelsome, impatient of all authority. He urges Titus to tell them to be law-abiding, active in service, careful in speech, tolerant, kind, gentle with temper under control, renewed by Christ. Living on a higher plane. Better family life. Better life in general. Self-control. Right living. And it's the grace of God that teaches this.

Grace also **works**. They were to be zealous of good works. Paul said to the Corinthians, that he was what he was by the grace of God, that he labored more abundantly than did all the others, and then he adds this thought: "Yet not I, but the grace of God which was in me" (I Corinthians 15:10 ASV). It was grace that was working in him. Grace is active. It works.

Grace strengthens. It enables us to live upright, disciplined, and godly lives. Luke quotes Paul at Miletus as follows:

"And now I commend you to God, and to the word of his grace, which is able to build you up, and to give you the inheritance among all them that are sanctified" (Acts 20:32). Grace is able to build you up! It helps you to stand (Romans 5:2). It gives you mercy and grace to help you in time of need (Hebrews 4:16). It strengthens your heart (Hebrews 13:9). My favorite illustration of God's grace is that of Paul with his "thorn in the flesh" (II Corinthians 12). As you recall, Paul asked the Lord three times to remove the thorn only to be denied his request. Instead, God said to him, "My grace is sufficient for thee: for my power is made perfect in weakness." Paul's response was, "Most gladly therefore will I rather glory in my weakness, that the power of Christ may rest upon me." I'll admit that I never expect to grow to his level of spirituality, but I admire people who do. Paul went on to say, "Wherefore I take pleasure in weaknesses, for Christ's sake: for when I am weak, then am I strong" (II Corinthians 12:10). As Philip Doddridge and John Logan express it in the hymn "God Moves in a Mysterious Way":

> Judge not the Lord by feeble sense,
>   But trust Him for His grace
> Behind a frowning providence,
>   He hides a smiling face.

> His purposes will ripen fast,
>   Unfolding every hour;
> The bud may have a bitter taste,
>   But sweet will be the flower.

Faith. Grace that strengthens. Spiritual solutions. That's what I'm talking about.

Grace also **hopes**. It "looks for the blessed hope and appearing of the glory of the great God and our Savior, Jesus Christ; who gave himself for us, that he might redeem us from all iniquity, and purify unto himself a people for his own possession, zealous of good works" (Titus 2:13-14 ASV).

Justified by grace. Heirs according to the hope of eternal life (Titus 3:7). Spiritual solutions to ultimate questions.

You may be wondering what all of this has to do with building better homes. Well, here's the answer: Spiritual development is at the very heart of building better homes. Just about every survey of healthy families, including the extensive one done several years ago by Nick Stinnett and others at the University of Nebraska, finds that spirituality is one trait common to healthy homes. I realize that families differ in their definition of spirituality, but they agree that it is important. Families need a bigger cause on which to focus. God's will. God's word. Grace. Forgiveness. Strength. Comfort in time of need. It's the way I function. So, I'll share it now with you.

JESUS CHRIST, CRUCIFIED

There is another Scripture that has significantly helped form my spiritual vision: I Corinthians 1:18-31. The cross was a stumbling block to Jews. They thought it meant condemnation (Deuteronomy 21:22-23), and they expected special signs such as the parting of the Jordan River or the making of walls around a city fall. Jesus was a suffering servant (Isaiah 53) instead. The cross was folly to Gentiles. They thought that God was beyond feeling; yet, God was said to love us so much that his son came in the flesh and died for us. They sought wisdom which had come to mean a man with a clever mind, a cunning tongue, who could spend hours discussing hair-splitting trifles. Jesus was wise but not like that. For the most part, they rejected him.

Yet, Paul says that we are "being saved" by him. That by God's initiative, we who are nothing, have become children of God in Christ. A close relationship, with God himself. Though guilty, acquitted! Though enslaved by sin, redeemed! Though enemies, reconciled!

You see, I believe that Jesus died for our sins (I Corinthians 15:1-4). He was sinless, yet made to be sin on our behalf (II Corinthians 5:21). We are healed by his stripes (I Peter 2:24). I don't understand all of this, but I appreciate it very much. I accept God's love and am grateful. "While we were yet sinners," Paul writes, "Christ died for us" (Romans 5:6-8).

Several years ago, my brother Don and I were driving through the beautiful hills of Northeastern Kentucky to a small schoolhouse where Don was to preach that night. As we made our way around a mountain road, Don told me that a school bus had run off that road down the steep hill into a river, swollen by recent rains. The front of the bus went into the surging river, while its back remained on the bank out of the water. While the bus was in that spot, some of the students opened the back door and escaped to dry land. One boy, a senior in high school, escaped to safety and then noticed that his little six-year-old brother was still on the bus. Making his way through the crowd, he finally found his little brother being trampled under a bus seat toward the front of the bus. Getting his brother and holding him in front of him, he made his way to the back of the bus and pushed him to safety. But at that very instant, the strong current of the swollen river carried the bus, the brave older brother and several other precious children downstream to their death. Several weeks later, Don said that the little boy whose life had been saved by his loving older brother, was still telling all who would listen what "my big brother did for me. He saved my life."

That's the story of grace and the cross of Jesus Christ. Our big brother saved us. In him there is freedom from death, freedom from sin, freedom from the law, and freedom from condemnation (Romans 5-8). Abundant life! It was Jesus himself who said, "And ye shall know the truth, and the truth shall make you free" (John 8:32). We are more than conquerors through him who loved us (Romans 8:37-39). Victorious. Abundant living! We may cast all of our anxiety upon him because he care for us (I Peter 5:7).

Paul spoke of Jesus as "our peace," who reconciled Jews and Gentiles in one body through the cross. He broke down barriers that separated them (Ephesians 2:14-16). Peace! Unity in Jesus. At the foot of the cross!

So, the cross has become the heart of my Christianity. Love. Sacrifice. Grace. Unity. You decide. But I hope the cross means something to you as well.

KINGDOM CITIZENS

Sounds strange doesn't it? Kingdom citizens. Yet, I believe that's what Jesus described in his world-famous Sermon on the Mount (Matthew 5-7).

He actually described what he wanted his followers to be like. Kingdom citizens. Christians.

They were to be poor in spirit; they were to mourn for their sins. Be meek, hungry and thirsty for righteousness, pure in heart, peacemakers, and even strong enough to stand persecution for righteousness. They could even rejoice when persecuted and accused falsely. You see, people of integrity have been persecuted for a long time.

They were to be salt and light to the world. Add flavor to their environment. Be pure. Genuine. They act as a preservative of that which is wholesome. Salt. Light. They shine, guide, warm, call people from their sleep to do better, and reveal Christ to others. They are a healing influence. At least, that's what Jesus wanted.

They are called on not to hate but to love. To be a friend. Reconciled to God and to others. They are to control their lust, not let it control them. Have a single purpose. Think good thoughts. Take right action.

You see, the attitude of heart is crucial. Hate may lead to insulting words or harmful actions such as murder. Love leads to reconciliation and peace. Work it out! Prolonged cultivation of lust in one's heart may lead to adultery. Some go so far as to say in their heart, "If I ever get a chance, I'll go to bed with that man's wife or that woman's husband." Thus they commit adultery in their heart. The only thing between such a person and adultery is the opportunity. A certain, pure, single-minded purpose of will leads to constructive action. A good tree bears good fruit. A corrupt tree bears corrupt fruit. Good people speak good things. A good attitude leads to a good life.

Jesus does not try to make it sound easy. He teaches against divorce. Such might cause your mate to commit adultery. He tells his followers to tell the truth. Don't deceive people by making tricky oaths as was the custom of the day. Tell the truth under oath or not! Turn the other cheek. Go the second mile. Give to the needy. Love your enemies. Good-will to all. Genuine love. Maturity.

I read once about how a mother eagle teaches her young ones to fly. She flaps her wings over them until they fall out of the nest. They are forced to fly, she lets them fly as long as they can. Then, she flies under them and lifts them up. Then, when they are rested, she dumps them off to fly again. This process continues until the young eagles learn to fly on their own. This illustration has its limitations, yet I believe it illustrates well how God helps us to meet our worthy goals in life. He lets go. We try. We fail. He comes up under us. Lets go again. Then, he lifts us up again and we eventually learn to fly without as much failure. We never get to the point where we can fly alone, however.

We are not to make a show of our religion to be seen of men. Good actions must have good motives! We are to forgive others, and God will forgive us. Lay up treasures in heaven. It's safe there. Don't worry. Trust God. He'll take care of you. Get your priorities in order. Don't borrow trouble!

Then Jesus gets even tougher if that is possible. Don't judge, he said, or you will be judged. How often I have violated this one! Don't project your problems onto someone else. You look for the speck in his eye and do not even see the plank in your own eye. First, get the plank out of your eye, and then you can see clearly to help get the speck out of your brother's eye.

Judge not. We are not to have a censorious, critical spirit. Not major in criticism. Not attribute motives. Not tear down.

There are at least three reasons why we should not judge others. First, we do not know all of the facts. Therefore, that which we do not know might cause us if we knew it to refrain from criticism. For example, I once heard a story of a certain poorly dressed man who visited an official of Harvard University and expressed a desire to build a building on campus there. Because of the way he was dressed, they did not take him seriously and thus told him that he would be contacted at a later date. He then became interested in building a college on the West Coast and did so by building Stanford University! If they had only had all of the facts!

Second, we should not judge each other because it is impossible for us to be impartial. It is almost impossible not to lean one way or the other because of our own baggage. It is almost impossible to listen to others without becoming entangled and threatened ourselves. Our prejudices, our problems color our vision. It's hard to be correct or fair in our judgments of others.

Third, we should not judge others because we are not qualified to do so. Jesus was without sin and is a righteous judge, but we aren't Jesus. We may have a beam or plank in our eye as we try to get a speck out of our brother's eye. Thus, it is impossible for us to see clearly how to take the mote or speck out of his eye. Jesus in this humorous statement is saying that a censorious, critical, judgmental person looks ridiculous in trying to correct others because he is worse off than they.

So, we need to quit judging. We may be able to tell good fruit from bad, but we can't judge motives. Leave that job to God. He's able to handle it.

Ask, seek, knock. Our Father in heaven knows how to give good gifts to his persistent children. Do unto others as you would have them do unto you. No, might does **not** make right. Let God help you reach for a higher ethic. The Golden Rule is not just a negative rule such as the Silver Rule: "Do nothing to others that you would not have others do to you." It takes positive action out of loving concern for others. If we went by the Silver Rule, we would not set fire to a person's house, but we might pass by their house when it is on fire and not stop and try to put it out though possible to do so. We would not kill our neighbor, but we might see him in a burning house and not try to save him. We would not deliberately do harm to our neighbor's good name by saying harmful things about him, but we might be silent when someone falsely accuses him. The Golden Rule in each case goes beyond the Silver Rule and causes us to do something positive. Help our neighbor. Protect his or her good name.

What a difference the Golden Rule could make in our home! What if the husband tried to feel what his wife feels? What if he tried to put himself in her shoes and try to understand? What if the children tried to feel what their parents feel? What if we all practiced the Golden Rule in our home? What changes we would see!

Jesus concluded his great Sermon on the Mount by calling us to his kingdom. Enter in at the narrow gate. It leads to life. The wide gate leads to destruction. The masses go in that direction.

Beware of false prophets who come to you in sheep's clothing. Look at their fruit, their lives. Good trees bear good fruit. Do God's will. Don't just talk a good religion; **walk** a good religion. Then, you'll be a wise builder. Your life will be built upon a rock. It will stand the storms of life because it is founded upon the rock.

The teachings of Jesus, as summarized in this sermon, have given me a star to reach for and a plan for my home. I haven't gotten as close as I would like in living according to his ethic, but I am still trying. And, while falling short, I am better for my efforts to reach a star.

Here are 11 resolutions I have made for myself from my study of this sermon of Jesus. I resolve:

1. To continue my efforts to grow toward greater maturity as a person.
2. To influence others in my own way for Christ.
3. To live with integrity.
4. To strive to glorify God rather than self.
5. To lay up treasures in heaven.
6. To worry less and trust more.
7. To judge not lest I be judged.
8. To pray more and complain less.
9. To do unto others as I would have them do unto me.
10. To build my life and my home upon the rock.
11. To show grace to others as grace as been shown to me.

CHRISTIANITY AND FAMILY VALUES

Family support. Values that will keep your family together. Christian principles will help you build a better home.

In an extensive review of religion and mental health, Payne, Bergin, Bieleman, and Jenkins in *Psychologists Interested in Religious Issue NEWSLETTER*, Summer 1991, said that there was a strong positive relationship between religion and good mental health. The religion under study was basically Christian in its broad definition. The particular kind of religion that was usually most positively correlated with good mental health was what social scientists call "intrinsic religion": internalized, with high commitment, maturity, unselfish living, principles that are not only accepted but also closely followed, with great concern for moral values, discipline, consistency, conscientiousness and resistance to external pressure to deviate from one's principles.

There was a positive correlation between such religion and quality of family life: good adjustment, happiness, and satisfaction. Religion was found to be a deterrent to divorce. Church attendance was positively correlated with marital stability. Very religious women reported greater happiness and satisfaction with marital sex than did moderately religious or nonreligious women. Religious women were less likely to report marital dissatisfaction because of a low level of sexual gratification in their marriage. Religious women were also found to be more conservative in reference to extra-marital sex. They concluded that religion clearly did not have a negative effect on marital sex, as commonly assumed. Religion was also positively correlated with less premarital intercourse and pregnancy, less alcohol and drug abuse. People who were active in a religious group drank substantially less alcohol, especially those with membership in a religious group that took a strong stand against its consumption.

Other positive relationships included: church attendance and less drug abuse, conservative religion and less substance abuse, deeply internalized religious values and less substance abuse, religion and non-experimentation with drugs, and religion and less drug addiction. Some additional research demonstrated that divorce went down significantly when a family attended church together, and prayed together.

On the negative side, a twisted religion and dysfunctional families are correlated with incest. Such religion is often used by the family to justify themselves. It seems to be an extrensic type of religion: selfish, closed, status-seeking, a kind of religion used as a means of obtaining selfish ends.

A daughter involved in incest with her father often takes the role of her mother in ways other than sexual: she looks out for him, waits on him much as his wife would normally do. A father involved in incest with his daughter often denies the sexual nature of sexual actions such as massaging his daughter's back, stomach, breasts, or genitals. He may say, "There was nothing sexual about it. I never did penetrate her. Or, I never had intercourse with her. Or, I never deposited my 'seed' in her. Or, I did it to express my love for her."

Most of the time I have a few clients who are or have been involved in incest. Most say they are Christians. But their incestuous behavior is far from Christian. It's a twisted sort of religion. Or, it may be that they have a religion in word but not in deed. Often fathers who have committed incest with their daughters, sisters, nieces, or granddaughters say they can't remember it. Right now I have two such clients. In one case, seven relatives say that he had sex with them over a period of some 25 years. My judgment is that they sometimes repress such ugly behavior and can't remember it. In practice, it often comes out a little at a time in counseling sessions. It usually has to come out before any kind of forgiveness and healing can take place.

My counseling experience confirms most of what Payne and his colleagues found. I'm not sure about how Christianity affects our sexual enjoyment. I believe that our basic beliefs affect our behavior. Christianity historically has taught values consistent with good family life: marital permanence, marital fidelity, love and respect for everyone, forgiveness, kindness, and self-control in relationship to alcohol and other drugs. All of these teachings if followed will help you to build a better home.

SOME SUGGESTIONS

I believe that religion can get twisted and cause damage in families. I get turned off when I am around such people. They're just too much for me.

But religion usually has a very positive influence. I remember my Pa Way's prayers of thanks before meals. I remember when my Dad began doing that. I remember my Mom as she got her Bible lesson for Sunday School. She filled in every blank in her workbook. I remember parents and brothers and sisters who loved the church and loved the Lord. Not perfect, but good people. Going in the right direction. I remember reading Bible stories to our children and grandchildren. I remember praying together as a family. I remember good direction given me by preachers and Christian friends.

Whatever I am, whatever my home is, these good people and their habits helped me along the way. I thank them.

Spiritual development. Think about it. I believe it's a vital part of building better homes.

A SELF-EXAMINATION EXERCISE

1. Write a one-page story of your spiritual development. Reflect on where you are and how you got there.

2. Discuss with your spouse the meaning of "Judge not." Do you judge each other? When? Give examples.

3. What place does grace have in your religion?

4. Does it relieve you of human responsibility? Why? Why not?

5. How does the cross of Christ fit into your religion? What implications are there in the cross for your life?

6. What changes would you have to make in your life to live by the ethics of Jesus? In your home?

7. Why can't Christians unite? What causes sects to form within the church? Why do we reject each other over differences of opinion? How does all of this affect your life? Your home? What changes do you need to make?

8. Do you live with integrity? Do what you really believe is right?

9. Are you kind and loving to every member of your family?

10. Do you have relationships you need to mend? Which ones? What do you need to do to mend them?

Five

Love and Affection

Some can love but not accept love. Others can accept love but not give it. Both cause real relationship problems in the home. An emotionally, mentally, and spiritually mature person can give and take love. Such persons can build good homes.

Love is a central principle for building better homes. Love that is given; love that is received.

The reason that I mention love after the other principles is that it is so easy to convince yourself that you have fallen out of love. At least what people call love. That's when commitment holds the marriage together. Yet, if we understand what love really is, it too would hold on during crisis times. When you've gotten to the end of your rope, love ties a knot in the end of the rope and holds on for dear life to preserve the family and improve it if possible.

Is this romantic love? Yes, and much more. Is it companionship love? Yes, and much more. Is it caring love? Yes, and much more!

Perhaps a definition of marital love would help. Paul wrote, "Let love be without hypocrisy. Abhor that which is evil, cleave to what is good. In love of the brethren be tenderly affectioned one to another; in honor preferring one another" (Romans 12:9-10 ASV).

"Love" in verse nine in the Greek text is *agape* love. Many use the term *agape* for the Christian ideal of love, like "God's

85

love." Although this is not entirely correct—since *agape* is also used for men's love of darkness—it is true that *agape* is often used in the New Testament for the Christian ideal, and I will use it that way here. *Agape* is thus a love that cares, a love that sacrifices, a love that does what is best for the object of it's affection.

Here are some verses of scripture that use this same word. God so loved the world that he gave his son for us (John 3:16). A fruit of the Holy Spirit is love (Galatians 5:22). Husbands are to love their wives as Christ loved the church and gave himself for it (Ephesians 5:25). Older women are to teach younger women to love their husbands and children (Titus 2:4). A love that cares, a love that endures, a love that is not self-centered. Christians are told to be imitators of God as dearly loved children and live a life of love (Ephesians 5:1). God loves. We live a life of love.

It seems to me that Ruth expressed this kind of love for her mother-in-law when she said, "Entreat me not to leave thee, and to return from following after thee, for whither thou goest, I will go, and where thou lodgest, I will lodge; thy people shall be my people, and thy God my God, where thou diest, will I die, and there will I be buried: Jehovah do so to me, and more also, if aught but death part thee and me" (Ruth 1:16-17). Her husband had died. Her sister-in-law had returned to her own people. Naomi told her to do likewise. Ruth refused, stayed with her mother-in-law, and later married Boaz, a wealthy relative of Naomi, who had left extra grain in his fields for Ruth to glean. Love. Loyalty. Caring. Sacrifice. All of these are involved.

Paul gives us a very clear definition of *agape* love in I Corinthians 13:4-8 (NIV). Apply what he says to your home.

> Love is patient, love is kind. It does not envy, it does not boast, it is not proud. It is not rude, it is not self-seeking, it is not easily angered, it keeps no record of wrongs. Love does not delight in evil but rejoices with the truth. It always protects, always trusts, always hopes, always perseveres. Love never fails.

Pure love can change you. It can change your family. It can change the world.

John uses this same word when he writes that love comes from God and that God is love. Everyone who loves is born of God and knows God. Then John concludes by saying, "Dear friends, since God so loves us, we also ought to love one another. No one has ever seen God; but if we love each other, God lives in us and his love is made perfect in us" (I John 4:7-12 NIV).

God is love. He lives in us. Thus, as we give way to him, *agape* love takes over and rules our spirit and our lives.

"Love" in verse 10 of Romans 12 can be thought of as friend-ship love or unselfish love (since *phileo* is also used of God's unselfish love for people). "In love of the brethren be tenderly affectioned one to another; in honor preferring one another." *Phileo* love (in the Greek text). Companionship, friendship, unselfish affection. In honor preferring one another.

This concept is used many times in the Bible. Jesus spoke of both *agape* and *phileo* love in John 15:12-17. "Love one another as I have loved you." *Agape* love. "There is no greater love than this that a person lay down his life for his friends" *(phileo).* Then, he says that we are friends of his if we do what he has commanded us. Service. Responsiveness to each other. Friends continue to love and serve each other in unselfish ways. Jesus is our standard of such friendship, and what a standard! He laid down his life for us. He wants us to be friends like that. He shares with us as friends: takes us into his confidence, tells us what the Father told him.

Friends of Jesus do what he commands them. Love that ignores the wishes of another is a weak and meaningless love. Friends are responsive to one another, emotionally there for each other.

Friends of Jesus **know** him. They do not follow in blindness. He **communicates** with them. He is their comforter.

Solomon said a lot about friendship. A friend is dependable, sticks closer than a brother (Proverbs 18:24). A friend loves at all times and is there to help in times of adversity (Proverbs 17:17). A friend is honest, gives constructive criticism careful-ly (Proverbs 27:6). A friend gives good counsel (Proverbs 27:9). As iron sharpens iron, so one person sharpens another (Proverbs 27:17). In all of this, remember that a friend is also tactful. He doesn't even joke with someone if it hurts his friend (Proverbs 26:18-19).

I believe that husbands and wives should be good friends. God made Eve to be Adam's help-meet, companion, partner, friend (Genesis 2:18). When Eve arrived, Adam was no longer alone. Intimacy. Closeness. Bone of my bones and flesh of my flesh. She was called woman because she was taken out of man. Therefore, Adam was to leave father and mother and cleave to his wife, and the two became one flesh (Genesis 2:18-24).

Caring. Friendship. Passion. One flesh.

Love in marriage includes romance and passion. Eve's **desire** was to be to her husband (Genesis 3:16). God made genitals, sex glands, and minds. He also said afterward that what he had created was good! He never condemns passion in marriage. People are never criticized for being attractive.

Solomon criticized men for having sex with loose women. Though her lips drip honey and her speech is smoother than oil, in the end her steps lead straight to the grave. Her paths are crooked, and she knows it not. Keep far from her. Don't go near her house. If you do, at the end of life, you'll groan when your flesh and body are spent. Such a person will say, "How I hated discipline. How my heart spurned correction" (Proverbs 5:1-14).

Then, Solomon says for the man to love his own wife, "to drink from his own cistern." Rejoice in your wife. "A loving doe, a graceful deer—may her breasts satisfy you always, and may you ever be captivated by her love" (Proverbs 5:5-19 NIV). Captivated, ecstatic! "You fill up my senses," is the idea. God must enjoy fun more than we think!

The Song of Solomon in the Bible is a story of love. I believe it's between a man and his wife, a lover and his beloved. It gets very erotic.

Beloved, 2:4-6 NIV:
> He has taken me to the banquet hall,
>> and his banner over me is love.
> Strengthen me with raisins,
>> refresh me with apples,
>> for I am faint with love.
> His left arm is under my head,
>> and his right arm embraces me.

Lover, 2:14:
> My dove in the clefts of the rock,
>> in the hiding places on the mountainside,
> Show me your face,
>> let me hear your voice;
> for your voice is sweet,
>> and your face is lovely.

Beloved, 2:16-17:
> My lover is mine and I am his;
>> he browses among the lilies.
> Until the day breaks
>> and the shadows flee,
> turn, my lover,
>> and be like a gazelle
> or like a young stag
>> on the rugged hills.

3:4:
> Scarcely had I passed them
>> when I found the one my heart loves.
> I held him and would not let him go
>> till I had brought him to my mother's house,
>> to the room of the one who conceived me.

Lover, 4:5-7:
> Your two breasts are like two fawns,
>> like twin fawns of a gazelle
>> that browse among the lilies.
> Until the day breaks
>> and the shadows flee,
> I will go to the mountain of myrrh
>> and to the hill of incense.
> All beautiful you are, my darling;
>> There is no flaw in you.

The story proceeds. They are captivated with each other: soul, lips, breasts, mind. He takes off his robe, and washes his feet. Then thrusts his hand through the latch-opening. Her heart pounds for him. His body is like polished ivory decorated with sapphires! She admires his legs and his mouth is sweetness itself. He is her lover (Song of Solomon 5).

They are carried away in ecstasy with each other. Mouth, breasts, eyes, lips, head, hair, all are admired. They filled up each other's senses like a night in a forest! Actually they go way beyond that.

Why is it that we seldom if ever hear anything about this great book at church? Are we afraid to teach what the Bible teaches about the beauty of romance and sex? Shame on us!

Jesus blessed a wedding in Cana by his presence and assistance. He showed its significance by teaching its permanence. He knew that the two were to become one flesh (Matthew 19:1-9).

Paul said that in marriage our body belongs to our mate. Don't hold out, he says. It might cause your mate to commit fornication. It's better to marry than to burn (I Corinthians 7).

One point I get out of this is that sex in marriage is ordained of God. He got it all going. Feeling sexy is okay. Not wrong. Just channel it in marriage toward your mate. Cultivate it!

I notice in all of this too that sex is to be enjoyed by women as well as men. The lover and the beloved. Not too many headaches.

I've found out in marital counseling that women often resent it when their husbands don't recognize **their** sexual needs. Judy was 55 and had been married for 35 years. "He threw me down on the bed on our honeymoon night and just sort of raped me," she said. No romance. No foreplay. He didn't even touch her much as he had sex with her. Satisfied himself, then got up. Then acted like he didn't even like her after that. And, Judy said, "It's been like that ever since. I tried to talk to him. I told him that I needed affection, romance, hugging, time to work up to it, but he wouldn't listen. Acted like he knew everything. I tried to tell him several times about my clitoris. He said, 'What's a clitoris?' But then he wouldn't listen to me as I explained its sensuous function in sex. I gave him books, but he wouldn't read. He has spanked me, pushed me, and insulted me over and over. I finally moved out of the bedroom. I went to our elders. They said, 'You made your bed. Now sleep in it. Obey your husband.' He says I'm not a real Christian or I'd move back in and let him do what he wants. But, I tighten up when he gets near me. Intercourse is painful. I don't seem to be **able** to have sex with him."

Well, that doesn't sound exactly like the Song of Solomon story, does it? We can't command our mates to feel sexy. We have to cultivate the marital relationship. Love, friendship, passion. It all goes together and is beautiful, ecstatic, uniting, terrific! I'll tell you more about how to get there later.

MARITAL LOVE

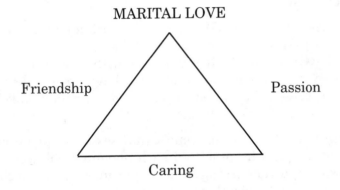

Friendship

Passion

Caring

Marital love is always heterosexual. It is ordained of God. It involves caring, friendship, and passion.

Fornication is improper sex, sexual immorality: between two single persons, a single person and a married person, two divorced persons, two widowed persons, or sex that is not between two heterosexual marital partners. It's improper sex: sex outside of heterosexual marriage. It's condemned in the Bible (Matthew 19:9). Those who continue to practice fornica- tion—"their place will be in the fiery lake of burning sulfur. This is the second death" (Revelations 21:8). Paul says they will not inherit the kingdom of God. They can repent and do so, but they can't continue in that lifestyle and do so (I Corinthians 6:9-11).

Adultery is sex between a married person and someone other than his/her spouse. "Thou shalt not commit adultery" is one of the 10 commandments (Deuteronomy 5:18). If a man commits adultery with another man's wife—with the wife of his neighbor—both the adulterer and the adulteress must be put to death" (Leviticus 20:10). Hard words to our ears but indicative of the seriousness of adultery. Call it an affair. Call it whatever. It's serious business. It's wrong! It causes lots of pain!

HOMOSEXUALITY

There are five biblical texts that deal explicitly with homosexuality: Leviticus 18:22, 20:13, Romans 1:26-27, I Corinthians 6:9-11, and I Timothy 1:8-10. Each of these texts will now be studied:

> Leviticus 18:22 NIV: "Do not lie with a man as one lies with a woman; that is detestable."
> Leviticus 20:13: "If a man lies with a man as one lies with a woman, both of them have done what is detestable. They must be put to death; their blood will be on their own heads."

These texts teach that homosexual sex is an abomination and that people who practiced such abominations were to be put to death, a very strong punishment indeed! And such people are responsible for their own death. These texts cannot be brushed aside by the claim that such prohibitions were because of cultic taboos of human origin in early Jewish culture. The Bible is inspired of God. Thus, these passages are God's word. The question then is whether or not God would have one executed for violating a custom. The answer is obvious. Levitical legislation prefigured the work of Christ and Christian behavior. The fact that Levitical material resembled other legal and religious systems of the Near East does not negate its divine inspiration.

These practices were condemned because they were wrong in themselves, not merely because they were associated with idolatrous cultures in Egypt and Canaan. Homosexuality is mentioned in the immediate context of adultery, bestiality, and child sacrifice, all acts wrong in themselves. The point in context is that such practices were a part of the surrounding culture which Israel was being warned **not to adopt!**

Others dismiss these passages because they were a part of
the law of Moses which was replaced by Christ. Yet, much of
the law of Moses was reinforced by Christ and his apostles,
and this is true of God's law on homosexuality (Romans 1:26-
27). The rest of the Bible confirms and reiterates the teachings
of Moses which prohibit homosexual acts (Leviticus 18:22;
20:13; I Corinthians 6:9-11; I Timothy 1:8-10).

Still others refer to different types of homosexuality. Biblical
writers made no such distinctions. If sex was between male
and male, or female and female, it was sinful.

The text in the New Testament that perhaps most clearly
condemns homosexuality is Romans 1:26-27, which reads as
follows:

> Because of this, God gave them over to shameful
> lusts. Even their women exchanged natural relations
> for unnatural ones. In the same way the men also
> abandoned natural relations with women and were
> inflamed with lust for one another. Men committed
> indecent acts with other men, and received in them-
> selves the due penalty for their perversion.

In this passage, Paul condemns both male and female homosexual acts. He seems also to see homosexual passions (shameful lusts) which lead to these acts as sinful though the condemnation in verse 32 is upon those who **do** these things, not
merely upon those who **think** such things.

The force of this passage has not been successfully evaded.
What is unnatural here is homosexuality—men with men and
women with women. "Against nature" means against God's
intention for human sexuality as seen in nature. For example,
in the intended function of male and female sexual organs. The
severity of Paul's language shows that the seriousness of the
offense goes far beyond a mere violation of custom. They had
repressed from their minds the awareness of the true God. As
a result, God abandoned them to inverted sexual desires and
practices. No doubt Paul was aware of the various types of
homosexual relationships in the Greco-Roman world. Yet he
does not make a distinction here: men with men and women
with women is wrong in itself. It is an example of what hap-

pens when humans worship the creature rather than the Creator. One's homosexual orientation does not justify homosexual acts, even though it be "their natural inclination." The "nature" of many heterosexuals is to have sex with numerous persons of the opposite sex, but as Christians they cannot do so (Galatians 5:16-22). They must submit to God through Christ and let him come in and help take control of such evil desires. That such desires are deeply rooted and subconscious does not alter these behavioral demands. That homosexuals today are not depraved in all of the ways mentioned in Romans 1 does not make modern homosexuality right. Homosexual sex is wrong in itself (Romans 1:32).

The question is not whether God loves all people. He does love all people including adulterers, thieves, and homosexuals. But this does not mean that he endorses these practices. Such people are told to repent (I Corinthians 6:9-11). Some **were** like that, but they changed.

Our next passage is I Corinthians 6:9-11, which reads:

> Do you not know that the wicked will not inherit the kingdom of God? Do not be deceived: Neither the sexually immoral nor idolaters nor adulterers nor male prostitutes nor homosexual offenders nor thieves nor the greedy nor drunkards nor slanderers nor swindlers will inherit the kingdom of God. And that is what some of you were. But you were washed, you were sanctified, you were justified in the name of the Lord Jesus Christ and by the Spirit of our God.

This passage clearly teaches that a practicing homosexual who does not repent has not yielded to the lordship of Jesus Christ and cannot enter the kingdom of heaven. Some try to avoid the force of the passage by saying that the same would be true of covetous persons. "We are all sinners," they proclaim. While this is true, there is a difference between a sinner who repents and then experiences relapses and one who denies that he sins and therefore does not repent saying, "There is nothing wrong with me." Paul indicates that unrepentant fornicators, idolaters, adulterers, the effeminate, homosexuals, thieves, covetous people, drunkards, revilers and swindlers shall not inherit the kingdom of God. This may not agree with our logic but it is what Paul says. We are not to continue in sin that grace may abound (Romans 6:1).

Some argue that the two words used here for homosexuals (*malakoi* and *arsenokoitai*) simply mean the self-indulgent and homosexual prostitutes. Not true. *Arsenokoitia* (Sodomite) designates the male who engages in sex with another male and *malakoi* (effeminate person) is the male who allows himself to be used for sex by another male. Even if these homosexuals of I Corinthians 6:9-11 were self-indulgent and male prostitutes this would not prove that loving homosexual acts are approved of God. This kind of reasoning would be like saying that since heterosexual prostitution is condemned in the Bible (Proverbs 5) that loving fornication and adultery are approved. Such is not the case! The fact is that sex outside of marriage is **never** approved in the Bible. Some of the Christians **were** homosexuals, but they changed and were saved. The same can happen today.

Our next text is I Timothy 1:8-11 which says,

> We know that the law is good if one uses it properly. We also know that the law is made not for the righteous but for lawbreakers and rebels, the ungodly and sinful, the unholy and irreligious; for those who kill their fathers or mothers, for murderers, for adulterers and perverts, whatever else is contrary to the sound doctrine that conforms to the glorious gospel of the blessed God, which he entrusted to me.

The word for homosexuals here is *arsenokoitai,* a male homosexual, a sodomite, a male-bedpartner. Male with male sex is again condemned as in I Corinthians 6:9-11.

Some scholars put this passage aside because it is in one of the pastoral letters supposedly written when Christianity had become hardened and doctrinal instead of spontaneous and full of the Spirit. Yet, for Bible believer this is not an adequate maneuver. **All** Scripture is inspired of God, and this text is Scripture. And its message is quite in line with earlier passages written by Paul (Romans 1:18-32, I Corinthians 6:9-11).

In addition to these texts which **explicitly** condemn homosexual sex, other passages imply the same message of judgment. Genesis 19 gives the account of the men of Sodom who were blinded and eventually destroyed because of their wickedness which included homosexual behavior. II Peter 2 and Jude 3-23 confirm this interpretation of Genesis 19.

These interpretations are in line with the broad scope of what the Bible teaches on sexuality. What God had in mind was one man and one woman living together (Genesis 1,2). Though Paul indicated that sex in marriage may help prevent fornication, its primary purpose was closely connected with family and reproduction.

This view has been held throughout the history of Christianity. Luther in his *Large Catechism* saw Paul's arguments in Romans 1:18-27 as a punishment as well as a sign of idolatrous religion. He did not negate law by reference to grace as do some today. He spoke of the Ten Commandments as not trifles of men but the commandments of the most high God. His sexual ethic included avoidance of "every form of unchastity" and helping one's neighbor do the same. The basic view of Christianity from the first century until about 1950 is that homosexual sex is against God's purpose. And even since 1950, those who go toward a contrary view have been in the decided minority. They have been influenced greatly by humanistic philosophy and liberal theology and have rejected the Bible as God's fully inspired message to us. Such a view should be rejected.

I support these conclusions regarding homosexuality from a biblical and psychological point of view:

1. God created sexuality.

2. God's word places the expression of human sexuality within marriage and connects it closely with reproduction and the prevention of fornication.

3. Sex outside of marriage is condemned.

4. Homosexuality is abnormal and in opposition to God's will.

5. The church should make a distinction between homosexual orientation and homosexual action—Christians must, by the help of God, control their inclinations toward undesirable actions.

6. Homosexuals can, by the help of God and perhaps well-prepared professional counselors, learn to control their behavior.

7. We need to rely heavily upon God, his Spirit, Christ and his word.

8. We should be kind and compassionate to all people.

So, you can see why I am not for homosexual marriages. It's abnormal. It is contrary to the Christian religion which I hold. It's wrong!

IMPROVING FAMILY LOVE

When I speak of love as a principle in building better homes, I speak of much more than sex. I speak of caring, sacrifice, unselfishness, friendship, companionship, romance, a demonstration of affection, intimacy, and passion. I speak of a willingness to share feelings, thoughts, and beliefs. Of flexibility, responsibility. Of acceptance and a sense of permanence. I speak of trust and dependability. Of willingness to see things from a new perspective, to look at things from different angles. Of the willingness to negotiate, to share positive emotions and the abundant life (John 10:10). I speak of self-respect and self-esteem. Belongingness. Success. Control over your own life. Empowerment, and the ability to handle anger. Communication, good times, fun. Realistic expectations, collaboration, and conflict resolution. Closeness, self-disclosure, partnership, and compromise. Enjoyable lovemaking, and compatibility. Autonomy, expressiveness, and togetherness! All of these are needed for a good description of a loving family, a family that has learned to **love and be loved.**

Sex belongs only in marriage. Caring, friendship, good self-esteem and most of the other aspects of love apply to the whole family. Parents love their children. Children love their parents. Grandparents share in the love, friendship, and concern for everyone in a healthy family. One of the last things I do before I go to sleep each night is to pray for my wife, our children and grandchildren, and our parents. I mention each of them by name. I want what is best for them with all of my heart!

Spiritual development, health, protection, prosperity, and a place of service and usefulness. Love. Caring. Closeness. Family. That's what love is all about.

I remember one husband, James Mitchell, age 30, who made a very enlightening remark in a marital counseling session one day. His wife, Jean, said she loved him but she also was extremely possessive of him. He said she was extremely jealous, yelled and threw things at him; and was almost never pleasant to be around. No fun to be with. She spoke of their two children as "hers," never as "theirs." She "cut him down" in front of the children and took the children's side when he tried to correct them. At night, she usually had a headache or was tired, turned her back to him and went to sleep. All the while she told him that she loved him. I believe she did in her own way. She just had lots of emotional problems. His response to her expression of love for him was, "You have a strange way of showing it!" You see, she didn't **show** that she loved him by the way she acted. And that's what counts most! How could she act much worse toward him if she **didn't** love him?

If you have sexual problems in marriage, begin by working on your relationship. Sex is an extension of a relationship in marriage. It's difficult for sex to be **good** if the relationship is **bad,** more so for women than for men. Most women need closeness, intimacy, consideration, affection, responsiveness, a sharing of deep feelings, and romance for sex to be enjoyable. Men need a **place.** Well, maybe that's an exaggeration, but it makes a point that is generally true. Relationship and sex go together like a horse and carriage for most women and for many men as well. It's hard for a man to approach his wife for sex after she has criticized him all day long. Criticism in front of others is especially hurtful. Criticism of how he performs sexually is even more devastating. You see, most men think that they are great lovers. Be gentle as you tell them otherwise. Something like this might work: "I like it when you do this but not when you do that. I really love you and enjoy being with you." Be careful. Male egos are sometimes fragile.

If your husband has an erectile failure, be sure not to criticize him for it. It's not intentional. It's not **your** fault. It's not **his** fault. It just happens at times, especially after age 40.

How to handle it? Hug him. Tell him it's okay. Be gentle and understanding. You see, he may think he is not a man anymore. Not so! This has nothing to do with being a man. It's very common. It's just something that happens.

Bill and Lorene were in their 60's. They had not had sex in four years. He could not maintain an erection. They would try to make love. He would **get** an erection; then it would subside. She would get "all excited" and then be "left hanging." This happened over and over again. She would criticize him rather severely: "What kind of a man are you? You don't love me anymore! You're over the hill!" Ouch! This, though perhaps understandable, caused **performance anxiety** and made the problem worse. Just being around her caused tension for him. On days when he thought she would initiate sex, he began to wonder how he would do. His self-talk was all negative. "I'll bet the same thing will happen again. If I were really a man, I could satisfy my wife. I'll try harder." All of this created more tension and his performance got worse. After a while, he had self-esteem problems and quit trying.

They went to medical doctors for physical examinations, but they found no medical problem. They said it was probably performance anxiety. It was. And, believe it or not, they began performing well after only a few sessions. I kept telling them that nobody was "at fault," that it was a relationship problem, quite understandable under the circumstances. He was **still a man,** very concerned about his wife and his problem. He was really worried about himself and certainly not doing this on purpose. She was a **normal woman.** Frustrated, but meant well. When they began to **reframe** their behavior along more positive lines, their sex life flourished. Really! One week they told me he had had another failure. I had told them to expect this. When I asked how often they were having sex, they said, "About three or four times a week." Wow! My reply, "What do you expect? It would be hard for a couple in their twenties to keep such a pace." I told them that once every two weeks would be great! Don't put so much pressure on people! It may cause performance anxiety. They soon leveled out to a "normal" schedule of every 12 days or so, and are still doing well after several years. I guess they had some catching up to do. Then, they could proceed on a more realistic schedule.

I'm sure you can see **their** problem. But you may not be able to see yours. **How** can **you** tell when **you** are headed toward relationship problems? Here are some important questions to help you:

1. Do you find it hard to spend time with each other?
2. Are you addicted to food, work, or drugs?
3. Do you focus on your children to the neglect of each other?
4. Do you find it boring to listen to each other?
5. Are you overweight?
6. Have you unintentionally lost more than 10 pounds lately?
7. Do you neglect personal hygiene?
8. Do you criticize each other?
9. Do you neglect your appearance?
10. Do you dread going home or seeing your mate come home?
11. Do you find it hard to express your feelings to each other?
12. Do you seldom compliment each other?
13. Are you unwilling to compromise?
14. Do you fantasize about some other person while you are having sex with your spouse?
15. Do you constantly desire more space for yourself?
16. Do you avoid affection? Romance? Sex?
17. Do you hold grudges? Find it hard to forgive?
18. Do you find yourself either pursuing or closing off from you mate?
19. Do you dislike your mate?
20. Do you still care for your mate?

GROWTH EXERCISES

1. Ask your spouse if you are a closed or an open person.
2. Discuss what you need to do to improve.
3. Do you **give** love?
4. Are you able to **receive** love? Discuss these questions with each other.
5. Tell your mate what he/she does to "make love all the time" with you, different ways he/she **shows** love.
6. Tell your mate how you would like him/her to show their love to you.
7. Tell each other what you will do in the future to show your love.
8. Discuss as a couple how you can show affection to your parents and children. Children, ask yourselves how you can show love to your parents.
9. Discuss how you can create an atmosphere of love in your home.
10. Tell each member of your family what you appreciate them for.

Six

A Healthy Family Structure

Principle Number 6:
A healthy family structure will help develop healthy
individuals within that structure.

A healthy family structure is essential to the building of healthy families. One-parent families, two-parent families, blended families, and other family forms all have structure whether healthy, unhealthy or in-between.

Structure has to do with organization, function, and boundaries. Some structures have been found to be more healthy, more functional than others. I want to discuss what I have learned about both healthy and unhealthy family structures from the Bible, other family therapists, and my own experiences.

BIBLICAL TEACHINGS

The first couple, Adam and Eve, are mentioned in Genesis 1 and 2. Adam was made first and then Eve, designed to be his partner. Both were made by our Father in heaven. Eve was to be his partner. Help-meet or partner does not indicate inferiority. Both were set apart as distinct from all other forms of life God had created, and they were to rule over them. They are on the same level. They would find companionship in each other. She was bone of his bone and flesh of his flesh, taken out of man. They bonded together to form the first family. They were united, and became one flesh.

103

Their sin in the garden of Eden is recorded in Genesis 3. They ate of the forbidden fruit: first Eve, then Adam. Because of their sin, God said that he would increase her pains in childbearing, her desire would be to her husband, and he would **rule** over her. She would submit her desires to her husband, and he would rule over her. Certain conditions that existed previous to sin would be worse. Adam's specific punishment was **increased** toil for food. He would have to work especially hard for food: Wrestle with thorns and thistles and eat of the plants of the ground. And he would return to dust and die. Adam and Eve became the "parents" of us all. They knew good and evil. The relationship of Adam and Eve before their sin seemed to be mutual and complementary, a relationship of love, respect, and partnership, not a relationship where one dictates to the other. But their sin brought punishment. Their marital relationship would be changed. Eve had not discharged her responsibilities as a helpmeet and was put under the "control" of her husband because of it. She gave him the forbidden fruit and encouraged him to eat it.

There is no indication here that would suggest a harsh and authoritarian abuse by her husband. Surely she was not to be his possession or slave, common in the ancient Near East. Sounds strange to us, but it's like God is protecting the woman from herself, which brings up the question to our minds: Who is going to protect the man from himself? He was an adult. He did not have to eat of the forbidden fruit. She didn't **make** him do it. He has to take responsibility for his own actions.

Let's take a look next at I Corinthians 11:3 NIV:

> Now I want you to realize that the head of every man is Christ, and the head of the woman is man, and the head of Christ is God.

There are two lines of interpretation on this verse. One is that "head" *(kephale)* means "source." Thus, God is the source of Christ (since he was made wisdom by God, I Corinthians 1:30), Christ is the source of man since he was the agent in creation (Colossians 1:15-20, I Corinthians 8:6), and man is the source of woman (since she was taken out of man, Genesis 2:13-24). The tension spot in this view is that God is not really the source of Christ since Christ is described by John as eternal. He was in the beginning with God (John 1:1-14).

The other interpretation is that "head" means "authority over." This goes against the grain with us today. We don't like to think of a chain of command that puts man over woman. That seems to have caused so many problems. Man has so often been arbitrary and domineering in this family role. You decide. But, before you do, read further.

Let's look now at I Timothy 2:11-15:

> A woman should learn in quietness and full submission. I do not permit a woman to teach or to have authority over a man; she must be silent. For Adam was formed first, then Eve. And Adam was not the one deceived; it was the woman who was deceived and became a sinner. But women will be kept safe throughout childbirth, if they continue in faith, love and holiness with propriety.

This passage is not any easier, is it? Let's try though. The woman is not to create confusion by insubordinate conduct toward men who are charged to lead. The reason Paul gives for this doctrine is that Adam was formed first, and Adam was not the one deceived. It was the woman who was deceived and became a sinner. Paul surely is not saying that Adam was not as great a sinner as Eve. He acknowledges Adam's sin in Romans 5. He may be emphasizing the tempter's subtle nature and Eve's vulnerability to the temptation of the serpent. Her salvation was not in spiritual leadership or in being the master of men but in submission to sound doctrine, "faithful, no slanderers, but temperate, faithful in all things" (I Timothy 3:11). She had a special place of service and authority in the home. She would be saved in this context. "Bearing children" means more than giving birth to children. It implies the raising of children. She is to love her husband and her children (I Timothy 5:14; Titus 2:4,5). Both she and her husband are to be concerned about pleasing each other (I Corinthians 7:32-35).

Another text that seems strange to us is I Peter 3:1-7 NIV:

> Wives, in the same way be submissive to your husbands so that, if any of them do not believe the word,

they may be won over without talk by the behavior of their wives, when they see the purity and reverence of your lives. Your beauty should not come from outward adornment, such as braided hair and the wearing of gold jewelry and fine clothes. Instead, it should be that of your inner self, the unfading beauty of a gentle and quiet spirit, which is of great worth in God's sight. For this is the way the holy women of the past who put their hope in God used to make themselves beautiful. They were submissive to their own husbands, like Sarah, who obeyed Abraham and called him her master. You are her daughters if you do what is right and do not give way to fear.

Husbands, in the same way be considerate as you live with your wives, and treat them with respect as the weaker partner and as heirs with you of the precious gift of life, so that nothing will hinder your prayers.

This message may seem unfair to you if you are a woman. Just grapple with it and see if you can get the entire picture. Men need to grapple too because there is a message also for them!

What is Peter saying? Just as Christians are to submit to governmental authorities and slaves to masters, wives were to submit to their husbands whether they were Christians or not. Obviously there are some limitations on such submissions. Wife abuse is never justified!

The wife is to be beautiful inside: gentle, quiet, mild, in control of her temper, not harsh and disrespectful. She is to be concerned about these inner qualities of personality rather than the outward flaunting of expensive jewelry and clothing along with outlandish hairdos. Such is not important and shows the wrong spirit. She respects her husband and shows him what being a Christian is all about. He may even become a Christian because of her way of life!

Notice this: However you interpret these verses, they do not justify mistreatment of wives by husbands! Wives **can't** control husbands! They **can** control themselves. Thus, they are to be kind and gentle. Not provoke their husband. He's bigger than they are. Be kind, Peter says. It's the right thing to do. Show everyone how to live the Christian life in your difficult situation.

Rather than being told to be dictators who always have to have their way about everything, husbands are told to give loving protection to their wives. Wives are physically, not mentally, weaker. Be considerate. **Her** feelings are important. Treat your wife with respect. She is an important individual in her own right. She is not your property. You don't own her. She has ideas and values of her own. Respect them. You are on the same level before God. Joint heirs of the gracious gift of the abundant life in Christ. There is neither male nor female in Christ (Galatians 3:26-30). We are all one in him. So, don't get puffed up about your position. A servant leader in Christ is not a one-upmanship type position. If you are not considerate of your wife, if you do not show her proper respect, your prayers will be hindered. You'll have difficulty praying together as a couple, and your prayers won't get any higher than the ceiling!

Ephesians 5:21-25 is probably the best-known passage in the New Testament about the husband-wife structure. Here's what Paul says:

> Submit to one another out of reverence for Christ.
> Wives, submit to your husbands as to the Lord. For the husband is the head of the wife as Christ is the head of the church, his body, of which he is the Savior. Now as the church submits to Christ, so also wives should submit to their husbands in everything.
> Husbands, love you wives, just as Christ loved the church and gave himself up for her.

Verse 33 says, "However, each of you must also love his wife as he loves himself, and the wife must respect her husband."

There is a question about whether verse 21 goes with verse 22, is a separate paragraph, or is part of the previous paragraph. Generally, it has been thought to go with the previous paragraph. All Christians are to submit to each other out of reverence for Christ. After all, Christ is supposed to be living in them (Galatians 2:20). The least I can say here is that husbands are to submit to their wives as they would submit to other Christians. The most I could say is that submission in marriage is mutual, equal. We observe though that wives are specifically instructed to submit to their husbands as though they were doing it for the Lord, as a Christian duty. In everything. Strong language! Doesn't that set the stage for male cruelty? In a way, but that's not what Paul wanted. He wanted husbands to love their wives as Christ loved the church and as they loved their own bodies! That kind of unselfish caring is not a set-up for abuse. Such love is patient, kind, does not boast, is not proud, is not rude, is not self-seeking! Not easily angered. Always protects, always trusts, always hopes, always perseveres! Remember this passage in I Corinthians 13?

What shall we say to all of this? I believe that the husband and wife are both in the executive branch of a healthy Christian home. They love each other, respect each other, are polite and considerate of each other. What about submission? I believe there are times when I need to submit to Louise. I hate to say this, but I'm not always right. It's hard to apologize and give in, but we as husbands need to do that at times. We all have the same master in heaven. There are times, perhaps too often, when Louise gives in to me.

I believe the husband has a certain leadership role to take in the home. Paul calls him the head of the family. He leads. He provides. He protects. His unique role seems to be that of a spiritual leader in the family. Yet, his wife is also a leader in the executive branch of the home. She is in charge of some aspects of home life. Together, they establish policies for the home. Both carry out those policies. When they disagree, they talk it out and hopefully reach a concensus. If they can't, there has to be some way to make necessary decisions. Perhaps this is where the husband makes the final decision, but he does not do it in a selfish way. Often he will decide to go **against his wishes** and do what his **wife prefers.** Servant, loving, leadership! Considerate. Not self-centered.

I want you to know that I had difficulty writing that last paragraph. Why? Because I have seen in my counseling practice so many men abuse their wives! I am afraid they will misuse what I have said! Please don't, men. Look at Jesus as your model. Unselfish, gracious, intimate empowering love. Love that does not misuse others for our own advantage.

I am also aware of the spirit of our age. Some wives hate men and will not submit in any way to them. If you are such a woman, I think I understand your attitude. You've been mistreated by men and are afraid of getting too close to them. I don't blame you. I'd be careful too! I've seen men almost totally destroy women. Even their personalities were disintegrating! **I know** that **it is not God's will** for women to be treated **this** way! But, let me say to men-hating women that there is no gain without risk. There is no real intimacy without some submission. There is no togetherness without a sacrifice of some individuality. Be cautious, but try.

Now, to complete the family structure, we must look at the in-laws and the children. The man is to **leave** father and mother and to **cleave** to his wife (Genesis 2:24). To leave does not mean to completely cut off one's roots. That's unhealthy. Emotionally immature. Like, I'll never speak to them again. Never visit them. Such action is not advised. **To leave** today means to **grow away from** your parents and in-laws. To grow up. To be a separate family unit with new boundaries. Distinct lines between the generations! You can ask them for advice if you wish; then make up your own minds. Parents can share ideas when appropriate but should not expect their married children to feel obligated to do what they advise.

A minister-professor friend of mine once shared this story with me. When his daughter was about to get married, he took his future son-in-law for a little walk and said to him: "You're about to marry my daughter. She is very precious to me. I expect you to treat her right. I may have something to say at times to you, and I expect you to show me enough respect to listen to me. But, after you listen, I expect you to do what you think is best." Not bad, huh?

A couple can show immaturity by not listening. Too threatened to do so. They are not sure of their boundaries yet. They can refuse to visit, not have anything to do with their parents or in-laws, and cut off emotionally. But, remember, that's a sign of emotional immaturity. Agreed, there my be times when you need to distance yourself, but that's not the same as an emotional cut-off which I would call a neurotic reaction. "He's mine now, not yours." Childish! Such a person needs to mature emotionally, to grow up.

Let me mention two other scriptures to complete our survey of biblical material on family structure.

Colossians 3:20-21:

> Children, obey your parents in everything, for this pleases the Lord.
>
> Fathers, do not embitter your children, or they will become discouraged.

Ephesians 6:1-4:

> Children, obey your parents in the Lord, for this is right. Honor your father and mother—which is the first commandment with a promise—that it may go well with you and that you may enjoy long life on the earth.
>
> Fathers, do not exasperate your children; instead, bring them up in the training and instruction of the Lord.

Honor and obey. Parents are the adults; children are simply children. They should listen to their parents.

Parents, don't be harsh. Be gentle but firm. Train them. Continue to bring them up to respect and obey you. Let God's word guide you. Teach your children over and over again. Be patient. Show them the way to live a good life. Encourage them. This "pleases the Lord." He knows the value of a healthy family structure that functions well.

MARRIAGE AND FAMILY THERAPY MATERIAL

Thus far, I have given a brief survey of biblical material on family structure. However we interpret this material, we have all probably been influenced by it as well as various twisted distortions of it. I'm not the Pope. Make up your own mind about it. What the Bible says about family structure has helped me, I think, to be a better family man. It's hard to imagine how ineffective I would be otherwise. I hope it can help you too.

In addition to this biblical material, I want to share with you some of what I have learned about family structure as a marriage and family therapist. This body of material is also very helpful to me.

Salvador Minuchin is the family therapist leader who has had the most profound influence on family structure and its importance to a healthy family. If the structure is healthy and functional, persons within that structure will tend to become healthy and functional. If dysfunctional, disfunctional. If sick, sick. Structure influences individuals within the structure.

There are several key words to understand in family therapy:

1. Structure: the manner of family organization.
2. Unit: an individual within the family system.
3. Family systems: the manner in which family units interact. Interdependence. The family context.
4. Sub-system: a part of the family system such as children or parents.
5. Feedback: self-correcting behavior of the system. She does this, he does that, then he does something else. . .
6. Communication: All behavior is considered communication. Communication defines relationships and establishes roles in the family system through the setting of rules. One cannot not behave. One cannot not communicate. Communication can be used to change family structure.
7. Stability and change: Feedback loops promote both stability and change as families accommodate to new input and thus become self-regulating. They establish self-perpetuating patterns which are hard, though not impossible, to break.
8. Process: movement or function.
9. Enmeshed: Too close, fused.
10. Disengaged: Too distant, disconnected. Both extremes are to be avoided.
11. Parentification: Parents train one child, usually the oldest, to be a parent substitute. Not usually healthy.
12. Scapegoating: Parents "make" one child guilty for all bad behavior in the family. Not healthy.
13. Nuclear family: Your immediate family, parents and children.

14. Boundary: An imaginary line, wall, or fence around your immediate family that separates your family from all others. There should be reasonable boundaries between the generations of a nuclear family and between a nuclear family and the extended family.

15. Inclusion: Those to be included in the boundaries. Some are in, others out.

16. Extrusion: What is being extended from the marriage and to whom. A wife may intrude into her sister's marriage, for example. It's not healthy!

17. Intrusion: Someone outside the marriage may intrude into the marriage. Illustrations are many: another man or woman, a job, or a parent.

18. Alliances: Special pairing and support systems within the family. For example, the mother and children may form an alliance against the father.

Lots of words, right? Right! And some of them may be difficult to understand. Let me highlight just a few to help you.

Boundaries. Unhealthy families have unhealthy boundaries. Either too diffuse (open) or too closed (too high and too wide with not enough doors and windows). An incest family is usually too closed. Boundaries are high and wide, almost like a wall between the family and the community. Lots of secrets to protect! The boundaries of extremely gregarious, community-minded, helpful people are often too open. Hard to tell where the family ends and the community begins. People are in and out of the house all of the time. Can cause feelings of overexposure, insecurity.

Enmeshment-Disengagement. Either extreme is unhealthy. Immature couples are likely to become enmeshed, fused. They would look somewhat like this:

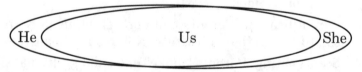

Such couples often feel in conflict with each other. They need space. There's too much togetherness, and not enough individuality.

112

Disengaged couples look like this:

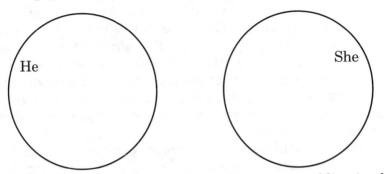

They don't touch bases much at all. Just sort of live in the same house. They need to work on **knowing** each other. Friendship. Overlap their lives more and give up some individuality for the sake of more togetherness.

Healthy couples overlap significantly but still have room to be themselves. They do not become submerged into one another completely. In a sense they become one; yet in a sense they are still two. The trick is to learn how to be united in purpose, in heart, and still allow each other the right to be an individual, with unique tastes, values, thoughts, feelings, and actions. A more healthy model might look somewhat like this:

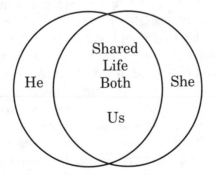

Intrusion and Extrusion. When there is too much of either, the family becomes dysfunctional. Don't let people intrude into your nuclear family too much no matter who they are: Grandparents, parents, uncles, aunts, friends, children, or others. Most decisions are matters for you to settle. Don't extrude into other people's business: parents, friends, or others. Be careful about giving advice unless it is requested.

Generational lines. There are different generations in a family: Grandparents, parents, and children. Keep a clear-cut line between each generation. Otherwise, individuals will get twisted and become dysfunctional, unhealthy. Grandparents should stay on their level, parents on theirs, and children on theirs. Otherwise grandmothers may control mothers, and children may control parents.

Unhealthy Alliances. The primary bond in a nuclear family should be between the husband and wife. It brought the family together, and it can keep it together. When that becomes weakened and other alliances become stronger, it is usually unhealthy and dysfunctional. A common unhealthy alliance is a wife and her mother against the husband. In such a case, the wife should spend more time with her husband and less with her mother. She should let her mother know that she loves her, but that her husband and new home are very important to her. Wife, don't let your mother come between you and your husband. In fact, it may not be your mother's problem. It may be yours. You may be clinging to your mother. Cut the umbilical cord. Grow up. Then, you can have an even better adult relationship with both your mother and your husband.

Step-families usually have unique problems with family structure. His children. Her children. His ex. Her ex. Some children live in the household, some don't. The bond between the husband and wife has to be strong and continually cultivated to keep unhealthy alliances from forming between parents, children, and ex-spouses, and to keep these from ruining the marriage. It's difficult for the most mature couples. As a rule of thumb, I advise the natural parent in blended families to do the rule-setting and enforcement if the child is 10 years old or older. The step-parent should be supportive of the parent. She or he administers these policies (rules, guidelines) when the natural parent is not present. If the children are under 10, many parents and step-parents have been able to establish a fairly effective, almost traditional, two-parent family. In such cases, children and step-parents **learn** to love and respect each other.

SUMMARY

Let me see if I can pull it all together on family structure. I'll try by illustrating a few different family structures I have discussed.

A Dictator Family Structure

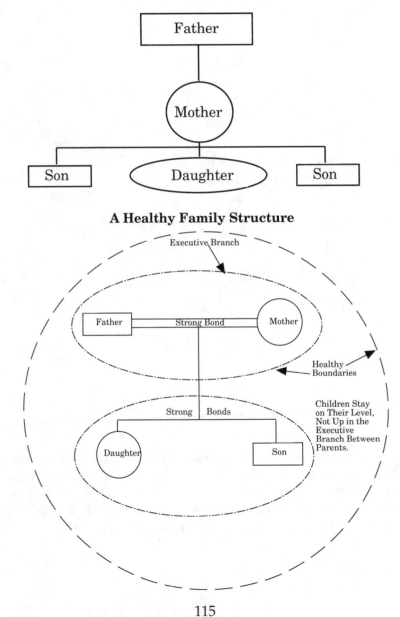

A Healthy Family Structure

An Unhealthy Step-Family

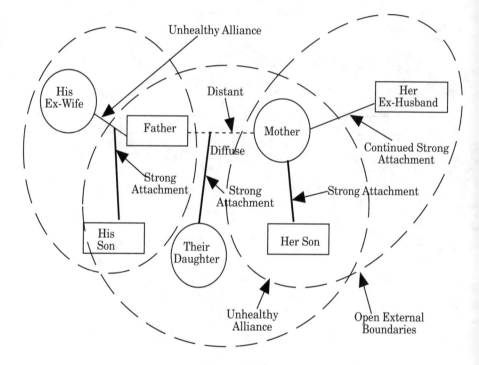

I'll let you guess at their typical problems. To give you a start: Mother is still seeing her ex-husband, mother and son side against father and his son, father is justifiably jealous of wife's ex-husband, their daughter is resented by both his son and her son. She feels that she needs more space, more privacy.

A Healthy Extended Family

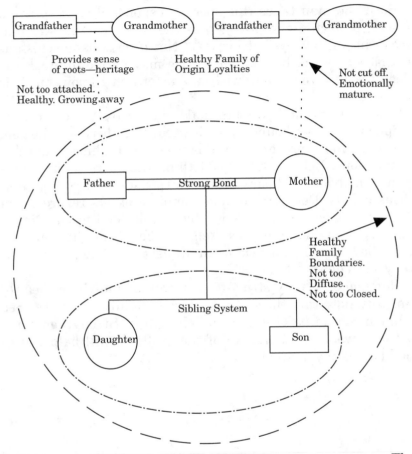

In summary, I think we need to guard against extremes. The man is a dictator; the woman rules the roost. I believe that if both husband and wife did what they ought to do that each would be heard, that many decisions would be made by each, and that most other decisions would be made through consensus. In a good marriage, I don't think the idea of pulling rank comes up often. Power plays are unnecessary.

Balswick and Balswick say in their book on the family that research shows that a family works best when either the husband or wife has a **little** more power than the other but **not**

much more! If they have the same power, deadlocks can't be broken. If one has most of the power, he/she steps on the other. Makes sense to me.

So if the man takes this special responsibility of spiritual leader, protector, and provider, as the Bible teaches, will that mean he will always get his way? Not if he is as unselfish as Christ was when he died for us! He may decide to break the deadlock in favor of **her** wishes. Far-fetched I know, but it is possible.

The main point I want to make on family structure is to emphasize proper boundaries, clear-cut lines between the generations, and a proper balance between enmeshment and disconnections. Believe it or not, I think that personality determines the balance of power between spouses more so than religious beliefs. Dominant people dominate others regardless of sex. Intelligent and knowledgeable people tend to have influence. And on and on it goes. Religious beliefs are just one factor. They should influence us in all aspects of family life, but they often don't.

Remember, family structure determines individual health. So, why not start there. Look at your family structure. See what needs to be changed and change it. Strengthen some actions, weaken others. All of these efforts will help you to build a healthy family.

A GROWTH EXERCISE ON MARITAL ROLES

Please circle True or False and Then Discuss with Each Other.

T F   1. The husband is the head of the wife.

T F   2. The wife is the head of the husband.

T F   3. The husband should make all of the decisions.

T F   4. The wife should make all of the decisions.

T F   5. Most major decisions should emerge from a consensus.

T F   6. Leadership should be shared.

T F   7. The husband and wife should discuss all major purchases before they are made.

T F   8. All major decisions should be made jointly.

T F   9. The husband's job should be given more consideration than the wife's job.

T F 10. The wife's job should take precedence.

T F 11. Decisions in a family should be made democratically—one person, one vote.

T F 12. The man is the primary bread-winner in the family.

T F 13. The woman's role is primarily in the home.

T F 14. Both parents should be involved in the discipline of the children.

T F 15. Parents should spank children at times.

T F 16. In a single-parent family brought on by divorce, the parent with custody should never consult the other parent about parenting policies.

T F 17. A couple should consult their parents before all major decisions.

T F 18. The mother should be a mediator between the father and their children.

Seven

Effective Parenting

Principle Number 7:
Effective parenting empowers children to
be all that they can be.

"Train up a child in the way he should go, and when he is old, he will not depart from it" (Proverbs 22:6 KJV). I've heard this verse of scripture all of my life. I've heard hundreds of parents blame themselves for what their children did even after they had left home because of what they thought this verse teaches. Many such parents needlessly whip themselves with guilt for actions of their children that they could not help. They did not teach their children to behave inappropriately; they taught them just the opposite of what they are doing, but they think their children's behavior is still their fault. And, they say, it's all because of this verse of scripture. Their interpretation of it. It's like children are **robots** to be controlled, **plastic** to be molded. They are passive; parents are all powerful molders. The **child has no choice** but to do what the parents want. Not so.

The childrearing process is more of an **interaction** kind of thing. Parents are very influential in the process but not almighty. Children are different. Wired up differently. Born that way. Not just molded but developed via an interaction process between themselves, their parents, and others. Interactive from birth. About 10 percent of all babies are born sad, another 10 percent happy and pleasant. Others are various degrees of in-between. They act and respond differently to parents and others and thus affect the interaction process. As

121

they grow older, they make more choices. Not just molded. Developing. Being influenced, not controlled. They have a choice. I agree with Ann Landers when she says that blaming parents for every bad behavior from shiftlessness to drug abuse, crime, and promiscuousness is a cop-out! A way to avoid responsibility! It's not set in concrete. You can grow out of it!

If this is true, does it rule out the importance of parenting? By no means. It underscores its importance. Parents are the **primary influence** in a child's life. They can give the child **a good chance** to live a good, productive, happy life. Proverbs 22:6 is a general principle that is true. Children tend to go in the direction of their training. Not always, but usually. It's similar to a general principle taught in Proverbs 12:21: "There shall no mischief happen to the righteous; But the wicked shall be filled with evil" ASV. Always? No. Usually? Yes. Or Proverbs 14:11: "The house of the wicked shall be overthrown; But the tent of the upright shall flourish." Always? No. Usually? Yes. It's the nature of proverbs. General truths. And they are very valid. Usually children go in the way they are trained, and parents are their primary trainers. Take your charge very seriously. Do what you believe is best.

I was hesitant for many years to speak on parenting. I was a parent, and I knew my own limitations and shortcomings as a parent. I made mistakes. I sometimes got my feelings hurt, and it affected my parenting behavior. But I had a lot of good help from Louise. We had good children. Not perfect, but good, and we somehow with God's help got through it all. They seem to be functioning well as adults. Now, I know that I don't know it all, but I believe I have learned some facts and skills that can help you as parents. A lot of what I know comes from the Bible. Some from personal experience. Some from my counseling experience with families in distress.

Let's look at the Bible then for some direction. Deuteronomy 6-10 describes **Israel's relationship with God,** their spiritual Father in heaven. **How he interacted with them** in their journey from bondage in Egypt to the Promised Land becomes **our model** for effective parenting. This model is not a perfect analogy but nevertheless a helpful one. Some principles of parenting are revealed to us in this model.

Like what?

1. **Teach** your children. God teaches his children. We teach ours. Israel was given commands, decrees, and laws to observe in the land beyond the Jordan River so that they, their children and grandchildren might fear the Lord their God and keep his commands as long as they lived. It would help them also to enjoy long life (Deuteronomy 6:1-2 NIV). Such results would require **continual** teaching. They were to love God with all of their heart, soul, and strength. God's commands were to be on their hearts. They were to impress them upon their children, talk about them when they sat at home, when they walked along the road, when they went to bed, and when they got up in the morning. They were to tie them as symbols on their hands, bind them on their foreheads, and write them on the doorframes of their houses and on their gates (Deuteronomy 6:4-9). Teach continually. Teach as you have opportunity throughout the day. Look for opportunities to teach. The magic moment. Teach them what they need to know. Use your voice. Use visual aids.

Let me share some personal illustrations with you. The television is on. You can't switch it every time a commercial entices your child to drink beer or go to bed with someone else's wife. So, use the moment to teach, to correct what is being taught on the tube or by some other means. No, they don't tell about disgusting black stuff on your lungs when they talk about cigarettes. They don't mention illness or early death for yourself and others who breathe your smoke. They don't tell about the damage it causes unborn children or the breathing problems it causes. Tell them! They don't tell the whole story about alcohol. How that it can cause wrecks, crime, family abuse, and brain damage. Tell them! Tell them the damage it does to your liver and other parts of your body. Tell them that the abuse of alcohol is one of our greatest problems. Tell them how it is impossible to serve God and be enslaved to alcohol at the same time. Tell them about unwanted babies, abortions, venereal diseases, AIDS, genital warts, herpes and other diseases that can be transmitted by sexual intercourse. Tell them about all of the heartache in families that sexual promiscuousness can cause. Tell them at the appropriate moment all of this, and also be sure to tell them about the rewards of living a healthy lifestyle. Of the beauty and fun of sex in marriage. No, it's not wrong to let them know this! God is not against our having fun. He just regulates it so that it may go well with us, that we might live good lives ourselves, and teach our children to follow us. They probably will anyway.

Recently I was in our backyard with Kevin, our three-year-old grandson. He pointed up to a beautiful full moon in the sky and said, "Look, Pa Pa." I said, "That's the moon. God put that up there." He said, "No. Jesus did." I said, "Yes, I think he did help. God and Jesus sort of did it together. They did a good job, didn't they?" Kevin replied, "Yes." Well, that was an opportune teaching moment as we walked along the yard. Reminds me of what a good friend of ours, Mildred Christmas, told me once about our son Steve. He was in her Bible class. She told them that God put the moon up in the sky. Steve replied, "No, Daddy did." He had me overrated, and I'm glad Mildred explained it to him. Teaching moments. Teach while the iron is hot. Teach continually.

We especially need to teach our children to take personal responsibility for their actions. They are **responsible** for what they do. **Not** someone else. Start this early. Hold them responsible for **their** behavior. **Talk** to them. Don't let them excuse themselves by blaming someone else for what **they** did. God gave his children responsibilities. He told them to break down the altars to false gods they found, cut down the Asherah poles, and burn their idols. Only he was to be served (Deuteronomy 7:5).

To be an effective parent, you will need to confront your children at times. God confronted Israel, told them that they had been rebellious against him ever since he had known them. He told them to circumcise their hearts and not be stiffnecked (Deuteronomy 9:24; 10:16). Confrontation of children is not always pleasant. It's especially hard as they get older. But you need to do it at times, even at the risk of "making it worse." They often need to hear what you have to say. They sometimes need to be corrected. With firmness and gentleness, but still corrected.

2. You need to **lead** your children. God led Israel out of bondage and into the land he promised Abraham, Isaac, and

Jacob to give them—a land with large flourishing cities they did not build (Deuteronomy 6:10). It was God who went across the Jordan ahead of them like a devouring fire. He drove out and subdued their enemies ahead of them. Then, he told them to drive them out of the land, to finish the job he had begun (Deuteronomy 9:3). He was their leader.

In scripture, a man named Lot is presented as a bad leader. In his one big opportune moment he was given a choice by Abraham, and he goofed. He chose to take his family and live in a wicked city. Many bad experiences followed: drunkenness, incest, children by his own daughters, destruction of the city along with his family who wanted to stay there in spite of warnings from an angel that the city was going to be destroyed (Genesis 13, 19). Lot was not totally responsible for his family's sad plight, but he did not lead them in a wholesome direction. I imagine many other bad choices were made by them as well. One bad choice often leads to another.

My point on leadership is this. Don't act like a child. Lead! **You** are the **adult; they** are the **children**. Don't get down on their level and fuss with them. Lead them. Take charge. If the television needs to be turned off, see that it gets turned off. Unplug it and lock it up if that is what it takes to get the job done. It's your house. Just do what needs to be done.

Lead them in the formation of their **values.** They usually value what you value. Here's a vivid illustration. Rachael Cooper, age 5, begged us to let her go with us to conduct Bible studies. Unusual, right? But she was the daughter of Dan and Kathryn Cooper who were also involved in such work. My brothers, Leamon, Don, Dowell, and I, were in a campaign for Christ in their community in Vineland, New Jersey. **We** were going. **She** wanted to go.

Lead your children in the formation of ideas about **romance and sex.** It's not just a no-no, you see. Many yes-yeses too! Positives as well as negatives. **No,** outside of marriage. **Yes,** inside. Model affection for the children. Hug your spouse. Give him/her a little kiss in front of the children. Explain love to them with all of its aspects and responsibilities. Children find out what it means to be a man and a woman from parents. Older women were told by Paul to train the younger women to love their husbands and to love their wives (Ephesians 5:25). This is a starting point for teaching children about romance and love.

I have probably counseled more than 100 homosexuals over the years. Most of them were from Christian homes. Most thought that homosexual sex was wrong and wanted to go straight. Several were from homes of ministers and other church leaders. Many have told me that they were taught not to touch a person of the opposite sex before marriage but were not told anything about the same sex. They knew all of the heterosexual no-nos, little or nothing about homosexuality, and nothing about the positive side of heterosexuality in marriage. They felt guilty hugging or kissing a person of the opposite sex, but did not feel guilty having oral or anal sex with a person of the same sex. Often such parents keep their children away from the opposite sex, even encourage the church to separate boys and girls if they talk about sex. It's a dirty subject. They often discourage dating. No wonder their children get confused. I know that the development of one's sexual orientation is not that simple, but I can also see that we often do not come to terms with our own sexuality and often lead our children in similar and other mixed-up directions.

Lead your children in the development of their attitude toward **others.** Children are aware of how we treat others: the mailman, waitresses, teachers, coaches, janitors, police officers, ministers, and others. They often **catch** our attitude. Jesus would have us do unto others as we would have them do unto us (Matthew 7:12). Good principle. Healthy for you, your children, and others.

Lead your children in the formation of their attitude toward **God and the church**. Show them that your faith is important to you every day: in crises, at other times. Show them that **you** are genuine. Don't just put on a show. Don't criticize the church and its leaders in front of your children. Express appreciation and love. Paul encouraged love out of a pure heart and a good conscience and a genuine faith (I Timothy 1:5). Real people. Solid. People with integrity. People of a good conscience. Strong faith.

Lead your children toward effective **interaction skills** with others. You can't make them learn such skills. Their personalities are a vital part of the process, but you may be able to **help** them in the process. **Interact** with them. **Play with** them. **Work** with them. **Communicate** with them. If both parents will do this, it will help their children to learn how to interact with both sexes. Invite children of **both** sexes into your home for parties with your children. Take your children to **Sunday School.** Encourage teens to get involved with youth groups at church. The scouts may also help. Perhaps **Little League** sports. Or **extra curricular activities** at school. Discourage overloading, but utilize others to help you teach your children to interact well with others. To be friendly. To talk. To listen. To smile. To show interest in others. To make friends. In doing this, you will be doing them a big favor.

3. Protect your children. God protected his children by driving many nations out of the land he had given them. He delivered their enemies over to Israel and told Israel to destroy them and not to intermarry with them. Why? Because if they did, they would turn their sons and daughters away from God to serve other gods. Then, the Lord's anger would be turned against them and destroy them (Deuteronomy 7:1-4).

Maybe it's hard for us to understand the ways of the Lord, but perhaps we can still learn some valuable lessons from all of this. God did what he did to preserve his special people, people whom he loved dearly as his very own.

Let's apply this principle to our children. There are child abusers, drug dealers, bullies, movie producers, and many others who may harm our children severely! We can't stand by and let it happen. Some may teach our children warped values: sex outside of marriage is okay. Homosexuality is just another legitimate lifestyle. Adultery is exciting and can actually help save a boring marriage. Racial discrimination is moral if it helps your race. Values are relative. All lifestyles are equally moral. Abortion is only a political issue. No so! I doubt if most people can believe all of this. Surely Hitler's lifestyle was not equally moral with all other lifestyles. Surely incest and rape are wrong! Surely pornographic literature and some movies are destructive. We need to grab hold of some valid moral principles and teach them to our children. Protect them from harmful people and warped principles no matter who says what.

A few years ago I was counseling with a young man, age 30, who had been convicted of raping an eight-year-old boy. He was in prison. Got seven years. During one session he asked me for some good reading material. I thought of a book that I had enjoyed. It was good in many ways. Good for self-esteem and depression. He needed help in those areas as well as in his sexual-power-exploitation problem. Then I remembered one often repeated statement in the book and didn't suggest it to him: "Avoid shoulds and musts." I'll admit that certain perfectionistic people major in minors and have too many shoulds and musts in their lives. "My moma had a Ph.D. I must get one too!" "My daddy was a very prominent man, made lots of money. I must do that too!" Such musts and shoulds can be destructive. Where are such musts and shoulds written in stone? Who says we **must?** But, the book went too far. Not what he needed to hear. "Avoid all musts and shoulds." No! This young man needed to **learn** some musts and shoulds. He **must not** let this happen again. He **should** stay away from boys for the rest of his life. And on and on we could go. He needed therapy over several years, and children needed to be protected. He needed to learn what was right and how to control himself and behave in a proper manner. And, he did! He continued in therapy, became a Christian, served his time, and is now living a productive Christian life. No more such incidents.

4. **Love** your children. **Tough love** sometimes, but nevertheless **love.** God loves his children. He did not choose Israel because they were more numerous than other peoples. They were the fewest. He chose Israel because he loved them and was loyal to his oath made to their forefathers. Thus, he brought them out of Egypt with a mighty hand and redeemed them from the land of slavery, from the power of Pharoah, king of Egypt. He thus kept this "covenant of love to a thousand generations of those who love him and keep his commands" (Deuteronomy 7:7-9 NIV).

We are to love our children. Care for them. Sacrifice if needed for them. Take care of their needs. The Bible tells us that God so loved the world that he gave his Son for us (John 3:16). Jesus loved us and gave his life for us (John 10). We love our children and do what is best for them. Not always what they want, but always what is best.

My parents loved me enough to say no to me. They loved me enough to take me to church from my youth up. They loved me enough to teach me what I needed to know as we lived and worked together. They loved me enough to clothe me and feed me. They loved me enough to walk through snow to get a doctor for me when I was sick. They loved me enough to teach me how to work hard. They loved me enough to not do "what every parent" was doing. They loved me enough to demonstrate honesty before me. They loved me enough to send me to school when they needed me to work on the farm. They loved me enough to support my teachers who corrected me. They loved me enough to discipline me. They loved me enough to teach me to love my country and to respect its leaders. They loved me enough to teach me that all people are created equal. They loved me enough to bid me God's speed as I left home at age 18. They loved me enough to keep in touch while I was away in Detroit, New York, Biloxi, Bremerhaven, Germany, and other places. They loved me enough to welcome me back home. They loved me enough to give good advice. They loved me enough to respect my autonomy as an adult. They loved me enough to inspire me to be all that I can be. And, I love them for it!

5. **Show** your children how to live. Be a good model for them. They learn more by what you **are** than by what you **say.** God demonstrated his faithfulness and his love to his children. (Deuteronomy 7:12).

There are several incidents that stick out in my mind about my parents who modeled a good life before us. I remember a mother who would say she didn't want any pie when we were one piece short. I remember a mother (we called her Moma) who worked in the garden, canned food for her family of 10, then got the children ready for church at night when we had a gospel meeting at the old schoolhouse at Union Hill. We would then walk to church together. I can still see her sitting on the porch getting her Bible lesson for church. I remember her stories about her father who when out on horseback in freezing weather, returned home frozen stiff, and she would help get him off the horse and into the house and thaw him out before the fireplace. I can remember her encouragement to preach the gospel. I can remember her wanting us to have things we could not afford. I can remember her encouraging me to go to school, "You need to get a good education." I can remember her brave struggle with rheumatic arthritis and congestive heart failure. I can remember what evidently were her last words. Don was sitting up with her that night. She was in a coma and went into a convulsion. She was very uncomfortable. Don, trying to help her toward comfort, began talking to her. He said, "Moma, just listen."

> The Lord is my shepherd.
> Mom said, "I shall not want."
> Don said, "He maketh me to lie down
>   in green pastures."
> Mom said, "He maketh me to lie down,
>   peacefully."

She then relaxed peacefully and went to sleep in the arms of Jesus the next night. What memories! I think of her almost everytime I get up to speak.

A few years ago, I was given the honor of being named "Fellow" by the American Association for Marriage and Family Therapy. We were in Washington, D.C. in the ballroom of a fancy convention hotel. Very nice. Very expensive. They called me up to the front of 10,00 people along with a few other senior therapists who were also given this rather distinctive honor. As I was standing there looking at the vast crowd I wondered how I ever got there. "I don't deserve this," I thought. I thought of Moma, straightened up, stood a little taller, and thought, "She would think I deserved it! She would be proud."

I just now stopped to wipe the tears away from my eyes and face. She still has that kind of effect on me.

My parents named me Billy Way Flatt. "Way" was Moma's maiden name. Somehow the "Way" part of my name did not get on my birth certificate, and as a child, I did not like my middle name. It sounded sort of different, and children were kidded for being different. But when I was in my twenties, I had it added to my birth certificate, especially in honor of Mom and her family. Most people call me Bill now, but I gave them a note that night in D.C. that my name was Billy Way Flatt. And that's what they read out as I walked forward to receive the honor. That's who I am.

My father is equally a good Christian man. He served as an elder of the church for some 35 years. Well respected in the community as a hard worker and a good man. I'd like to share a few incidents that indicate his good character. He once was offered $50 more for a mule that he had just sold. No money had changed hands. No contracts signed, but he had given his word and would not go back on it. I remember gathering corn in the fields with Daddy. We rented extra land and paid a third of the crop to the land owner. One wagon load for him, two for us. What I remember is that he would always round up the load for the landowner a little bit more than he would the loads for us. He showed us what it means to be fair, to be honest.

Dad fell and broke his hip some six weeks ago. Even in such pain, he started figuring out what to do. He told my brother-in-law, Jimmy Anderson and his brother: "Go get the truck, one of you get on one side of me, and one on the other. Pick me up and put me in the back of the truck." Lots of grit! He was laughing and talking when I visited him in the hospital. "Doing just fine," he said. He shows us how to live a good life. "Be honest. Pull your own weight. Take responsibility. Be a good neighbor. Do what is right." It's hard not to learn from parents like I had.

Someone wrote, "Children are natural mimics who act like their parents despite every effort to teach them good manners." If I mimic my parents, I'll be going in a good direction.

Several years ago I read that two little boys visited the wildcats at a local zoo. One of them asked, "Wonder why these cats are wild?" The other boy replied, "I guess they are wildcats because their father and mother are wildcats." It hurts us as parents sometimes to be reminded, but there is a lot of truth in that statement.

One poem I read when our boys were little influenced me a great deal. I don't know who wrote it, but it's a good one. It caused me to quit smoking years ago.

A LITTLE FELLOW FOLLOWS ME

A careful man I ought to be,
A little fellow follows me;
I do not dare to go astray
For fear he'll go the selfsame way.

Not once can I escape his eyes;
Whate'er he sees me do, he tries.
Like me he says he's going to be
That little chap who follows me.

He thinks that I am good and fine;
Believes in every word of mine.
The base in me he must not see—
That little chap who follows me.

I must remember as I go
Thru summer sun and winter snow,
I'm building for the years to be
For that little chap who follows me.

My favorite poem on the effects of modeling was written by Dorothy Doke.

If children live with criticism,
They learn to condemn.

If children live with hostility,
They learn to fight.

If children live with ridicule,
They learn to be shy.

If children live with shame,
They learn to feel guilty.

If children live with tolerance,
They learn to be patient.

If children live with encouragement,
They learn confidence.

If children live with praise,
They learn to appreciate.

If children live with fairness,
They learn justice.

If children live with security,
They learn to have faith.

If children live with approval,
They learn to like themselves.

If children live with acceptance and friendship,
They learn to find love in the world.

Remember that it all starts by showing love to your children. Psychiatrists Michael Kerr and Murray Bowen in their book on *Family Evaluation* say that depression in human infants can be triggered by a lack of adequate physical contact, comfort, and stimulation. Infant rhesus monkeys who were denied access to their mothers had difficulty forming affectional ties in later life. If this is true for monkeys, I'm sure it is also true for humans as well. A lack of demonstrated love can set us up for trouble.

On the other hand, Kerr and Bowen found that when parents were emotionally close themselves, that their child improved as a psychiatric patient. When they were more emotionally invested in their child than with each other, their child regressed. All hospital management approaches worked well when the parents modeled emotional closeness before their children. Strange research but impressive! Bonding. Modeling. Children catch on. They tend to feel secure in a good, loving environment. They learn love. They learn how to live when we **show** them.

6. **Discipline** your children. The Bible tells us that God disciplines his children as a man disciplines his children (Deuteronomy 8:5). Though it's an unpleasant task to do, we are to discipline our children. The root word for discipline is

the same as the root word for disciple. So, discipline includes teaching and learning as well as appropriate punishing. Not child abuse, but punishment appropriate to the behavior, age level, and temperament of the child.

A man named Eli is mentioned in the Old Testament. A godly man who had wicked sons. They despised the Lord. Had sex with the women who did service at the tent of meeting or tabernacle (I Samuel 2:12, 17, 22). God said he would punish the family of Eli for the iniquity which he knew, because his sons brought a curse upon themselves, and he did not restrain them. God expects us to discipline our children. They need discipline to protect them, to keep them out of trouble, and to help them internalize values they will need to live in a civilized world.

The discipline of children by parents is taught throughout the Bible. Paul encourages parents to not provoke their children to anger but to bring them up in the nurture and admonition of the Lord (Ephesians 6:4). He tells fathers not to embitter their children lest they become discouraged (Colossians 3:21). This reminds me of Solomon's idea that a broken spirit dries up the bones (Proverbs 17:22) and that by sorrow of heart the spirit can be broken (Proverbs 15:13). So, do it, but don't overdo it! God chastens those he loves (Proverbs 3:11-12). Solomon says that by withholding discipline we demonstrate hate to our children (Proverbs 13:24). Discipline brings hope, and a lack of discipline leads to destruction (Proverbs 19:18). Discipline drives out foolishness in the heart of a child (Proverbs 22:15). The right kind of discipline will not harm children but will deliver their "soul from death" (Proverbs 23:13-14). Discipline gives wisdom, but children left to themselves cause shame to their parents. Correction brings delight (Proverbs 29:15-17).

So, what is appropriate disciplines for children? Let me suggest some of the following principles that seem helpful to me:

a. Don't go to extremes either toward no discipline or too much discipline.

b. Discipline small children immediately. They probably won't connect the correction with the inappropriate behavior if you wait.

c. Set expectations for your children and communicate such expectations clearly to them. Change the expectation as needed as the children get older.

d. Make a list of rewards and punishments for various desirable and undesirable behaviors. A reward can be as simple as a compliment and a punishment as simple as verbal communication of disapproval.

e. Make a distinction between the children and their behavior. Show that you disapprove of their bad behavior but not of them.

f. Try your best to be consistent from one time to the next and between parents. Children are often damaged emotionally when one parent says one thing and the other parent another. Values get confused.

g. Spank with a light paddle. Not hard. Not too many licks. You can reinforce your point without really hurting the child much. Use other methods such as "time out" with small children.

h. Stop spanking children at age 10. After that, it may do more harm than good. Research shows that the effects of such spankings are hard to predict. I know this for sure: Every client I have had with excessive anger had been whipped with a belt or switch or hit with a fist or hand as a child! They bottle up the anger inside, and it explodes onto others throughout their lives. And believe me, it's hard to change even in extended psychotherapy. Be careful. Think of what is best for the child, not what is best for you when you are mad.

i. Don't make idle threats. Be reasonable, and do what you say you will do. It's better to withdraw privileges for one day and stick to it than for a month and give in.

j. Let the parent who has disciplined a child console him/her. And sometimes you will need to explain why you did it.

k. The "natural consequences" approach to discipline can be very effective. A four-year-old goes into the street. You do not let him play in the yard again for a few days since he has not handled such freedom well. A seventeen-year-old gets a DUI. You take away his car keys for three months since he has not handled driving responsibilities well. In this approach to discipline, the parent logically connects the punishment with the crime. A teen-age girl runs up a $200 long-distance phone bill. You take away her long-distance privileges for two months or require her to work and pay the $200 phone bill. Tough love!

l.   Be creative. Hugs, praise, gold stars. Pleasant words are sweet to the healing of the bones (Proverbs 16:24).

m.   Don't yell. Employ negative consequences. Speak firmly, and back up what you say. If you get into the habit of yelling at your children, they'll think you don't really mean it unless you yell.

n.   Parents must stick together in discipline. Underscore this!

o.   Withdrawing privileges often works well with teenagers. Don't be fooled if teens say they don't care if you take away television, telephone, dating, or driving privileges. They do! Just do what you need to do. You know what they like to do. So, use that knowledge in deciding what privilege to take away. And don't overdo it.

p.   Reinforce your children for good behavior. Compliment. Praise. Most of us tend to do that for which we are reinforced. Once, for example, I was in Maine. Went home with a minster for lunch. A mother and her little boy, age three, were also there, along with several other people from church. The little boy cried all during Sunday School and church and for some 20 minutes at the preacher's home. Everybody was getting a bit on edge because of his crying. His mother tried everything, but nothing worked. The boy was lying in his mother's lap, she was patting him on the back, and he was crying. I looked at this scene and thought of B. F. Skinner and his theory of reinforcement. "People tend to do what they are reinforced for." She seemed to be reinforcing him for crying. I got an idea. Wondered if it would work. I didn't know, but it was worth a try. I turned to the little boy and said, "I'm sorry you don't feel well. You have been crying for a long time. I was just thinking, you could cry just as well sitting over there in the floor as you can in your mother's lap. So, get down and go over there and cry as long as you want to. Then, when you get through, come back over here and get in your mother's lap and she'll pet you some more. You'll deserve being petted then." He and his mother complied with my request, and he stopped crying within 10 seconds. She took him back on her lap and reinforced him for not crying. This was hard to believe for the whole roomful of people, including me, but it worked! Watch what you are reinforcing! If your child wants candy, you refuse, she throws a fit, and you then give in; you have taught your child that if she will throw a fit, you will get her some candy. If your child throws his clothes on the floor, you fuss but finally pick them up and put them where they belong, he learns that if he throws his clothes on the floor that you will pick them up. Reinforce only behavior that you wish the child to repeat!

q. Be sensitive to the temperament of your children. They don't all need the same discipline. Each child is "wired up" differently. What is appropriate discipline for one may not be for another.

r. Trust teenagers, but do not always trust their judgment.

s. Expect good behavior from your children. When asked about how he was sculpting a beautiful angel out of a huge stone, Michelangelo replied, "There's an angel in that rock that wants to come out. It's my job to help it do so." And, he continued chiseling!

t. Do what is best, not always what is pleasing to your children. King David's son Adonijah exalted himself and wanted his father's position as king. The Bible tells us that his father had never displeased him (I Kings 1:5-6). Perhaps this was part of the problem. Do what you think needs to be done, not always what you think will make your children like you.

u. Live disciplined lives yourselves: disciplined diet, sleep, work, and play habits.

137

   v. Be willing to deal with conflict. It's good practice for the children. Teach them how to resolve conflicts.

  w. Don't offer children a choice unless you intend to allow them to make a choice.

7. Spend time with your children. The Bible says that God spent time with his children (Deuteronomy 6-10). He led them through the desert for 40 years. We need to spend time with our children, be there for them.

8. Be a blessing to your children. God blessed Israel with manna to eat, water to drink, and clothes to wear. He even protected their feet from swelling (Deuteronomy 8:3-4). He gave them the ability to produce wealth (Deuteronomy 8:18). He also blesses us with life, liberty, and the pursuit of happiness. In him we live, move, and have our being (Acts 17). We need to be a blessing and not a curse to our children. What we do should help them, not hurt them. Help them by providing for them: useful training, educational opportunities, healthy food, shelter, medical and other needs.

9. We need to **listen** to our children. Moses wrote that God listened to him as he prayed for Aaron and Israel (Deuteronomy 9:19-20; 10:10). God's wrath turned away because Moses prayed. God listens to us, and we need to listen to our children. Unless we listen we cannot communicate. If we cannot communicate, we cannot teach. If we cannot teach, they cannot learn what we wish them to learn. If we do not listen, we will be ineffective parents.

10. We need to be **patient** with our children. God, our model parent, was patient with Israel. He wrote the Ten Commandments once, Moses threw them to the ground in an angry outburst of disgust at Israel's idolatry; he went back to the mountain, and God wrote another set of tablets containing the same Ten Commandments (Deuteronomy 10:4). Patience. God was continually patient with Israel and is continually patient with us. We need that same kind of patience with our children.

Jason was only four. His parents were furious with him because he wouldn't sit still and eat meals politely. They yelled, they threatened, they spanked, but nothing worked.

"We tell him to sit still and eat his food, and one minute later, he is fidgeting and trying to get up from the table again," they reported. "What is wrong with him?" My response to Jim and Laurie, Jason's parents, was to be patient. Remember that Jason is only four. They don't sit very long at age four. Their attention span is short. They forget quickly. Be firm and loving. Loosen up. Remember that he is not a **little man** but a **little boy.** Teach him to do what he is capable of doing. Teach over and over again with kindness and firmness. Don't yell. Don't get mad. Be patient. He'll learn as he grows and is more capable of acting like an adult.

What I'm suggesting is that God as Father is a good model for us as parents. There are some principles we can learn from God as Father that will help us to be effective parents. Remember Principle Number 7: Effective parenting empowers children to be all that they can be.

PARENTING EXERCISES

1. Do you and your child's other parent agree on parenting policies? These principles are valid for both married and divorced parents.
2. Do you have a clear sense of what you expect from your children?
3. What are you teaching them?
4. Do you wish them to have roots and also wings? What do you think this means?
5. Do your children know what you expect of them?
6. Do they know what will happen if they do not meet your expectations?
7. If they meet your expectations?
8. How would you describe the atmosphere in your home?
9. How will you make changes that need to be made?
10. What are you going to do differently to become a better parent?
11. What does it mean to empower children?
12. Do any of your children irritate you? How does this affect your parenting behavior?

13. Do you undermine each other's authority as a parent in front of the children?

14. Are you in competition for the children's attention?

15. Do you compliment your mate in front of the children?

16. Do you use your children to get even with their other parent?

Eight

Effective Communication

Principle Number 8:
Effective communication promotes problem
solving, intimacy, personal and family growth.

Suzie told her younger brother her desires for her mother's funeral. They agreed. But, in the meantime, their older sister had already made funeral arrangements for their mother. Feelings were hurt but nobody expressed them. The problem: Communication broke down.

Both Lorene and her husband, Frank, had had affairs: He several, she one. Their marriage had been "bad" for years. He had several affairs before she had hers. When they counseled with me, she felt very guilty about her affair and wanted to know what to do about it. She was anxious and depressed and had told Frank that their marriage had to change or she would divorce him. This motivated him to come for counseling when 10 years of begging by his wife and 15 years of a dysfunctional marriage had failed to do so. They were stuck in a dysfunctional pattern that fed upon itself. He dished it out: She swallowed it. Depression and anxiety symptoms followed. Communication had broken down.

She decided to tell him of her affair, and apologize. They both confessed to each other. Their marriage got worse at first. He was indignant that she could do that to him. Wanted every detail. Tried to make her drop her career, drop her friends, and quit going to church. Sort of wanted to lock her up. His finger of blame was always pointed at her. He minimized the plank in

141

his own eye and maximized the sawdust in her eye (Matthew 7:1-5). They were stuck again. She was afraid to say what she thought because "it would just make things worse." She did not want a divorce but was willing to allow her husband to get one if the marriage didn't improve. She "couldn't stand" the situation anymore. Communication had broken down again. He would pursue and escalate; she would withdraw and absorb the tension, then get depressed and anxious. What next?

Lorene decided to assert herself. She told Frank that she did not want a divorce but would get one if the marriage did not improve. She wanted to be treated with respect, not talked down to, not continually criticized. She wanted to be able to make her own decisions about employment, church and friends. She was not going to live "in a box." They had to learn to trust each other again. They needed to learn to communicate.

Frank didn't like his "new" wife at first, but he went along because he "loved her and hated to lose her." She learned to verbalize her feelings, and he learned to listen and respect her decisions. He began to accept responsibility for his **own** behavior including his affairs, and they began to develop much more intimacy than they had ever experienced before. He still yells at times, and she absorbs the tension, but that is not their typical pattern now. She is still working part-time, socializing some with her friends, and going to church. He has begun going to church with her at times. Their marriage is much better. They are communicating better and solving more conflicts over various issues.

Effective communication. A beginning point for a healthy home.

Over the last several years I have collected statements such as the following from many unknown sources about the value of communication:

> Just because many couples harp at each other does not mean their marriage was made in heaven.

> If a man has enough horse sense to treat his wife like a thoroughbred, she will never grow into an old nag.

One minute of keeping your mouth shut is worth one hour of explanation.

Be careful of your thoughts; they may become words at any minute.

Those who say the least often say the most.

Swallow your pride occasionally. It's non-fattening.

The person with a closed mind usually has an open mouth.

No one is too big to be courteous, but some are too small.

Treat rude people with kindness and respect, not because of who they are, but because of who you are.

Temper is a valuable possession. Don't lose it.

To speak ill of others is a dishonest way of praising ourselves.

Silence is the best and surest way to hide ignorance.

Nothing is so often opened by mistake as the mouth.

In order to have a happy marriage, the wife has to be blind and the husband deaf.

Sam Rayburn, for many years Speaker of the House of Representatives in Washington, D.C., used to admonish young congressmen by saying, "When you are talking, you are not learning." A lot of emphasis on silence. Wonder why? Maybe we often say the wrong thing. And, maybe we don't listen well.

A certain woman came to her minister to counsel with him about her marital problems. She wanted a divorce. The minister asked, "Do you have grounds?" "Oh, yes. About five acres," she replied. "That is not what I meant," he continued. "Do you have a grudge?" "No," she said, "but we have a carport." The minister tried again, "Is there a charge?" "No, that's one of my complaints. He cut my charge cards all up," she rejoined.

Knowing that he was not getting anywhere, the preacher tried again. "Does your husband beat you up?" "No," the woman replied, "I get up before he does every morning." Making just one more attempt to communicate with her, the minister finally posed this important question, "Lady, just what is your problem?" She angrily responded, "You just can't communicate with some people no matter how hard you try."

Very true! And we always think it's the other person's fault.

Effective communication is very difficult, yet extremely significant. Beech, Sandeen, and O'Leary reported in their book on *Depression and Marriage* that there is a 25-fold increase in the risk of depression associated with being married and not being able to talk to one's spouse! Someone has to swallow the tension in the family system since it doesn't get solved. And **that** person is the one who gets depressed. I've seen it over and over again.

A group of faculty members in the Family Studies' Division at the University of Denver have done some enlightening research on marital communication. They have found that there are certain dysfunctional communication patterns in marriages that lead to divorce. In fact, they report that they can predict divorce with a 90 percent accuracy by a study of communication patterns in marriages. People don't usually divorce as much over issues as over an inability to solve issues. Issues control them! They don't control issues. And issues don't get solved when couples don't communicate.

Here are four of the dysfunctional communication patterns they discuss:

1. The female pursues, the male withdraws (pouts, clams up, stonewalls, is poker-faced).

2. Arguments escalate. Get louder and louder.

3. Couples invalidate each other. They expect to be validated (complimented. . .) but get invalidated (criticized).

4. They give negative interpretations to each other. Twist what the other says to make it mean something negative.

What I want you to do is to look for such patterns of communication in your marriage. Then, do something different! When you quit playing your role in the pattern, the pattern has to change. Your changes throw the pattern into a different orbit. The change may be bad or it may be good, but there will be a change. And, when the pattern is dysfunctional, such action is worth a try. Change what you are doing! And if your change makes sense, the change in pattern has a good chance of being positive.

Remember Lorene? She needed to change her pattern of swallowing whatever cruel comment her husband made. She did, and he changed for the better.

But, what if the pattern becomes worse? Keep doing what is **healthy.** The alternative is to continue being a part of a sick marital pattern. You need to try something better.

Let me get to some specifics. Some **keys** to effective communication in the family. I have found these to be very effective personally and in counseling with families.

1. Be a decent human being. It all starts with your heart, your motives, you intentions. Jesus Christ has become my model. Though I fall short of his perfect example, thoughts of him and what he would do have helped me to be better than I would have been otherwise. I try to follow in his steps (I Peter 2:21). I want his spirit to live in me (Galatians 2:20). If I listen with his attitude of concern, I will hear. Then, if I speak from the heart, my message will be wholesome. And if I act in response to what I hear, my actions will be helpful.

Remember what James, probably the brother of Jesus, said? We bless God and curse people with the same tongue. It shouldn't be that way! A spring does not send forth both sweet and bitter water. A fig tree does not yield olives, nor a vine figs. So, the point is that a good heart (person) will communicate with goodness. Not with sarcasm or hurtful messages, verbal or non-verbal (James 3:1-12).

Others agree. Jesus said, "Ye offspring of vipers, how can ye, being evil, speak good things? For out of the abundance of the heart the mouth speaketh" (Matthew 12:34 ASV). A person who loves transgression will transgress in various ways (Proverbs 17:19). Strife and destruction follow.

Start with yourself. Is your heart right? Do you have a good attitude? Do you treat others as you want to be treated? (Matthew 7:12). Good questions. A good starting point. What

I'm saying is that your communication is no more wholesome and upbuilding than your heart. A good person is likely to communicate a good message; a "rotten person," a rotten message. So, what kind of person are you? Are you willing to change for the better? To grow?

2. **Guard** your mouth. It's so easy to say the wrong thing. Your tongue has the power of death and life (Proverbs 18:21). If you are wise, you will say the right things; if foolish, your mouth will pour out folly (Proverbs 15:2). Leave off contention before there is quarreling. If you don't, it will be like trying to hold your finger in a hole in a dam (Proverbs 17:14). It's smart to spare your words and be of a cool spirit (Proverbs 17:27). It shows that you are a person of understanding. If you guard your mouth and your tongue, you keep your soul from trouble (Proverbs 21:23). There is more hope for a fool than for a person who is hasty in his/her words (Proverbs 29:20). It's an honor to keep aloof from strife, foolish to argue (Proverbs 20:3). Not foolish to solve conflicts, but to **look for** an argument. To **seek** strife. Why? The tongue, though small, can cause lots of damage. Just like a match can set fire to a whole forest (James 3:5).

I've seen it many times. We get mad and say too much. Anna May was suffering from depression and low self-esteem. What she "could not forget" was a statement from her mother when she was only four years old. In a moment of anger, her mother yelled at her, "I wish you had never been born." She apologized later, but her daughter never forgot. This statement "made her feel" "insignificant, not wanted, in the way." She later wondered if she really belonged to her mother. Maybe she had been adopted.

Carol was upset at her husband because he was "just using me." He got upset and said she was frigid, no good in bed. "Just lay there like a log during intercourse. Never moved." Carol cried and yelled, "I don't love you. I **never** loved you. I get sick everytime you touch me." They calmed down later, talked it out, and apologized. But, he "could not forget" that she said she never loved him.

I tell families that people say extreme things when they are at their worst. Let them take it back. Apologize. Better still, guard your tongue if you want to build a healthy home.

No wonder Paul said, "Let your speech be always with grace, seasoned with salt, that ye may know how ye ought to answer each one" (Colossians 4:6). We can also see the wisdom of James' message when he said, "Let every man be swift to hear, slow to speak, slow to wrath" (James 1:19).

3. **Listen carefully**. There's the rub! It's hard to do. We hear, but we don't listen. We read and "listen." We watch television and "listen." But what we hear is often garbled, much like code messages I used to copy in the United States Air Force. A lot of static made it hard to hear the message!

I read an extremely helpful book on marital communication recently on *Love Is Never Enough* by Aaron Beck, M.D. In it, Beck applied cognitive therapy to marital therapy. He specifically pointed to the self-talk of both mates to explain how we miscommunicate! The wife gets a promotion. Comes home excited. Says to herself, "We'll celebrate tonight. My husband will be so proud of me!" But he has just been told by his boss that if he makes one more mistake he will be fired. He's worried. Says to himself, "When my wife gets home, I'll talk to her about this. She always makes me feel better."

Scene two. The wife comes in and happily shares the good news: "Guess what? I've been promoted. I feel like I'm finally successful in my career. Let's celebrate!"

The husband says without enthusiasm, "That's good. I'm glad to hear it."

She goes into her bedroom thinking, "He's not happy for me. I expected him to be excited. To help me celebrate! He doesn't care about me. Our marriage must be on the rocks." She pouts the rest of the night.

Meanwhile, he is saying to himself, "She's so self-centered. Didn't even ask me how I'm doing. She's not even concerned about **my** job. Just hers. She must be tired of me."

Our own agenda gets in the way of effective communication. We need to take time to ask questions and to clarify what we are hearing. Otherwise, I don't see how we will ever meet minds, stay close, and deal constructively with issues.

Misunderstandings happen in all marriages. Louise and I went to a football game at Memphis State University recently. It was very hot. I bought a program and looked up various num-

147

bers of key players and then put the program down on my lap. Momentarily, Louise picked up the program. I thought to myself, "I'm glad she is taking such an interest in football. I didn't think she really enjoyed it." Then what? Rather than looking up numbers, she began using the program as a fan. Not completely in sync after 37 years! When we guess at what each other is thinking, we are wrong about 50 percent of the time.

Here's another illustration. To understand the story, I need to tell you some of our habits. Louise is a tremendous wife, shows her love to me in lots of ways. Anticipates my needs. This incident happened one night at 9:30, when I usually take a bath. I had just gotten settled in my easy chair to watch a football game for about 15 minutes before bathtime. Louise peeped into the den at 9:30 and decided that she would not bother me, would instead just go ahead with her bath first. She went into the bathroom and turned the water on in the bathtub, then proceeded to our bedroom to get ready for her bath. When I heard the water running, I thought, "She is really something! Getting better all the time, sensitive to my needs. I don't really expect her to turn the bath water on for me though." I turned the television off, went into the bathroom and got into the tub. What next? She came into the bathroom to take her bath, saw me in the tub, looked puzzled, and went back into the bedroom. Later I found out what she was saying to herself: "What in the world is going on? He is using **my water**."

Different wavelengths. It happens all of the time and often causes damage to a relationship. But not usually if both mates feel loved and supported!

Don't fret, women. I turned her bath water on the next night!

Biblical writers have much to say about speaking and listening. There is a time to speak and a time to be silent (Ecclesiastes 3:7). If a person **answers before** he hears, it is his/her folly and shame (Proverbs 18:13). I've done that lots of times, and it causes trouble. Butt in when the other person pauses. Miss the mark. Get corrected. "No, that's not what I meant," they say. And I start listening again.

Once in marriage counseling, J. T. said that his wife was prudish, uptight about sex. I was thinking to myself, "I know the kind of woman she is, have counseled with many just like her: frigid, ashamed of the way she looks, super modest, won't undress in front of her husband. . ." But, instead of following my hunch, I asked, "Can you give me an example?" Nancy, his wife, spoke up, "*I* can give you an example! We have two teen-age daughters and two younger boys. **He** takes off every stitch of his clothing the minute he gets home. Walks around in front of all of us like that all of the time. Then, calls me prudish about sex because I want him to keep his clothes on. I get sick of looking at him! I'm afraid of what his odd behavior will do to our daughters." I was glad I asked for an example. I shared her fears.

In order to learn, we need to **focus** on the person who is talking. We need to hear counsel and receive instruction that we may "be wise" (Proverbs 19:20). I have also found the following tips to be useful:

a. Avoid cross-complaining. Just concentrate on one issue at a time. Don't bring in everything but the kitchen sink. Take time for other issues later.

b. Don't interrupt. I've noticed it many times. The husband is talking. He thinks and talks a bit more slowly than his wife. She butts in to help him out. He gets irritated. She complains that he never says anything in-depth to her. He clams up. She is part of the dysfunctional pattern. She needs to let him have time to finish his thoughts.

c. Empathize. **Feel with** the other person. Try to put yourself in their shoes. Judy complained about Joe. "He just is not on my wavelength. We're not close. He has no idea about what I am feeling. He intellectualizes everything," she says. Joe then intellectually analyzed her complaint and organized it into three main points. True! Judy threw up her hands and exclaimed, "What can you do with a guy like that?" On personality tests, men are often high on indifference and logic; women high on compassion and feelings. Men complain that women are fuzzy in their thinking, and women complain that men can't feel. "It's just like talking to a computer talking to them," they say. Men need to improve in empathic ability; women in their ability to follow the logic of men and look for feelings expressed by them indirectly. Both would be more completely developed in such a case.

d. Be tentative in what you think others say. If you are puzzled, check it out. You need to get it straight.

e. Don't mind-read. When you do, you'll be wrong about 50 percent of the time. Your wife may be turning on her **own** bath water instead of yours.

f. Draw others out. Solomon said, "Counsel in the heart of man is like deep waters; but a man of understanding will draw it out" (Proverbs 20:5). When he clams up, ask questions. Help him express what is bothering him. He may have gotten to the point where he thinks that his ideas don't matter. Let him know that they do.

Speak softly. "A soft answer turneth away wrath; but a grevious word stirreth up anger," Solomon stated (Proverbs 15:1). And again, "A man hath joy in the answer of his mouth; and a word in due season, how good it is" (Proverbs 15:23). How helpful it is to express yourself well at the appropriate time! Just as we can't know God unless he reveals himself to us, we can't know each other unless we talk (I Corinthians 2:11-13). The point Paul is making is that we can know God because his Spirit has revealed him to us. We need to reveal ourselves to our family. Listen. Talk.

Solomon has much to say about the attitude we need to have. He mentions that the contentions of a wife are like a continual dripping of water (Proverbs 19:13). He says it's better to live in the corner of a housetop than with a contentious woman in a big house (Proverbs 21:9). Or he would prefer to live in a desert land than with a contentious and fretful woman (Proverbs 21:19). Makes me wonder which of his 1000 wives and concubines were getting on his nerves! He also mentions at least once that men can have an attitude problem: "As coals are to hot embers, and wood to fire, so is a contentious man to inflame strife" (Proverbs 26:21). A man or a woman looking for a fight will find one. One who is slow to anger is more likely to overlook a "transgression" (Proverbs 19:11). If our attitude is positive, we will try to avoid "breaking the spirit" of others (Proverbs 18:14).

I'd like to share some other tips on talking that I have found helpful:

a. Don't hog the conversation. Not if you want to communicate. Such action indicates a defensive posture.

b. Don't put others down. They can't communicate well in that posture. Ask yourself, "Why do I need to do that?"

c. Give feedback. Reflect. It helps them examine their own feelings and helps them know that you are listening.

d. Clarify. If it is unclear to you, it probably is to them as well.

e. Initiate conversation. This is an indication of openness. A willingness to communicate, to get to know someone, to be friends.

f.. Respond and add comments. Did you ever talk to someone who would not answer? And if they answered, they only answered the specific question? Chances are, they are a **closed** personality. Hard to get to know. Keep everybody at a distance. Skeptical of people. They drive people away from them. It's not worth the effort, they decide. Open up. Take a risk. No risk, no gain.

g. Paraphrase. It lets others know that you are listening and grasping their message.

h. Don't overgeneralize. "You never do anything I like," one man told his wife. Surely that is an overstatement! Other examples: "Nobody likes me. I can't do anything right. I'm a total failure." And on and on it goes.

i. Don't attribute motives. You'll probably be wrong if you do, and you will usually hinder conversation by doing so. I have heard in counseling such statements as the following: "You are just doing that to make me mad. You never want to please me. You're just wanting to get rid of me. You're just wearing that dress to attract other men. You only touch me because you want sex. You don't value me as a person. You just want to use me." You get the drift. Check yourself. You probably attribute motives more than you think you do. Judge not. Ask. It's better for communication.

j. Summarize. At the end of a lengthy discussion, summarize your conversation. Look at feelings as well as content. Remember the main points and give then back to the other person. It allows for correction or confirmation. It shows you are taking the other person seriously and that you have been listening. All of this will help you communicate more effectively.

5. Learn to cope with anger constructively. Jesus got mad, but he did not sin (Mark 3:1-6). Paul says, "Be angry, and sin not: Let not the sun go down upon your wrath" (Ephesians 4:26). Paul continues by saying to not let unwholesome talk come out of your mouth but only what is helpful to build others according to their needs. Our talk should benefit those who listen. Thus, we are to get rid of bitterness, rage and anger, brawling and slander, along with every form of malice (Ephesians 4:29-31). All of this is indicative that you have put off the old, corrupt, deceitful self and put on the new self with a new attitude toward God and people (Ephesians 4:20-24).

Here's my point. Anger gets in the way of effective communication. An angry person seldom communicates well. She clams up or blows up. Seldom finishes a conversation! Issues remain unsettled. Love erodes. Relationships are broken. Try to talk it out. Lower your voice. Slow down. Imagine that you are talking to your boss at work. Show respect. Be courteous. Speak of feelings if you need to do so. Weigh whether or not what you want to say will help or hinder. You don't need to be a martyr. There's no future in that. Be a mature person. Talk. Listen. Work it out. Learn to cope with your anger. It's a sign of emotional maturity.

Anger operates out of our mid-brain. After it becomes full-blown, our mid-brain takes over and sort of short-circuits our upper brain and frontal lobe where our thinking and reflecting occur, and we seem to lose our ability to think. Murray Bowen says it **fuses** with our upper brain so that we can no longer program our emotions by our thinking. That's trouble! Anger then controls us instead of the other way around. We need to control our anger.

Part of our problem may be tied up in an incident I once heard about Leonard Bernstein, famous orchestra conductor.

When asked what instrument is most difficult to play, he replied without hesitation, "Second fiddle. I can get plenty of first violinists, but to find one who plays second violin with as much enthusiasm or second French horn or second flute, now that's a problem. Yet if no one plays second, we have no harmony." Not selfish, not conceited, but in humility, counting others better than self. Consider their needs as well as yours (Philippians 2:2-4). It's hard to do, but important for close, meaningful relationships.

6. Be **kind** to each other. Tenderhearted (Ephesians 4:32). Once in a sensitivity training class in graduate school we decided to share our **real** feelings with each other. Just what we thought about each other. We decided that we were graduate students in psychology and that we could handle it. It would demonstrate our maturity. What happened? **All** of us got our feelings hurt. We destroyed in 30 minutes good feelings that had built up over a semester or more. We were not as mature as we thought. We don't want people to be brutally honest with us. We want kindness, compassion. We need it, and so do others. Be kind one to another, tenderhearted.

7. **Forgive** each other. Paul writes, "And be ye kind one to another, tenderhearted, forgiving each other, even as God also in Christ forgave you" (Ephesians 4:32). Jesus taught us to pray, "And forgive us our debts, as we also forgive our debtors" (Matthew 6:12). He also said, "Blessed are the merciful: for they shall obtain mercy" (Matthew 5:7). If I want mercy, I must give mercy. If I want forgiveness, I must forgive. Forgive each other. God in Christ forgives you. Simple words. Sometimes hard to do.

When someone has really done you wrong, that's when forgiveness is hard. Lies. Deception. An affair. Betrayal. Hard to forgive. We often **say** we forgive, but we haven't. We're still **full** of resentment!

I have learned that people who forgive too fast often have not really forgiven. They may have huge vested interests in the relationship: dependency needs of a wife with no job skills, low self-esteem, unworthy feelings, and guilt feelings. Whatever the reason, I encourage people to face the hurt before they say they forgive. To express their pain. To work through their questions. To be honest with themselves and with the person who has wronged them. **Then** forgive, and ask God to help them to let it be in the past so that it is no longer a factor in their relationship. It's hard to do, but not impossible!

I have counseled with hundreds of couples who got stuck on grudges. Not willing to forgive. Then, I've seen them become more intimate and go forward with their relationship when they forgave each other. I've had many clients who hate their parents. And, it's usually understandable, given the perceived abuse of their childhood. But, I encourage them to talk it out, to pray it through, to get a new perspective on it all, and to let it go. Then forgive. Don't let it ruin their lives!

And, that's what I want **you** to do. Forgive those who have sinned against you: parents, siblings, mate, children, and others.

One reason I think it's hard to forgive is that forgiveness means giving up an advantage we have over our foe. We've been wronged, and we don't want them to get off easily! We want to get even! We don't want others to think they are okay. We don't feel like acting as though nothing has happened. So, we hold on even though they repent. We may want to use what we know against them at some future date. So, we don't budge.

Remember, God forgives when we repent. Jesus Christ forgives. King David who committed adultery, the people who killed Jesus, Peter who denied Jesus, Saul of Tarsus who persecuted Christians—all were forgiven! Tremendous! It takes a big person to forgive. Reach for such bigness of character. Grow. Be divine-like. Forgive each other and start over. You'll be glad you did!

Remember, hurt feelings hinder effective communication. If we are mad at each other, it's hard to communicate. Forgive each other. Relationships are worth saving. Your marriage is worth saving.

8. Solve deep-seated foundational problems that hinder effective communication. Jim and Jenny had been married five years. Their main problem, they said, was communication. They just didn't talk. She couldn't stand him anymore! When I asked Jenny how long she had felt this way, she replied, "Oh, it has been about two years, I guess." What happened two years ago?" I asked. "That's when I began teaching school. Before

that, I was a full-time homemaker taking care of Lorrie." She then had a flash of insight. They stopped talking because she was angry at Jim for not helping her with the housework. She resented him. Didn't want to even look at him. She got up at five o'clock, got ready, got breakfast, got Lorrie up, got her ready, took her to a babysitter, went to work, picked up Lorrie, cooked supper, cleaned up, and fell into bed! Make you tired just to listen?

I have counseled with numerous women who are on such a schedule these days. Men, are you picking up on what I'm saying? It's not fair! If she has a career outside the home, you should divide the work around the house with her. Give yourself credit for mowing the lawn and taking care of the car if you do these chores. Then, do your share of the work inside the house including taking care of the children: dressing the little ones, feeding them, putting them to bed, and correcting them.

My Grandfather Flatt used to say rather proudly that there were three things he had never done: "I have never voted for a Republican; I have never taken a drink of whiskey; and I have never diapered a baby." Had 13 too!

Times have changed. A majority of mothers of small children work outside of the home. Fathers need to learn to diaper babies, wash dishes, and clean the house. And many people have taken a drink and voted Republican.

I feel like I need to pause and apologize to my grandfathers and father for having written such thoughts. I almost feel guilty. Like I've betrayed my manhood or something. I wasn't raised that way. But times have changed. Parents today need to train their sons to help around the house. They will need to know such things. They need to train their daughters to have a broad array of skills to live in today's world. They'll need them. Politics is a matter of judgment and drinking whiskey can cause trouble, but diapering a baby is a loving thing to do.

Almost every couple who has communications problems also have other problems. There is often a problem underneath the communications problem. Chisel it out and solve it, and then you can see more clearly how to communicate. Jim learned to help Jenny. He learned to work and to clean the house. He learned to take Lorrie to the babysitter's place. Jenny still picked her up on her way home from school. In helping Jenny, Jim grew a lot in my estimation. And, guess what? Jim apologized for his past mistakes. Jenny forgave him, and they communicated much better than before. They had solved a foundational problem that was hindering effective communication. Know what? You can too! It just takes a little humility and a lot of courage. Do it! You'll be glad you did.

Jesus must have recognized the significance of problems that damage relationships. He tells us how to solve them. If you brother has something against you, go to him and be reconciled. Then you can worship God more acceptably (Matthew 5:23-24). Or, turn it around. If you have something against your brother, go express your complaint and try to reconcile with him (Matthew 18:15). Helpful principle indeed! Take responsibility and seek reconciliation! A good general principle and an especially useful one in the family. Try to get along with other family members. Don't look for reasons to be hurt. Don't be a martyr. Be a peacemaker. "Blessed are the peacemakers: for they shall be called sons of God" (Matthew 5:9). Peacemakers know how to communicate. Be a peacemaker. Try to see the situation from the other person's point of view. Solomon says, "He that pleadeth his cause first seemeth just; but his neighbor cometh and searcheth him out" (Proverbs 18:17). Ask yourself: "Is my view the only way to look at it?" An emotionally mature person can often see other views as well. Such perspectives usually help solve problems and enable effective communication. Give it a try. You'll grow from the experience. Remember principle number 8: Effective communication promotes problem solving, intimacy, personal and family growth.

A COMMUNICATIONS EXERCISE

Read and discuss this with your mate, family or other special persons.

1. Do you butt in before others finish what they want to say?
2. Do you give an answer before you hear?
3. Can you express your real feelings in the presence of significant others?
4. Do you really listen?
5. Do you affirm significant others? How?
6. Do you watch television during meals? How does this affect conversation?
7. What is your attitude?
8. What changes will you make to become a more effective communicator?
9. Do you believe that significant others really understand you?
10. Do you understand them?
11. Do you pursue or withdraw?
12. Escalate?
13. Give negative interpretations? Mind read?
14. Invalidate?
15. Do you express your feelings well?
16. Do you speak softly?
17. Do you speak in "due season"?
18. Are you a closed person? If so, what can you do to open up more?
19. Are you kind?
20. Forgiving?
21. Do you cope with anger well?
22. Do you solve problems that hinder effective communication?

Nine

Growth and Change

Principle Number 9:
Healthy Families are able to grow
and change from one stage of development to another.

Louise and I met when my mother took me to see her mother and her new babies (twins) just after Louise and Ernest were born. I was only seven months old, but she must have made a good impression on me. I remember thinking she was cute in the second grade and dating her some in high school. Later, we dated more seriously and became engaged while I was on leave from the Air Force. I suppose she could not resist the uniform! About eight months later she took a ship to Rotterdam, I picked her up, and we got married in Bremerhaven, Germany.

About 16 months later, Steve was born. We returned to the States from Germany, I enrolled in college, and Tim and Danny were born.

Steve began school in Brownsville, Tennessee; Tim and Danny in Indianapolis. I remember the first day of school for each child. I still remember the particular way Tim looked back at us before he went into the school building that first day. Sort of a bit hesitant, somewhat apprehensive. He didn't cry; just turned and proceeded on to his classroom.

I also remember when each of them left for college. Louise and I took Steve and Danny. I took Tim. Steve's small room already had two boys in it. Already crowded. We left him, and I think we both cried a bit as we left Searcy, Arkansas and Harding University. He got a new room in a couple of weeks.

When I took Tim, Louise had just gotten home from the hospital after a long, serious illness. She was bedfast for the most part when we left for Searcy, which made it more difficult. I got Tim to Searcy, left him, and as I left town, I broke down, all alone, and cried. I felt especially sad when Danny, our youngest, left. I was glad for all of them. College for them was what we had worked for. Yet, such transitions are also tinged with sadness. Change can be unsettling.

Before Steve and Tim graduated from college, they both got married. I was very pleased with their brides; yet, when I was right in the middle of doing Steve's wedding ceremony, I choked up. Transition. Something gained but also something lost. For Tim's ceremony, I decided that I was not going to cry. So, I just concentrated on doing my thing rather than anything else. I got through it okay.

Danny finished college and returned home. He then moved into a condo, attended law school and graduated three years later.

The empty nest syndrome came next. All the boys were gone, and we were together in a different way than we had been in more than twenty years. Transition. Making adjustments.

A few years later, Danny sold his condo and moved back in with us. He works as an attorney and lived upstairs with us until he got married recently. More adjustments for all of us followed.

On June 28, 1985, Louise and I became grandparents. This brought more adjustments to make and additional family to love and receive love from. Babysitting. Ballgames. Children's museums. Hamburgers. Pizza. It seems in a way to be starting all over again. But, it's different too. Very wonderful! I never knew that being a Pa Pa could be so great. Grandchildren who run to you when they come in the door. Grandsons who walk with Me Ma to meet you as you come home from work and run and jump up into your arms as you jog to meet them! It's hard to describe.

Louise and I have already lost our mothers. Her Dad is extremely ill at this time and my Dad is recovering from a broken hip. Both are retired. I hope, Lord willing, to work six more years and retire at 65—well, mostly retire. I plan to counsel some, preach some, and write some. But, hopefully not punch a timeclock.

Family development and change. That's what all of this is about. Things don't stay the same. Refusing to change is unhealthy. Healthy families are able to proceed through the various stages of family development toward continued growth and change. Life-span family development. That's our topic.

The family system develops stability, yet it also manages to change. It adjusts. It generates new ways of responding to situations, of operating better with newly acquired patterns. It creates and reorients to new goals.

Families go through stages as individuals do. Obviously, different family forms will vary from the family stages of two-parent families with children. Thus, adjustments in thinking about family stages must be made as we think about such families.

Let's look at a typical family development profile with parents and children:

Stage	Major Task	Initiating Event
1. Marital	Differentiating from families of origin, establishing a new nuclear family, and adjusting to each other.	Marriage.
2. Family of children.	Adjusting to children.	Birth or adoption
3. School	Adjusting to children in school.	First child in school.
4. Adolescents	Flexibility and stability in family system.	Children's beginning to differentiate from the family.
5. Launching	Accepting and adjusting to the departure of children.	Children's leaving for college, careers, and marital partners.

6.	Settling Down	Readjustment to marital partner, life without the children and the aging process.	Departure of last child from home.
7.	Retirement	Adjusting to life without a career.	Ending of career.
8.	The Final Transition	Preparation for death.	Aging and Illness.

Louise and I are now at the stage of both five and six. Sometimes the transitions from one stage to the next are not once and for all. A child may leave and return several times. Families fit many shapes and sizes these days.

In all of this, healthy families exhibit cohesion, adaptability, effective communication, and role structure. There is room for both individuality and mutuality, flexibility and stability. There needs to be clear perceptions and effective communication. There will be some conflict over roles in most families, yet healthy families move toward agreement on such roles while remaining flexible. Generational boundaries are clear.

Balswick and Balswick in their book, *The Family*, stress **adaptability** by grace and **authority** by empowerment. Such adaptability leads to creativity and sometimes interchangeable roles as well as flexibility. Such families are not rigid, stilted, undetermined and chaotic. Both parents are involved at times in different roles. Child raising is an example. Sometimes the father feeds, bathes, dresses, and puts the children to bed. Sometimes it's the mother. Sometimes the mother works outside of the home. Whatever seems best is what is done. Healthy families today are making many adjustments.

Healthy marriages are relationship centered, not male or female centered, and not self centered. This leads to mutual submissiveness and interdependence. Both mates give love and go the extra mile. Family members submit to and serve each other. Mutual love. Mutual submission. Intimacy. Discussion. Negotiation. Fathers learn to be nurturing, to form bonds with children. Mothers learn to be all that they need to be. As children come and go, many adjustments and changes are affected. How? With priority given to spirituality, to relationship, to mutual empowerment rather than solely to material gain. With healthy boundaries around the family, family traditions, and solid spiritual and family values. With openness to people who are different, while holding on to individual and family values.

Change and stability don't go together so well in our minds, but we need to put them together to grow through necessary transitions in our families. As the family changes, necessary family functions may pass from one family member to another; but in healthy families, all necessary functions are performed.

Why is a study of family development so important? Research shows that most family dysfunctions brought to family therapists are dysfunctions that occur between various family stages. Marital problems are more likely to happen during the first few years of marriage and in the "settling down" stage after the children leave home. Sometimes problems have to do with school; at other times with teen-age problems, especially with the oldest child. Parents, you see, have not crossed that bridge before. They learn as they go. If we understand the family dynamics of each stage, we can learn to change and grow while remaining stable. Sounds easy, right? It's not always easy but most of the time possible with a lot of work, emotional maturity, encouragement, and prayer.

EMOTIONAL MATURITY

So, what are some of the individual and family dynamics that influence family development? First, I'd like to take you back to the concept of **emotional maturity** which I discussed previously and mention some relevant principles. The more mature you are emotionally, the more stress you can tolerate at each family transition. If you and your spouse are a 35 on a 0 to 100 scale of emotional maturity, for example, it won't take much to upset you. You'll have more than your share of initial marital adjustment difficulties. You may cry for days when your first child leaves for school. Your child's teen years may be too much for you. It's almost like a child raising a child. You may feel useless and worthless after your children leave home.

163

Nothing to live for. And who knows what other symptoms will emerge?

I'm not criticizing. I'm just saying that there is a correlation between **emotional maturity** and **healthy family development.** And, the reason I am saying this is to encourage you to examine yourself, learn to stand on your own feet, differentiate from your family of origin, and learn to guide your emotions by your thinking. You need to quit blaming others so much and take responsibility for your own life. You help create your own environment. Perhaps you even create some of the stressors in your life.

Let me point out some other ideas about emotional maturity and family development. There is a strong interrelationship between thinking, feeling and acting: each may influence the other. Thus, it's very difficult for us to be objective. Yet, thinking may be used to manage feelings and emotions. Mature people are able to distinguish between the feeling process and the intellectual process and to use that ability to direct their lives and solve problems.

Adaptation relieves anxiety while poorly defined relationships create it. If one mate overfunctions, the other tends to underfunction. It doesn't have to be that way but it often is. Anxiety can propel emotionally immature people into too much dependence upon others for brain-power and a lack of confidence in their own ability to think. Firmly held beliefs can reduce anxiety.

Three people spending time together usually gravitate to a process of **two insiders** and **one outsider**. Makes me think of the new mother and her child as insiders and her husband as the outsider. Emotionally mature people keep such triangling low-key and flexible. Thus, being the outsider is not disastrous. When one mate in a family triangle assumes more responsibility for his/her functioning, the other will often do so as well.

Key issues in conflict patterns are control and nurturance. The aloof-passive-aggressive person wants closeness, attention, and nurturance but often becomes aggressive and demanding and does not get it. He undercuts his own best interests. In marriages, individual behavior helps create many of the things we use to justify or condemn our spouses.

The emotional process in our family of origin helps determine how emotionally separate we will be as we leave home. Emotional distance between parents increases the mother's vulnerability to involvement with their children and makes it more difficult for her to separate from them. Anxiety by parents often stems from feeling overwhelmed by responsibilities for the child and feelings of inadequacy as parents. Parents who foster emotional maturity in children focus on their own functioning and not so much on the functioning of the child. Thus, modeling individuality. Parents lead the child toward accepting responsibility by being responsible and respecting boundaries as individuals themselves.

Emotional problems are often found in one or more of three family patterns: conflict between the mates, disproportionate adaptation by one mate to bring togetherness and preserve harmony, or the focus of parental anxiety upon a child or children. Denial of one's responsibility in a relationship process reduces one's options. If we are not responsible, we see no need to change. You see, the relationship process **within** people and **between** people are interrelated. And relationship disturbances may become self-perpetuating. Scary. Right?

There is an important difference between **breaking away** and **growing away** from one's family of origin. When one **grows away,** he or she gains more emotional objectivity. When one breaks away, he or she is still likely to develop the same type of intense relationship with others that they had with their family of origin. People who use emotional cutoff to deal with the past, often use emotional distance to deal with the present. How we leave father and mother is very significant. It's a barometer of our maturity.

The **thinking** you do about your family of origin can help you to change. If you know little about them, your parents may be cut off emotionally from their family of origin. There may be relationships in your family that have parallels in your family of origin. Inquire about these possibilities. It seems to me that we all have the responsibility to grow up emotionally as much as possible within our multi-generational emotional process. The bridging of emotional cutoffs with the past usually makes emotional growth more rapid.

Emotional growth is significant because it affects how we relate to others. Family life is affected. Emotionally immature people do not have an adequate sense of **self.** Pseudo self or borrowed self but not **solid self.** And why is this important in family development? Because significant changes in physical and emotional functioning occur as a result of more ability to be a **self** in one's most emotionally significant relationships. It is necessary to be **in contact** with others in one's family system and still be one's **self** in order to not be swallowed by the family system. Such a mature person can modify self and not be influenced by the irresponsible opinions of others. I believe we all have some vulnerability to believe what we "are supposed to believe" rather than what we ourselves believe. We hear through a fairly fixed screen that is mostly within us. We may sometimes hear very little and criticize the presenter, clam up or turn him off in other ways. We sometimes replace hearing with emotional reactivity.

Often in a family system, one child is more dependent and less differentiated, less emotionally mature than her parents, and more vulnerable to emotional, physical, and social illness. Such a person my grow by learning to know the difference between feelings and objectivity and to act on **knowledge** rather than **feelings.**

Another point I have observed in my professional practice is that a rigid, dogmatic person is rarely sure of himself. He acts as though he is, but he is not. He's just showing you a mask which covers up deep-seated doubts and insecure feelings.

This discussion about family of origin, emotional maturity (mental health), and differentiation is vitally important in family development. Why? Because individual mental health affects family relationships. **Individuals affect family systems, and family systems affect individuals.** So I stress both individual and family responsibility. If nobody is responsible, then nobody can fix it. If everybody is responsible, then everybody can fix it.

So at each stage of family development, both individuals and the entire family take responsibility to grow through the various crises often brought on by transitions between family stages of development. They make it work! Let either off the hook, and

somebody suffers, either the family **or** some individual within the family. What we want are healthy families and healthy individuals within families. And I'm saying that this is possible.

GROWING THROUGH STAGES

To make adjustment possible, we **apply** what we have learned, and especially so during transitions between stages of family development. Let's take **early marriage** first. After the marriage ceremony, romance sometimes turns into disillusionment. In a sense, we don't reveal ourselves to each other before marriage, and two strangers marry. After marriage comes the task of adjusting. Commitment, caring enough to understand, and considering the needs of each other carries us along. Closeness. Intimacy.

MARITAL

All of this can get complicated. All marriages are different. Different relationships, and this complicates matters. In certain types of marital complementarity, couples share the same insecurities but express them in different ways: bossiness-submissiveness, liveliness-shyness, or impulsiveness-cautiousness.

In marriages which exhibit positive complementarity, mates have similar problems but help each other. They grow and change together. They learn from each other without swallowing each other.

In marriages where there is negative complementarity, each emphasizes the other's imperfections. I often see this. They try to re-make each other. They criticize. They often are afraid of closeness but may express it in different ways: in a fight for power or in submissiveness.

In cases of extreme complementarity, each is a half person. Each lacks wholeness as an individual and is looking for someone to fill in the missing part.

With this as a background, I'd like to share some **keys** for adjustment during Stage 1 of family development:

1. Learn **how** to make decisions. **How** they are made is often more important than **what** is decided.

2. Try to make decisions that satisfy both partners. A win-win situation.

3. Avoid being enmeshed (too fused) or being disengaged (too much distance).

4. Learn a healthy sense of being together, yet still independent in a sense. Depend on each other. Be united. Not enmeshment or disengagement.

5. Do not avoid necessary conversations. Sometimes things need to be said to achieve real intimacy.

6. Do not **look for** fights. Such couples often cover up their need for intimacy and affection by fighting. **Compromise** does not mean surrender and loss of self-esteem. Winning is not always crucial. Couples who "always fight," seem to argue to have an excuse for making up, which leads to sex. It's a **vicious cycle**. They are often nasty, insensitive, withholding, unyielding, sarcastic, and mean. Not a good way to build a good marriage.

7. **Leave** father and mother and **cleave** to your mate. Separation from parents that is needed for independence in our world means financial, emotional, and social independence. You cannot depend on your parents for money and be completely independent at the same time. You cannot be enmeshed in your family of origin and have a healthy marriage at the same time. **New family rules** need to be established. **New boundaries** for family and friends. Each spouse is a one-some before he/she is a two-some.

8. Don't speak critically of your spouse to friends or extended family. See a counselor if you need help.

9. Do not recreate family of origin problems. You see, we tend to relate to our mate from our family of origin experiences. Establish a strong personal **identity.** You can then make choices rather than be ruled by compulsions established in the past.

There are some special challenges during this stage for those who have been previously married. Two families merge with one. Or maybe it's more like four families: his family of origin, her family of origin, his previous marriage, and her previous marriage. You could, of course, also take it back to four sets of grandparents. It's like being a citizen of several countries that permit dual citizenship. It gets complicated. The two spouses are often in two different emotional states (one just divorced, the other divorced for several years . . .). Each has loads of responsibility already. **New boundaries** and doors must be established. Parenting is difficult, especially with teenagers who may be withdrawn, sulky, aggressive, arrogant, or self-centered and preoccupied with their own baggage. Such couples need to take time to work things out: time with spouse alone, time with children, time with the entire blended family. It's difficult but not impossible for you to have a healthy family.

FAMILY

There are also adjustments to make in stage two, especially adjustments to children. Hopefully, at this stage, you have had adequate time for marital adjustment. Otherwise the first child will cause even additional adjustment difficulties.

Crises here can be many. I've seen these two more than any others: sexual difficulties, and marital relationship problems brought on by the arrival of the baby.

Before the baby comes, sex is usually spontaneous and unplanned. The wife is fresh and energetic. Sex can occur anywhere in the house, any room, just about any place. After the baby comes, both (especially the wife) are tired and may not feel up to it as often. They listen for signals of distress from the baby. Some wives **change their identity to mother** so completely that they ignore their role as wife. "The baby needs me more." They get turned off to sex. Some wives have told me in counseling sessions that they lost their sexual desires after childbirth. Seems to be connected with either the pain of childbirth which they connect with sex, or with their identity as a mother rather than as a woman and wife. Most respond well to therapy. Some husbands lose desire for their wife during pregnancy and after childbirth. Seems to be connected to a combination of being turned off because their wife is carrying a baby and is "overweight," and the identity problem I mentioned previously. She's not a woman and a wife now: **she's a mother.**

And you don't make love to mothers. Remember men, **she's still a woman and your wife.** And, though she is a mother, she's not your mother. Childbirth does not usually take away from her sexuality in the least. If you do not wish to have additional children, carefully practice birth control methods: take the pill, use a diaphragm, get a vasectomy, or use other methods.

After the birth of a child, **realignments** are made in the family system. One of the more common ones is for the mother to focus most of her attention on the baby and less on the husband. Sometimes this is accelerated by anxiety between the spouses prior to the baby's arrival. One way to handle the marital problem, you see, is to avoid it. Concentrate on the baby. It's socially acceptable, and it reduces marital anxiety. Yet, the marital problems remain. The **husband feels lonely and neglected** and sometimes turns to **someone else** for companionship and sex or buries himself in his work. Marital problems remain unsolved.

Keep your identity as persons, as mates, as well as parents. They are not mutually exclusive roles! Work on your marital problems. Spend quality time together, sometimes without the baby. Cultivate romance. Keep your appearance as attractive as possible. Build the relationship. "Be there" emotionally for each other. You can get through this important transition.

SCHOOL

When the first child begins school, you need to alter your personal identity again and not be lost in the family. Family patterns change at this transition also. Work it out. Change. Grow. Children become more independent, but they are still family. The healthy home helps launch each child into the larger world. It starts earlier as the parents encourage trust, autonomy, and initiative in the child during preschool years. Leaving him for gradually longer periods from birth leading up to school trains the child to know that you are dependable. They can handle it without your presence. Others can take care of them. And, they learn that you always come back. So school is not such a big change for them.

Boundaries change at this new stage. External boundaries open more to life outside the family system. Internal boundaries and the marriage are reaffirmed. You are still an individual and still a spouse (unless divorced, widowed, or a never married parent).

Disengaged families have problems with this transition. It's everyone for himself. No strong friendships or alliances within the family. There is little family support or cohesion at a time when it is needed.

Enmeshed (too close, too fused) families may have even more problems at this transition period. Everyone is in everyone else's business. Children don't want to leave Mommy. Mommy rescues them. Children come between parents. Many parent-child coalitions exist. External family boundaries are high and thick. The outside world is closed out. Too much dependency is approved.

Bryant, age 8, was brought by his parents to see me for counseling. He cried every time he had to leave his mother. Even at his grandmother's house, someone had to hold him while he screamed as they would leave him for perhaps less than an hour. Separation anxiety. Extreme! He cried when he left for school. Got sick almost daily! Mother came and got him, and he got better. Serious problems.

Where was his Dad in all of this! You guessed it, always at work, in retail sales. "Had to pay the bills," he said, during his one visit for family therapy. Both his wife and son were growing away from him. Weak bonding with both. I sympathized, but led them into a discussion of priorities: God, spouse, children, work, other concerns. I asked him to take his wife to dinner once a week, and to take his boy hiking in the woods as well as to help him each night with his homework.

But, there was another problem. The mother and son were enmeshed. I noticed a sign of this extremely close enmeshment one night in a family therapy session with the mother and son. When I would ask him a question, he would always glance at his mother and wouldn't answer until she prompted him. She was always attentive to his glance and sometimes would answer for him. As I caught on to these enmeshment dynamics, I smiled and asked him if his mother had his "thinker." He looked puzzled and glanced at her. She smiled, looked at him, but said nothing. As I got my point across, I expressed confi-

171

dence in his ability to think and gave her some assignments designed to push him out "of her lap." Really, it was almost as though he were still in her womb.

Their genogram at first looked something like this:

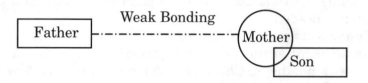

I tried to strengthen the bond between the spouses and between the father and his son and to get the mother to completely give birth to her son. To give him wings as well as roots. Perhaps she needed such closeness because of the weak bond with her husband, and she was still enmeshed with her Dad.

At his juncture, another complicating factor is that the husband and wife do not always grow in the same direction or to the same extent. Thus, the relationship must be redesigned, adaptations made. Mom may go to work, which may cause a shift in power and self-respect. The husband must adjust to her new role. The wife must also adjust to numerous changes: new attention by men, less time for homemaking, new complaints from children and husband, fatigue, and other matters. Not easy, but possible.

Remember as you deal with this transition of children in school that:

1. Marriage can give companionship (Genesis 1:18-27).

2. Marriage requires commitment (Genesis 2:24).

3. Sexual gratification is to be fulfilled in marriage (I Corinthians 7:1-5).

4. In marriage we can find acceptance (Ephesians 5:21-30).

5. In marriage, we try to please each other (I Corinthians 7:33)

6. Making a marriage good requires unselfishness (I Peter 3:1-7), purity (Psalms 24:4), respect (Ephesians 5:31), inner beauty (I Peter 3:1-6), and unity of purpose (Amos 3:3).

7. To build a better home, you must first build a good marriage. That's where it all starts. This means paying more attention to your spouse than to your children, though you should not neglect them.

8. Pay attention to your own needs without being self-centered. You can't be the kind of spouse or parent you want to be if you are unhealthy yourself.

ADOLESCENTS

When children become **adolescents,** parents need to help them to launch out while maintaining family cohesion. Letting go a little at a time requires a great deal of flexibility and emotional maturity. And a good life yourself. Not completely invested in them.

This is an especially critical stage to negotiate. While adolescents are bursting into adulthood, parents are usually in a mid-life crisis wondering if they are "losing it" and if their life really counts for anything important. Adolescent bodies are blooming; parents bodies sagging. Adolescents are growing intellectually and seeking good self-esteem. They often seek thrills: sexual experimentation, stealing, taking drugs, and defying authority. Parents sometimes live vicariously through their teenagers.

With all of this in mind, I'd like to give you some **keys to success** during this stage of family development:

1. Set reasonable limits and assert your value system. Communicate expectations and consequences clearly. Exert leadership, but do not be bossy. You do still have the final word, however. Teens often want all the freedom of an adult with none of the responsibility. Encourage them to take whatever responsibility they can handle (II Timothy 2:22). Allow them to **make more decisions** as they mature, some with which you may not agree.

I remember a teen named Tony. His parents were extremely rigid and ultra-conservative. To the right of me several notches. Tony was 16 but was not allowed to decide whether or not he would wear shorts while mowing the grass in 95 degree weather. They said shorts might tempt some girl sexually. They had similar conflicts over mixed swimming (boys and girls in the same pool), school socials, school dances, friends, and many other matters. He was compliant, went to church, and seemed to be a good boy although he was beginning to rebel. His parents meant well but were coming down on him with more rules everytime he did anything "wrong." He would ask why it was wrong, and they would say that their position was taught in the Bible. He would ask where, and they would show him. Only it didn't mean that to him.

He was getting into more and more trouble: the wrong crowd, drugs, and other problems. His Dad and he had a family therapy session with me. His Dad had taken driving privileges away from him for four months. He laid down the law to his son. Tony agreed readily. Too readily. He had been defeated. I told them before they left that I was afraid that Tony was agreeing but really not agreeing. Tony's father felt good about his son's agreements, and they left. That night, Tony "took" his Dad's car and ran off with a friend. It really, you see, had not been settled!

I believe there are times when parents should not answer the "why" questions of teens. They often are just trying to wear us down. "Why should I not drink and drive?" "That's our rule," may be a sufficient answer. Don't let them wear you down. Be like a policeman when they stop you for having run a red light. "Why is it wrong? Why are you giving me a ticket? I didn't mean to run the red light!" Just not enough! A well-trained policeman will not yell or get upset at such protests. He or she may not even answer your questions. Policemen will be nice in such circumstances, smile, hand you a ticket, and wish you a good day. Expectations. Consequences. That's okay.

But these parents were equally rigid on shorts and drugs. No sufficient answers for an inquiring mind, a young Christian boy who was trying to learn what God's will was for him. At least at first.

I'll stick my neck out. As a parent, I would not force my will on my teen-age children in marginal matters. I would let them have some practice in making decisions and living with the consequences. It's the best way for them to develop a faith or a set of moral values of their own. Such training will get them prepared for the next stage—life on their own. Try to protect them, be tough at times, teach them, show them, but encourage them to make decisions as well. Make less and less decisions for them as they mature.

Remember that during all this conflict with teens that parents are usually experiencing a mid-life crisis toward the end of this stage. Who am I? Where is my career going? Am I still attractive? What do I really believe? What are my priorities? Difficult questions are being asked by parents.

Their marriage may suffer with less sex and affection, fewer shared activities, less common interests, and the blahs. **Many get divorced** during this stage, and divorce of parents is **extremely painful to adolescents.** They become sad, angry, anxious, embarrassed, ashamed, and doubtful of their future as marital and sexual partner. They feel **cut down** as they go into adulthood. **Let down by their idols.** They usually withdraw and distance themselves against pain. Many fail in school. Girls get depressed or anxious. Boys get into trouble, while they assure their Dad that it is not connected in any way with their divorce. Tough times for everybody! A real crisis in family development.

During this ADOLESCENT stage, there are many family problems. Co-parenting after divorce for some. Single parenting for others. The mother usually keeps the children; the father adjusts to his pain and loneliness.

The enmeshed family avoids all conflict and refuses to release the children during this stage. One child often becomes a "traitor" as he breaks away (cuts off) in anger.

The disengaged family has no discipline, no leadership, no center of gravity, alienation, anti-social activities, loneliness, insecurity, and drifting in separate worlds. Parents are **split!** The **mother** often *indulges* the children while the **father punishes them.** The submissive parent may fight his or her mate through the teenager. The adolescent becomes trapped in the family. Many triangles and scapegoats appear. It's unhealthy. Too much guilt. Manipulation. Disregard.

During this turbulent stage, here are **some keys** to a successful transition:

1. Remember who you are as a person, a spouse, and a parent.

2. Give yourself credit for your simple accomplishments.

175

3. Learn that it's okay to get older. You're not in the grave yet.
4. Learn to enjoy each stage. Delight as your children mature.
5. Spend more time with your spouse. Strengthen that bond.
6. Stop affairs before they start. Nip it in the bud. Don't let it get started. It's wrong. It's not worth it, and it hurts too many people!
7. Take appropriate leadership. You still have rights as a parent. Don't be afraid to go against what you children want. You don't have to be liked every minute by your children.

All of this will prepare you to let your children go and to give them wings. Remember, children are born dependent, and they usually become independent before they become interdependent as mature adults. Don't think it strange when they oppose you as teenagers. That's when the independence streak begins to hit. It's normal. Help them grow through it in a healthy manner. With their cooperation, you will succeed. And, one encouraging fact I have learned is that parents can make many mistakes and their children still survive. Help them not only survive but thrive as well!

LAUNCHING

During the next stage of family development, our task is to let the children go and readjust to each other. Disengaged families tend to release children suddenly, enmeshed families slowly, and disturbed families trap their children indefinitely.

The traditional homemaker may experience a crisis at this point: with loss of central mother role, self-depreciation, depression, and loss of identity. "Not needed anymore." She needs to re-orient her life and revitalize her marriage: more time together, romance, and companionship. Learn to enjoy being without children. Louise and I, for example, eat out more now, and she travels with me more since our children matured.

Remember these keys to success as your family shrinks:

1. Support each other. Be considerate (I Peter 3:1-6).
2. Encourage children to pass the torch of leadership from one child to another as they leave home.
3. Let your children go. You'll have an especially difficult time in doing this if you are still enmeshed with **your** parents. Everybody holds on: "What could they do if **I** were not there?"
4. If family secrets are revealed, as they often are during this letting go stage, face them and deal with them in an open and honest way. Admit that your family is human and that humans make mistakes. Humans are also sometimes good at correcting mistakes and growing through difficulties.
5. Learn to really **listen** to your mate.
6. Be **emotionally present** for each other.
7. Treat each other as **equals** (Galatians 3:26-29).
8. Replace hatred with **love** (I John 4:20)! It's a good trade!

Now the **nest is empty.** You need to **rediscover close companionship** in your spouse. Give more attention to each other.

At this point, parents are usually in the mid-life crisis. One may stop living while the other expands his or her life and looks forward zestfully to the future. A time of self-development. Remember, you're not undesirable just because you are getting older. Keep your confidence. You're not a failure just because you have failed at a few endeavors. You don't have to achieve **every goal** in life to be successful. Look at **what is important. What is nice but not necessary.** Build a new, meaningful relationship with your marital partner. Enrich your friendship, your romantic life. Show that you care. Put yourself out for each other. Learn to like you children as adults.

Becoming in-laws is a challenge to most parents. Enmeshed families tend to absorb their children's mates; disengaged families extend a restrained welcome. Welcome them "into the family," but don't take them over.

Becoming a grandparent means continuity and heritage and more fun to share. It can provide energy for family unity. Yet, old conflicts, disappointment, and pains can be revived. Grandparents are often able to give more affection to grandchildren than they were to their children. Less conflict. Less responsibility. Maybe by that time, we're more mature and have more emotionally to give. Grandparents can help build confidence and self-esteem in grandchildren by giving "unconditional" love. I hope we have been able to do that with ours without undermining parental authority. That's what we want.

The empty nest also means **aging parents** and sometimes **role-reversals.** Children take care of parents and sometimes have to tell them what to do. It's hard for everyone but sometimes necessary. Children should share caring responsibilities for parents with each other. Being too burdened often leads to resentment. Contrary to popular myth, 80 percent of older parents live close to and interact with at least one child at least once a week. Aging parents means debts and hospital bills. Medicare. Health insurance. Home health nurses and caregivers. A handy telephone for emergencies. Changing diets and habits.

Consider these keys to success through the **empty nest** stage:

1. Treat your parents well. How you treat them is a model for your children (Matthew 7:12). Maybe they'll take care of you if you set a good example.

2. Rediscover your mate. It can be very rewarding!

3. Enjoy your children as adults. It was a special pleasure the first time Louise and I dined at the home of our children! We were **proud of them**. They were sort of giving back to us. Successful!

4. Give your **children wings** as well as **roots.**

5. Be supportive as parents and in-laws but not intrusive.

6. Don't allow your grown children to intrude excessively into your life. It's not healthy.

7. Be a loving grandparent and support the parents.

8. Return good for evil (Romans 12:20-21). Somebody needs to display **mature behavior.**

9. God loves you, and love makes a difference for good (I John 4:7-8; I Corinthians 13).

10. **Be faithful** to your spouse (Malachi 2:16). It feels good to do right, and it **is** good.

11. Learn to forgive (Psalms 86:5; Matthew 6:12-14). It keeps transitions and growth on the move.

RETIREMENT

Retirement comes next. Right now, I wonder why my older friends are having problems with retirement. My good friend, Dr. W. B. West, Jr., taught and preached until he was past 80. At 85, he would like to continue doing so. I think he deserves a rest, but he wants to work. It seems to be that way for most. My Dad was "piddling around at the barn" when he broke his hip recently. My grandfathers worked right up until they went on to be with the Lord. I may do the same.

With this in mind, I want to share with you **some keys** for getting through the retirement stage:

1. **Prepare** for the changes that take place as you age: decline in physical ability, not going to work and staying at home more, loss of social status, and sometimes a loss of family home. There is more to you than your body, your house, or your work!

2. Cultivate closeness with your spouse.

3. Find **new interests and purpose** and don't lean excessively on each other.

4. If you become a widow or a widower, work through your grief toward recovery and a new life with more independence and freedom.

5. Learn to **grow through difficulties** (James 1:2-4).

6. If you re-marry, consider pre-marital counseling. Really! Both of you are probably set in your ways and carry a lot of baggage! You will probably need to make a pre-nuptial agreement (as much as I dislike the idea) on money and property.

7. Learn to be close with your adult children but not enmeshed.

8. Don't move in with your children unless it's absolutely necessary.
9. Heal family wounds. Come together in peace.
10. Make a will. It's **your** property. Direct how it will be used.
11. Be a good example of a retired person. Not useless. Still alive with a purpose for living! Still useful as long as possible!

THE FINAL TRANSITION

After retirement, comes the **"going home stage."** Going home was the way Ma Flatt said it. Pa Way often talked about going to heaven during his latter years. He said he had "fought a good fight, had finished the course, had kept the faith. Therefore, there was laid up for him a crown of righteousness which the Lord God shall give me in that day" (II Timothy 4:6-8). I heard him preach it. I heard him talk about it. I think he had prepared well: had lived a good life! Ma Flatt had too!

Remember as you face your final transition **these keys** that should help you in the process:

1. Live the way you want to die.
2. Forgive. Don't hold grudges (Ephesians 4:25-26). Mend fences. Reconcile (Hosea 11:1-8; I Corinthians 7:10-16).
3. Build others up. Edify. Be a blessing. You have a lot to give (Ephesians 4:29).
4. Nurture the inner person. Such a one does not decline with age (II Corinthians 4:16-5:1) but grows!
5. Hold on to God. He never leaves us (Isaiah 41:10; Psalm 71:17-18).
6. In my life, I have found joy and inner peace in Jesus (John 14:27; 16:22, 33). I hope you can too.
7. Live **until you die. Function** as long as you can. Don't let others do for you what you can and wish to do for yourself. Hold on to as much **independence** as you can handle, then **let others take over.** You deserve it.
8. **Press on** toward the mark of the high-calling of God to which you have been called (Philippians 3:13-14).
9. **Look forward.** The best is yet to be.

10. Leave your children and grandchildren a good heritage, roots. Share old stories and information about genealogies. [Our son, Tim, who proofread this text and offered valuable suggestions, wrote "priceless" at this point!]

Family development. You move from one stage to another. Marriage, children, school, adolescence, launching children, settling down, retirement, and preparation for the final transition. It's normal. Natural. Couples who have no children and single parents do not proceed exactly the way I have described it with children included, but they will make many transitions throughout life as well. Transitions may bring crises, but crises can be overcome. Actually crises **present opportunities** for change and growth. And healthy family development comes from such change and growth. Hang in there when it gets rough. Your family is worth saving.

CHANGE AND GROWTH QUESTIONS TO DISCUSS

1. What are some of the conflicts you have experienced because of what you learned from your family of origin?

2. Can you see that such conflict is not always over right and wrong but over different traditions?

3. How would you rate your level of emotional maturity (mental health) on a zero to 100 scale?

4. How does this affect your family?

5. Can you see that individual mental health affects family dynamics?

6. How would you describe your family system? Who does what? When? Who talks? Who listens? Who gives in? Who always has the last word?

7. How does this need to change?

8. What are you going to do to change it?

9. In what stage is your family?

10. What will you do to make transitions proceed effectively?

11. What have you gained from trials in your life?

12. How would you like your life to look when you are in your final transition?

Ten

Anger and Conflict Management Skills

Principle Number 10:
Healthy Families are able to cope successfully with anger
and manage conflict well.

Audra was silently sobbing. Tears running constantly down her face. She would wipe them away with tissues we provided, but they kept coming. She said, "We've got lots of problems, but the one thing I can't deal with is Chris' temper. He gets mad and yells at me. He intimidates and bullies me. It's like he's trying to scare me."

Chris said that he came from a family like that. "My father, in fact **all** of my family acted like that. We just yelled until we got everything straight."

They had been married for 10 years before they came to me for counseling. The marriage had been "bad" almost from the start, but they thought they could work it out. "Why do we need to pay somebody $90 an hour just to talk to us?" they reasoned.

So, by this time, they were stuck. Never had worked out their marital problems! Their self-perpetuating pattern went something like this: He yelled; she cried. He pointed his finger into her face; she froze and cried more. He wanted sex; she tensed up and pulled away. He continued to pursue her for sex; she continued to refuse. He would proceed in foreplay almost immediately to her genitals; she wanted a better relationship and much more non-sexual touching. She held out; he got worse: went for her genital area more rapidly and yelled louder when he was refused, which was for months at a time by then.

Anger and conflict management. Relationship building. That's my concern at this point.

I've seen numerous families break up because they did not know how to cope successfully with anger and to manage conflict well. People get frustrated and angry. People conflict with each other.

It's okay to get mad. It's normal to have conflicts. Just learn how to handle it.

With our background, it's almost impossible for us to think of anger and conflict without thinking that it is bad. Bad in itself. Can't be good.

I suggest that it **can** be good. Stay with me. It depends on how it is handled. Something good can come out of anger and conflict.

We live in an angry age: an age of fighting, hijacking, murder, rape, and war. It's usually not constructive. It is a saboteur of the mind, a factor in the formation of many serious diseases, and a leading cause of misery. No matter what the problem, control of anger and conflict management are key factors in its solution.

Anger is usually destructive but can be constructive if handled properly. It's like fire. It can be used for good or evil.

SOME EXAMPLES OF ANGER

Cain, the world's first child, got mad, and this led to the murder of his brother, Abel. Sadness, loneliness, and endless wandering followed (Genesis 4:1-8).

King Saul's jealousy and anger prompted him to threaten to kill David and throw his spear at his own son, Jonathan. He chased David for months (I Samuel 20-31).

Yet, even Jesus Christ, who did not sin, got mad (Mark 3:2-6). He healed a man's withered hand on the sabbath, which the on-lookers thought was against the law. They criticized. Jesus looked at them with anger and was grieved at the hardening of their hearts. The Pharisees and Herodians went out and "took counsel" against Jesus. They planned how to destroy him. Oh, how I wish that the spirit of Jesus could come into our hearts (Galatians 2:20; Romans 8:1-17)! What a difference it would make upon the church as well as others. Jesus did not let criticism stop his good work. He got mad, but he channeled his anger into something useful. He controlled it! He did good, not harm!

Jesus seems to have been angry when he cleansed the Temple (John 2:13-17). The Passover was at hand. Those who sold oxen, sheep, and doves as well as the moneychangers were in the Temple. They all had a tendency to take advantage of the people. They rejected the animals **they** brought for offerings at the Temple in order to sell them theirs at a high price. Required payment in **their** money and charged the worshippers an inflated exchange rate. Jesus made a whip of cords, cast them out, poured out the changers' money, and turned over their tables. He said to those who sold doves: "Take these things hence; make not my Father's house a house of merchandise" ASV. What he did is sort of scary to me, but he knew what needed to be done and did it. He channeled his anger into constructive activity.

The Bible tells us that even God gets mad. Angry at evildoers. He sometimes speaks in his wrath and severe distress (Psalm 2:5). He in his wrath said that those who had been unfaithful to him would not enter into his rest (Psalm 95:11). His wrath is revealed from heaven against all ungodliness and unrighteousness of people (Romans 1:18). God is God, and he knows how to handle his anger.

When the magicians came to worship baby Jesus, they became afraid of King Herod and returned home another way. When Herod learned of this, he got exceedingly angry and killed all of the male children in Bethlehem from two years old and under (Matthew 2:16). Sick!

The prophet, Jonah, got mad at God because he spared the great city of Nineveh (Jonah 1-4). Jonah had preached to them but didn't want them to be spared. He was more interested in his own comfort than he was in their salvation! How sad.

The other 10 apostles of Jesus got upset and angry at James and John because they tried to get ahead of them in the kingdom (Mark 10:35-45). Position. Prestige. The more we change, the more we remain the same. It's hard to be humble.

Notice this, most of the time anger gets us into trouble. So, how does it arise, and what can we do to successfully cope with it?

SOME CAUSES OF ANGER

We need to know some **causes** of anger in order to help us successfully cope with it. Otherwise, it controls us!

Anger may be caused by **conditioning.** It may very well be a **learned** response. We learn from parents who will not let us talk out our frustrations. Conflict is always bad, you see. Good people don't have conflict. We learn from parents who are often angry. Lots of anger directed at everybody and everything. We may learn from watching so much anger and violence on television. It may desensitize us to think it's normal. We may learn from parents who administer incorrect discipline. They provoke their children to wrath by whipping, slapping, punching, and beating their children. Nurture them instead in the chastening and admonition of the Lord (Ephesians 6:4).

Let me say this. Every time I have ever counseled with a client who displayed excessive anger, that person had been disciplined **excessively** by his or her parents. It's true! Long switches! Many licks! Slaps, punches, fists, ax handles, wires, and the list gets sicker and sicker. Such people have anger problems with their mates and usually abuse **their** children. They don't have to, but many of them do. Remember, there's a big difference between a big switch and a little paddle. Between a belt and a small strap. And there is a difference in very young children and older children. Between children who don't understand and those who do.

Anger may be caused by **injustice.** The prophets often got mad at the injustice toward helpless people in their day. They were constructive in speaking out against such injustice.

I get mad when I hear of child abuse, of wife abuse, and of incest. It upsets me to hear widows tell of their disappointment with the companies their husbands worked for who go bankrupt, change names, and cheat them out of their husbands' provision for them earned over a lifetime of work. Same company. Different name. I think it's illegal now. Somebody chan-

186

neled their anger in the right direction. It makes me mad that insurance companies can legally cancel your policy if they have to pay off several claims. It happened to us on our house recently. It happens to many of my clients on their health insurance. Rates escalate first. Then, cancellation. You get older and have a record of illness. You get fired. You can't get insurance. No wonder our leaders are saying that something has to be done. Somebody got mad and channeled it in the right direction. Such solutions will not be easy, but the problems need to be addressed! Too many innocent, hardworking people are being hurt!

Anger may be caused by **frustrations.** Something stands in the way of our progress toward a goal. Car trouble. A breakdown of household appliances. Theft. Potential for anger increases as frustration increases!

Anger may be caused by **disappointments.** You do a good job, but your mate doesn't notice. Disappointment is followed by anger. You talk, but your children do not understand. Disappointment is followed by anger. Anger tends to increase as disappointment increases.

Threat and **hurt feelings** may lead to anger. As they increase, potential for anger increases. Your wife cuts you down; you're hurt and get mad. Your husband hints that you are stupid; you're hurt and become angry. Your children criticize you for not giving them what they want. You get hurt and upset. Unjust criticism between races of people inflames anger. The same is true of unjust gender criticisms. Threat and hurt are then followed by anger.

I recently agreed to speak at a certain large workshop. Of course, many other speakers were invited as well. Before the workshop, I got several letters asking, pleading, and "begging" me not to go because they thought there were speakers on the program who were liberal theologically.

I have always had a practice of saying yes or no to speaking invitations based upon my schedule. Most invitations come to me by phone. I have not had a practice of asking who else is on the program. I always figured that I am responsible for what I say, and they are responsible for what they say. I also remember that Jesus was often falsely judged guilty by association.

187

Jesus preached in synagogues, and Paul preached on Mars Hill, and I always thought we accepted them as models.

How to decide? I knew I couldn't please everyone, so I had to do what I thought was right. I went! I spoke on "Some Ingredients of a Healthy Christian Family." Even my critics did not disagree with what I said, but they didn't want me to say it **there.** Not unless all of the speakers on the program were "sound."

Louise and I heard several of the other speakers and enjoyed them. I wouldn't have said everything exactly the way they did, but I'm used to that sort of thing. We learn from each other.

At any rate, I got some letters of criticism after I returned home from the engagement. Same rationale. "You should have known not to speak on that workshop. If you were a sound preacher, they would not have invited you," were some of the sentiments. One letter especially hurt me. It was from a man I baptized during his teen years. He was very disappointed in me! I must not be preaching the gospel anymore because I spoke on that workshop. One church has cancelled a meeting because, according to them, speaking there has caused me to lose my influence with "sound brethren." Perhaps, they said, I can gain it back at some time in the future.

Threats and hurt feelings lead to a bit of anger over all of us at times. What I'm trying to do with my anger is to channel it into constructive activities. I teach, I counsel, I write, I preach, I try to share the good news of Jesus, and to help people develop good mental health and to build healthy families. I'm not infallible. My judgment may at times be wrong, but I've got to follow my own conscience. You see, I didn't agree with their logic; so, I went. I spoke. I don't see how we can influence each other if we don't talk.

About two years ago, I was cancelled out on a speech I was to deliver at a church on "Overcoming Grief." The elders had decided that such a topic was not a Bible topic. Sad! I grieved over their decision! You see, I was going to talk about how Abraham, Joseph, the nation of Israel, Job, David, Mary, Martha, and Jesus handled their grief. I got hurt and a little angry. There is plenty for me to do without these assignments, but such decisions by church leaders are disturbing to me. No wonder many people today think the church is irrelevant!

One morning the husband of a woman I had counseled the previous night came storming into my office. Didn't even say, "Hello," just said: "I've only got one question for you. Did you tell my wife last night that all of our problems are **my** fault?" I grinned and asked: "What do you think?" He hesitated and then replied, "No. I don't think you said that."

Sometimes it's not that easy to deal with misunderstandings. People get **faulty perceptions** and get mad. We often misunderstand each other and get mad.

Immaturity leads to anger. Children have temper tantrums. As we mature, anger usually decreases. We control it more by our minds.

Repression leads to anger. We get hurt, disappointed, insulted, or threatened and just swallow it. We "bite our tongues" and keep it to ourselves. Sometimes this is needed, but if repression becomes habitual, it leads to anger.

Feelings of **inferiority, insecurity,** and **low self-esteem** lead to anger. "Everybody has it better than I do. They have it made. They look down on me." These attitudes are not far from anger, which may be turned inward or outward. Explosions in inner-cities are expressions of anger. Feelings of inadequacy lead to fear which leads to anger.

For whatever reason—conditioning, angry parents, television, violent discipline, injustice, disappointments, threat and hurt, faulty perceptions, emotional immaturity, repression, or feelings of inferiority—we get mad. Then, what we do with anger becomes extremely important.

SOME EFFECTS OF ANGER

If we turn our anger **inward,** we hurt ourselves spiritually, emotionally, and physically. Anger turned inward often leads to tension, self-pity, self-destruction, increased blood pressure, adrenaline, and pulse rate; blood clots, stomach pains, strokes, angina pectoris, heart attacks, headaches, nausea, gastric ulcers, diarrhea or constipation, itching sensations, increased problems with asthma, and problem drinking. Such problems affect our family relationships negatively: dysfunctional communications patterns, increased fights or emotional distance. Thus, don't turn anger inward. Don't just swallow all of your disappointments and frustrations. There's a better way!

If you turn your anger **outward,** you usually hurt others. You attack the object of your anger or a substitute such as a spouse or a child. You may blame inflation on the grocery clerk. You spray the whole area with a shotgun approach in hopes of hitting someone. You may be angry about anything, and it can result in injury to others: physical or verbal. The husband gets mad, hits his wife and beats his children. The wife gets mad and insults her husband and scolds the children. Insults, ridicule, name calling, cynicism, and foul language follow. You get mad at your mate for aloofness, indifference, or insults and go have an affair with someone who "appreciates" you. You get mad and refuse to cooperate in any constructive way with other family members. Anger turned outward can even lead to murder. I've counseled with some 100 wives who have been hit, shoved, spanked, or thrown down by their husbands. Five have told me their husbands attempted to kill them. Of course, in such instances, they need to flee to safety.

Jesus condemns a "get even" approach to life (Matthew 5:35-44). Don't fight. Turn the other cheek. Go the second mile. Give more than is expected. Love your enemies. Pray for them that persecute you.

ANGER AND CONFLICT RESOLUTION

Conflict may come from anger, different viewpoints, pressures of daily life, different tastes, or other factor. Whatever the cause, healthy families learn to cope with anger and manage conflict effectively. Not easily, not without many ups and downs, but they manage it nevertheless. They don't let it control them. They control it!

How? Here are some keys to success in coping with anger and managing conflict.

1. **Identify** the source of anger and conflict. Is it frustration, different viewpoints or tastes, put-downs, or something else? Then deal with these problems, preferably before they increase to full-blown conflict and anger.

2. **Meditate** upon **God's word.** There is power in the biblical message to change the heart and life. It is living and active and sharp (Hebrews 4:12). It can penetrate to the bottom of your problem. It can help to get your will lined up with what is right. My experience has been similar to that of the psalmist who wrote, "Thy word have I laid up in my heart, that I might not sin against thee" (Psalm 119:11 ASV). My experience is that it won't overpower you but can guide you toward a constructive attitude which will help resolve conflicts and manage anger well. Again the psalmist writes, "Cease from anger, and forsake wrath: fret not thyself, it tendeth only to evil-doing" (Psalm 37:8). Solomon writes, "A hot-tempered man stirs up dissention, but a patient man calms a quarrel" (Proverbs 15:18 NIV). And, "An angry man stirs up dissention, and a hot-tempered one commits many sins" (Proverbs 29:22 NIV). He again cautions us, "Do not be quickly provoked in your spirit, for anger resides in the lap of tools" (Ecclesiastes 7:9). Cool it!

3. I have found that it also helps when I **pray about** my anger and conflicts. James writes, "Therefore confess your sins to each other, and pray for each other so that you may be healed. The prayer of a righteous man is powerful and effective" (James 5:16). Sometimes we're wrong and need to apologize, to confess our wrongs, to say we're sorry and really mean it. Real sorrow can lead to reconciliation. Praying is not just saying a prayer but pouring out our hearts to God. Getting specific about our frustrations, hurt feelings, anger, and conflicts. Resolving to work it out if possible.

4. Sometimes it's better to **keep our distance** from chronically angry and disagreeable people. I've done this a few times. But, it's not a very practical, permanent solution in a family.

5. **Be humble.** Peter teaches us to be likeminded, compassionate, loving, tenderhearted, humble-minded, and not to render evil for evil or reviling for reviling (I Peter 3:8-9). Insult for insult does not often lead to equitable solutions. But an attitude like Peter described points us toward such solutions. As much as we hate to admit it, we are not always right! Not always wise! Our emotions get in control, and we just react! Somehow, we must get beyond that type of animal reaction toward more mature behavior.

6. **Think** about things that are true, honorable, just, pure, lovely, and of good report (Philippians 4:8). Realize that your mind is very powerful, and transforming. **Renewal** can come through it (Romans 12:1-2). The mind controlled by the Spirit leads to life and **peace** (Romans 8:6).

7. **Reinterpret** what you are angry and in conflict about. Is there any other way of looking at it? Usually there is, and you just haven't seen it yet. Naaman thought he was right about how he should be healed, but the prophet Elisha suggested doing it another way (II Kings 5). "Go dip in the Jordan River," the prophet commanded through a messenger. Naaman thought that the prophet should come out to meet him, call on the name of God, and wave his hand over the spot and cure him of his leprosy. Not so. He just sent a message about dipping in a river. Enough to make any logical person angry! Why, he knew of rivers in Damascus that were better than the waters of Israel! So, he turned and went off in a rage!

Naaman's servants, however, went to him, and challenged him to rethink his position. Their logic convinced Naaman to look at the conflict in a different way. He then went and dipped in the Jordan River seven times and was healed! Reinterpret what you are angry about. Challenge yourself to view the conflict from different points of view. This has helped with many conflicts.

8. Communicate. Talk. Affirm. Don't clam up. Don't yell. Don't escalate. Don't mind read. Don't judge each other. Give the other person the benefit of the doubt. Validate each other. Healthy families remember that they are on the same team when in conflict. Make it a win-win situation, if possible. Give the other person room to **save face**. I like to call this "room to wiggle." That's in the opposite direction of "nailing them to the wall." Remember, it's possible to win a battle and lose a war. I'd rather build a healthy marriage and a healthy family than to win every battle. See my point? "We" versus "the problem" rather than "me" versus "you." Try to see the other person's point of view. Try to meet **their** needs. Focus on **issues** rather than personalities. "You're just like your father" is a focus on personalities and not usually helpful!

9. **Don't badger** the other one to agree with you. **Influence** but don't force. And, remember, **it's okay to have differences.** You can have many differences and still love and **support each other!** Try it! It'll help your family.

10. **Negotiate.** What does **he** want? What does **she** want? Maybe there is an in-between position that will satisfy both. Or at least it will serve as a workable compromise. Remember, it takes a mature person to **compromise** in matters of judgment. To be **flexible.** Rigidity is usually a sign of emotional immaturity. Grow out of it. Your way is not always right. I don't like to admit being wrong anymore than you do, but Louise's ideas are sometimes better than mine. And, I'm sometimes wrong. Every action I have ever taken with Louise and the children has not always been healthy. What little growth I have made mentally and emotionally has come from my recognition of these truths. It's humbling in a good way. Yet, rewarding. Cleansing. Growth oriented.

11. **Channel** your energies into **constructive activities.** Jesus did this: healed the man with a withered hand and cleansed the Temple. The apostle Paul gives us helpful instructions on how to do this (Ephesians 4:25-32).

a. Put away falsehood and speak the truth.

b. Being angry, sin not: Let not the sun go down on your wrath.

c. Quit stealing. Work and **give** to the poor instead.

d. Let no unwholesome talk come out of your mouth. Say only **what is upbuilding** to others according to their needs instead.

e. Get rid of bitterness, rage and anger, brawling and slander, and every form of malice. Be kind, forgiving, and tenderhearted instead. That's the way God is in Christ toward us!

Notice Paul's model for changing undesirable behavior. Get rid of the dysfunctional, sinful, hurtful, put-down types of behavior, but don't leave it there. Vacuums tend to get filled with something. **Replace bad behavior with good behavior. Replace anger with constructive activities.**

Albert rechanneled his anger into jogging and strenuous exercise. He was 42 and had been married to Pat for 15 years. He admitted that anger had always been his problem. He'd never been able to control it. Escalation was their usual pattern of behavior with conflicts. It didn't work. Pat had just about given up when they first came to me. She had distanced herself, tried about everything. Although he had never hit her, he yelled, pointed his finger at her, and slammed doors. Of course, when he was like that, he was always right: she was always wrong. They did not usually solve conflicts! Just **piled them up.** What to do? He learned to catch himself before his anger boiled over and to discuss his frustrations, hurts, and disappointments. You see, she often misinterpreted him. He didn't talk much. He learned to back off when his anger had gone too far, to jog, to mow the grass, to vacuum the floors, and to exercise. He also learned to return to his wife after he had calmed down and schedule a time when they could discuss their differences. If the discussion got too loud, either of them could call **time-out** and **re-schedule** the discussion.

One counseling technique that worked well with them was for me to choose an issue from their list and have them in turn talk about it. They faced each other, one spoke for a minute, and the other listened (not allowed to speak). Then, the other talked for a minute while the mate listened. One session I did this with Albert and Pat for 45 minutes. Got one conflict settled! And I think they learned something about conflict resolution that they can use with other conflicts. Remember, **it's better to talk it out than to act it out!**

Remember also to re-channel your anger. Control your behavior. Don't do everything you feel like doing. Don't yield yourself to sin (Romans 6). Don't follow every angry inclination you have (Galatians 5:16-25). Solomon says that a **soft** answer turns away wrath, but a harsh word stirs up anger (Proverbs 15:1). **Speak softly.** You can still say what you need to say. **Learn to overlook some things** that bother you. To not let so many things get under your skin. Learn to control your behavior (Proverbs 29:11). It's helpful to say a word in due season (Proverbs 15:23). How good it is! Don't get even; leave that to God (Romans 12:19).

12. **Learn to give in.** It's not a sign of weakness but of strength.

Obviously, sometimes you can't give in. I've counseled with several men who wanted their wives to allow them to have another woman on the side. And a few who wanted to have a continuing affair with other men. Wives in such circumstances need to **assert themselves,** to not be a doormat, to draw a line.

It's so important to **know when** to draw a line and where to draw it. Don't draw lines over every conflict. Don't argue over every difference on issues. Let them have their way if it's no big deal. Save your assertiveness for something important!

13. **Reduce stressors.** I went to an internist about eight years ago because I felt exhausted and wanted to be sure that nothing was wrong with me medically. My doctor knew my schedule: full-time faculty member and administrator with Harding University, minister at the Ross Road Church which I helped start, psychologist and marital and family therapist in private practice, supervisor of other professional counselors, and a speaker in about 12 week-end meetings and seminars each year. My doctor told me a story about himself: he told his wife recently after a 14-hour day at the office and hospital that he was tired "all of the time lately." She replied, "I wonder why!" He got the point, and so did I. I reduced my work load some not long after that.

Most people I counsel with are too busy, especially career women with children. Super women. While I admire their determination, their judgment is sometimes questionable. They always agree that they have too many stressors in their lives but fight me every step of the way as I suggest the elimination of some stressors. No, they can't drop that! No, not that either! People **expect** me to do that! What would they **think?** My friend does more than I do, and she can handle it! Maybe so, but **you're not she.** Think for yourself. Your family doesn't have to be just like theirs. And your friend may also be stressed out and hiding it well.

To reduce stress, you must do one of the following:

a. Reduce the number of stressors in your life.

b. Or don't allow so many things to bother you.

   c. And/or become more mature emotionally and thus able to handle more stress.

Don't fight me on all three points. If you do, you may be trapped into a lifestyle that you can't handle! It's not worth it.

14. **Grow spiritually.** Jesus as a boy grew in wisdom and stature, and in favor with God and people (Luke 2:52). Peter admonishes us to grow in the grace and knowledge of our Lord and Savior Jesus Christ (II Peter 3:18). Such growth, though perhaps gradual at times, will result in the fruit of the Spirit in our lives: Love, joy, peace, patience, kindness, goodness, faithfulness, gentleness, and self-control (Galatians 5:22-25). Such living is in step with the Spirit and pushes out a spirit of fighting, having our own way, and getting even.

15. Learn to **relax.** I trained my phobic and anxiety clients in progressive relaxation for years before I thought of using it with angry clients. One day it dawned on me that it might work. So, I began trying it.

Take a deep breath of fresh, soothing oxygen, and then let it out slowly. Do that over and over again. Breathe in relaxation, exhale anger and tension. Keep it up. Repeat the process for several minutes. Combine this with other silent self talk such as "calm, relax, cool it, and control yourself." Then, catch yourself getting mad and take a deep breath. . . talk to yourself. It stops the usual escalating anger cycle and allows you to control your anger by thinking with your upper brain.

Or if you really want to learn progressive relaxation well, go to a psychologist or other professional counselor who uses this therapy and have him or her teach you. Or you might rather order some audio tapes on progressive relaxation and listen to them over and over again while lying on your bed or reclining in an easy chair. My album on *Relax and Feel Better* is available through Harding Bookstore, 1000 Cherry Road, in Memphis.

16. **Get help** from a third party. Anger is hard to control. Not impossible, but difficult. If you try and fail, get help from a psychologist or some other professional counselor who shares your basic values.

SUMMARY

I've gone from examples of anger to some causes of anger, to some destructive effects of anger. I then gave you 16 keys to help you cope constructively with anger and to successfully handle conflicts. Ponder what I have said. I believe it will help you. I've had it work for me personally and have seen it work for others many times. I've shared with you in this chapter many of the ideas and techniques I use with my clients in therapy. Remember, healthy families learn to constructively cope with and to handle conflicts successfully. Good luck as you give it a try. It's not easy, but keep trying. You'll grow through the process.

GROWING EXERCISES

Discuss with Your Spouse
1. How do I handle anger?
2. What effect does that have on our family?
3. What hurts you the most about what I do when I am mad?
4. How would you like for me to handle my anger?

Catch Yourself Getting Mad:
5. And take a deep breath and say "calm." Repeat that procedure over and over again. Say to yourself: "Be calm, cool it, you'll just make it worse."
6. Back off. Take it walk and think.
7. Tell your spouse or children, "I'm getting mad again. Don't want to talk right now. I'll get back to you later."
8. Write down your thoughts. Read and edit them an hour later and share them with your spouse, children, or parents, if you still believe it will help.

Other Suggestions
9. Discuss each suggestion I made for handling your anger and conflicts with your spouse and agree to try one or more of them each week as appropriate opportunities present themselves.

10. Write a prayer about your anger and the way you handle conflict and then pray the prayer. Then let your spouse, children, or parents read it.

11. Face your mate and complete these sentences. Mention as many ideas as you can with each sentence stem.

    a. "I need you to . . ."

    b. "What I've been doing wrong is . . ."

    c. "What I'm willing to do to help us cope with anger and settle conflicts successfully is to . . ."

    d. "What I hear you saying is . . ."

    e. "I am proud of you because . . . "

12. Read the Bible together and discuss how it relates to your family and how the church can help.

13. Take responsibility for your own anger. It's you who gets mad. Deal with it constructively. Don't put the blame on others.

14. Allow your spouse to disagree with you.

15. Don't hit and run. Listen.

16. Commit yourself to spiritual growth together.

17. Discuss the meaning of koinonia (fellowship) in a marriage. How can you develop more meaningful fellowship?

18. Discuss the five things you want most from your mate.

19. Develop a **family night** in your home.

20. Communicate well. Practice when you are not angry. Consider self, others, and the context in which you communicate.

_____ **Eleven**

Ability to Cope With Crises

Principle Number 11:
Healthy families somehow develop
the ability to cope with crises.

Deborah became depressed when each of her children left home and got married. Cried sometimes for hours at a time. She accused her husband of not loving her anymore and resented his spending time with others. She needed him herself.

Howard, her husband, resented her efforts to control him. Crisis time! Serious depression. A strained relationship. It took months of psychological and medical treatment to help them stabilize.

On the other hand, Burl and Melissa went through many seemingly more severe crises, yet without serious consequences. Their daughter, Lynn, died in an auto accident at age five. Melissa had breast cancer, and Burl lost his job. Took him six months to find another. Of course, they hurt, but they seemed to handle it well. They continued to be active in church. They talked about seeing Lynn some day in heaven. Cried it out and talked it out with friends. Accepted help while Burl was unemployed. They said, "We grew closer to God, to the church, and to each other through all of this."

Different reactions to crises. Different people, different levels of emotional maturity, different situations. Different network of family and friends. And they handled crises differently.

Crises will come to all of us. Sickness, death, loss of job, divorce, and unexpected pregnancy, mental illness, a suicide in the family—all heavy stuff. All of us would hurt a lot and be shaken by such crises. Yet, healthy families find a way to cope with them. In this chapter, we will examine some major crises: suicide, divorce, and death.

SUICIDE

Jennifer Dawson, age 40, was married and the mother of two teen-age boys. She had been poor as a child, but was able with her husband to support their family well. Yet, she stole a large sum of money from her employer, was arrested, and attempted to kill herself. She was referred to me for counseling by her medical doctor.

We worked together for several months. She was convicted and went to jail for three years. She was sorry for what she had done, gave back most of the money she had left and "turned back to the Lord for forgiveness." Her husband, children, and mother forgave her and stuck with her. She is back out of prison now, and they seem to be doing well.

Why were they able to adjust? Who knows for sure? Family, church, and remorse were no doubt factors. When I asked her what helped, she replied, "I was able to get to the bottom of it. You helped me to see that I was not worthless as so many told me I was. There are no magical words. Just face it, and work through it."

Suicide is the eighth leading cause of death in America, one every 18 minutes, 30,000 per year. Five thousand of these are young people between ages 15 and 25.

There are some 20 non-fatal attempts for each completed suicide. That adds up to a lot of sad, frustrated, trapped people. Somehow if they could get through the immediate crisis, many of them would go on to live happy, productive lives. One statistic that impresses me is that of some 20 people who have jumped off the Golden Gate Bridge, all five of the survivors said they knew they had made a mistake and wished to lived as soon as they had jumped! I have been with numerous survivors of attempted suicide and most of them had similar feelings.

The Bible mentions six suicides: Saul and his armor-bearer (I Samuel 31:4-5), Zimri (I Kings 16:18), Ahithophel (II Samuel 17:23), Samson (Judges 16:19-31), and Judas (Matthew 27:5). All were in difficult if not trapped situations.

The Bible's influence is against suicide. God gives life, and it is only his prerogative to take it away. Job acknowledged this fact and praised the name of the Lord (Job 1:21). Paul recognized that we are God's servants (Romans 14:4). We are not our own: we've been bought with a price and are therefore to glorify God in our bodies (I Corinthians 6:18-20). Since we are not our own, we have no right to take "our" life. It belongs to God who gave it. Paul also recognizes the fact that it is normal to feed and care for our body and abnormal to hate it (Ephesians 5:29).

Suicide is hard to understand. It has been thought of historically as shameful, sinful, and criminal. The property of a person who committed suicide was forfeited to the King in 18th Century England. Survivors thus disguised the cause of such deaths to counter the abuse of the law.

Suicide has been equated with insanity which was thought to be inherited. Thus, survivors felt tainted and suffered in secret.

Today, suicide is seen as closely connected with clinical depression, pathological grief, mental illness, and situations in which the person feels trapped. Although there is no typical suicide, some facts concerning suicide include the following:

1. Males are more likely to commit suicide than females.

2. Older people are more likely to commit suicide than younger people.

3. People who talk about it are **more** likely to do it than those who don't.

4. White people are at greater risk than African-Americans.

5. Americans are at greater risk than people from other nations.

6 Also, people without an adequate support system or from a dysfunctional family.

7. Those unable to communicate effectively with significant people in their life.

8. People who feel trapped.

9. Those with low self-esteem.

10. People who are angry, lonely, isolated, and want to "get even."
11. People who feel rejected socially.
12. People who feel intense guilt and shame.
13. People who are in trouble with the law.
14. Those who have relatives who have committed suicide.
15. Those who have previously attempted suicide.

Some specific **warning signs** include:
1. Talking about committing suicide.
2. Giving away property in an uncharacteristic manner including prized possessions.
3. Eating and sleeping problems.
4. Drastic changes in behavior.
5. Withdrawal into a shell.
6. Loss of interest in just about everything.
7. Untimely preparation for death by making a will and funeral arrangements.
8. Unnecessary risk taking.
9. Recent severe losses.
10. A preoccupation with death.
11. A lack of interest in personal appearance.
12. Increased use of alcohol and other drugs.
13. Serious depression, anxiety, or other serious emotional disturbances.
14. Chronic illness and/or severe pain.
15. A specific plan and means to carry it out.

Although the research has shown that these are warning signs associated with suicide, they are not **sure signs** of it. A person may be white, male, American, unemployed, and mentally ill and not commit suicide. The idea from research is that **the more we have going against us, the more we are likely to commit suicide.** When we are carrying a heavy load, we need family, friends, and others to help.

How? Most of us are scared in such situations. Afraid we'll make it worse. But, in spite of such feelings, perhaps we can help. Here are some suggestions:

1. Do your best to **establish a meaningful relationship** with the suicidal person. Talk. Be honest. Communicate **acceptance,** listen carefully.

2. Accept their **pain** as real. It is! They hurt, feel trapped as though there is **no other way out.** Empathize with their pain. Then, perhaps they will listen to alternatives you may suggest.

3. Help them **clarify** the problem. Ask specific questions. Offer ideas. Inquire about obscure suicidal comments or actions.

4. Look for **warning signs** and evaluate suicidal potential: from demographic data, medical data, psychiatric data, situational factors, and suicidal plan. Remember, the more they have going against them, the more seriously you consider the risk.

5. Discuss alternatives: Individual competencies, other people who can help, support groups, hospitals, psychotherapy, previous successes with crises, and other alternatives. There is always a way of escape that we might be able to cope with trials (I Corinthians 10:13).

6. Point out that **life is worth living**—not always easy, but **worth living.** Pain can often be alleviated and/or tolerated with help. **Connect** with some professional who can help do that. The apostle Paul's life was **not easy,** but it was **very meaningful.** His thorn in the flesh must have been tough to handle, his being whipped must have been painful, but he lived a very significant life nevertheless. He discovered in pain that **God's grace was sufficient for him** (II Corinthians 12:1-10; 11:16-29). He ran the race that was set before him (I Corinthians 9:24-27). Perhaps he learned to find **meaning even in suffering.** He boasted in a sense in his sufferings. Learned to live with it, and **perhaps we can too.**

7. Be **patient.** Suicidal persons don't get where they are in a day, and they may need considerable time and help to recover. Life can sometimes be hard.

8. Help them **keep** their **dreams alive.** All of us need people to love, work to do, and meaning to find. Help them in such a quest. **Affirm them. Value them.** Be kind.

9. Promise to **participate in their life but not in their death.** A client of mine, Mary Jean, once wrote me a suicide letter in which she told me she was going to kill herself, and that it would be done by the time I got the letter. I made several calls including one to the police. They went and broke into her apartment, found her close to death, and took her to a hospital. When I visited Mary Jean in the hospital, we had a rather ineffective counseling session. She still wanted to die. She was sorry we found her.

At any rate, in the letter, Mary Jean had asked me to talk to her teen-age daughter, explain why she had to "do it," and tell her she loved her. She also left a message for her mother, told me where she wanted to be buried, and what to do with her possessions. While I appreciated her confidence in me, I told her not to write me any more suicide notes, that I would participate in her life but **not in her suicide.** Mary Jean is still alive and doing better. She now says she wants to live, that she was trying to "take the easy way out." She continued, "God has put me here, has given me life, and I'm going to somehow find courage to live it the best way I can." Incidentally, the phrase, "Life doesn't have to be easy to be meaningful" became very helpful to her. She sort of latched on to it to help her with some very painful experiences with both her job and her family. She said she had gotten to the end of her rope but had tied a knot in the end of it and was holding on! Encouraging!

10. Learn to look for **meaning in pain.** You can't see it readily but perhaps with a great deal of patience you can eventually. The idea here is that sometimes people become stronger in weakness (James 1:2-4).

11. Ask for professional help if you need to do so. Doctors, psychologists, other professional counselors, hospitals, churches, family, and friends will surely respond to your call. Let's learn to allow others to help us in time of need, to bear our burdens and so fulfill the law of Christ (Galatians 6:2).

Suicide is but one of many serious crises that families sometimes have to face. Divorce and grief over the loss of loved ones are two other crises that I want to discuss with you. I believe I've learned some things that can help you. Obviously, there are terrible crises that will almost crush any family, but with help, healthy families stagger, regroup, and somehow survive. Stay with me.

DIVORCE

I'll emphasize steps designed to stop divorce later on in this book. Right now, I want to deal with divorce. It happens in many good families today. They are thus put under tremendous strain—their family structure, their economic means of survival, their emotions—yet healthy families find ways to cope.

First, let's look at what happens to family structure after a divorce. Before the divorce, a typical nuclear family may look something like this:

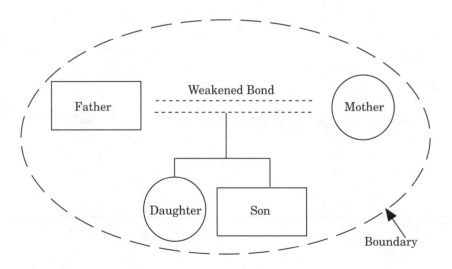

Immediately after the divorce, it may look like this:

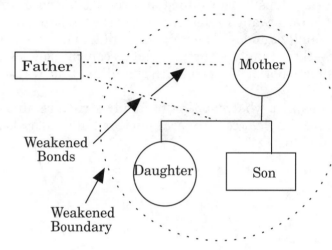

Not long after this stage, the family structure usually looks something like this:

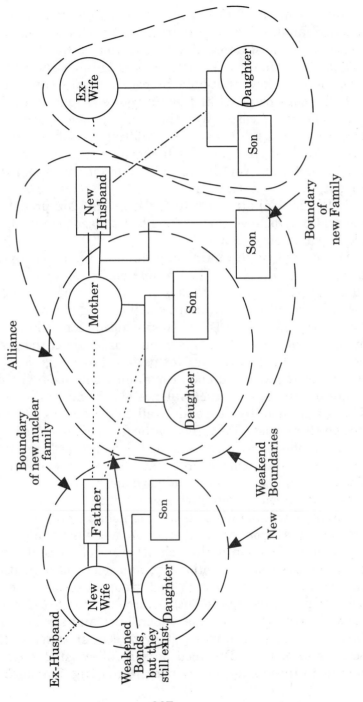

Get the picture? Can you see why divorced families and blended families feel so vulnerable? At best, it's a challenge. At worst, it is almost impossible for everyone to handle.

Thus how can divorced persons and families survive? Let me give you some keys that have helped many after divorce.

1. Take a look at **what has happened.** Talk about the marriage and the divorce. Was the marriage ever good and what was good about it? If there are children, pay attention to **their** needs. Ventilate feelings. Try to learn from your mistakes. Feel good about what you did to help your marriage and to try to save it.

2. Pay special attention to **feelings.** You are probably hurting and may believe that no one cares. Jesus cares about people in pain, and so do we.

The extent of the pain may depend upon the pattern of divorce that took place. The **enmeshed** (couples who are immature and too close) pattern may lead to extreme conflict, heated debate, a great deal of communication, and much ambivalence toward the divorce decision. The **autistic** (non-talking) pattern often exhibits no conflict or communication about the possibility of divorce. The **direct conflict** pattern has a high level of conflict with frequent and open communication about the divorce. There usually is some ambivalence about ending the marriage. This group usually responds well to counseling. The **disengaged** (little contact) conflict pattern is characterized by a low level of ambivalence about ending the marriage. The parties are not close; so they don't seem to care. These patterns affect emotional pain and post-marital adjustment.

Most divorced people hurt a great deal. The divorce process is usually a trauma which is distinguished by the experience of growing apart from each other, one's needs not being met, having little in common with each other, grief without flowers, a draining experience emotionally, and death of a relationship. Divorced persons are a high risk group in terms of social and psychological maladjustment. Divorce is often listed just below death in listings of trauma which hurt and shame a person. Divorced persons are more likely to commit suicide than are persons in general. Divorced persons often go through stages similar to those I list in my book, **Growing Through Grief,** experienced by persons who have lost loved ones by death: shock and denial, lamentations or anger, withdrawal from people, frustrations with everyday life, panic, depression, emotional detachment from the person lost, adjustment to life, reinvestment in life, and growth.

Kaslow in _Handbook of Family Therapy_ lists three stages and attendant feelings during the divorce process. During the pre-divorce deliberation period you may experience feelings of disillusionment, dissatisfaction, alienation, dread, anguish, ambivalence, shock, emptiness, chaos, inadequacy, and low self-esteem. During divorce, the litigation period, you may feel depressed, detached, guilty, angry, hopeless, confused, furious, self-pity, sad, lonely, and relieved. During post-divorce, the re-equilibration period, there may be feelings of optimism, resignation, excitement, curiosity, regret, acceptance, self-confidence, self-worth, wholeness, exhilaration, independence, and autonomy. How you feel is influenced by personality variables, time, reasons for the divorce, and many other factors. Even so, we need to try to understand how you feel and exhibit some sense of compassion and understanding. This in itself often helps, and it also enables us to be of further assistance.

3. **Formulate** your **problem** and go beyond just talking about the situation. A number of difficult questions may have to be answered. "I can't stand my wife, but I don't have a scriptural reason to divorce her." "My husband had an affair twelve years ago, I forgave him, but I never did get along with him after that." "I divorced my wife. She drove me crazy, but I still love her. What's wrong with me? Why can't I forget her?" "I know it's wrong to have sex outside of marriage, but what am I supposed to do? Surely God does not expect me to live without a woman!" "I married and divorced when I was fifteen. Does God hold that against me?" "How could God let this happen?" "How do we divide our property?" "How will all of this affect our children?" "Why won't the church use us anymore?" "Will God forgive me?" "How can I make a living? I don't have any job skills or experience." "Should we break up the children?" "What do you think about joint custody?" You need to answer these and other questions as best you can. Good decisions need to be made. You need to work through such questions toward

answers which you feel good about. Take your time. Remember, you are the person who has to live with each decision.

4. Learn what you can from your former marriage. It's okay to look at the faults of your ex-mate first. Yet, if you do not get beyond this stage in the divorce process, you do not learn from your mistakes. Your feelings of rejection and failure are so great that you may stay preoccupied with your ex-spouse's mistakes indefinitely. You need to proceed and look at yourself by asking such questions as the following: "What mistakes did I make in my previous marriage? Were I to live through it again, what would I do differently? Was I at fault at all? In what way? How would people who know me describe my personality? How will my experiences in this marriage affect my future life? Can I change? **Will** I change? These are very important questions. If they are not asked, history may repeat itself.

For example, if you were attracted to an abusive person the first time around because of low self-esteem, you will be likely to do the same the next time. I know of one woman who married seven times and six of the seven husbands beat her. I know of an abusive man who has married four times, and he abused all four of his wives. If you have a personality disorder (passive-aggressive, avoidant, anti-social . . .), you will likely not change very much following a divorce and may repeat the pattern of the previous marriage in future relationships. If you are depressed, you may be depressed with any mate you might choose in the future. The point is that **we help create our own environment.** You owe it to yourself to ask hard questions and to try to learn from and grow because of the past. You can even learn from your sins. Friends, family, and professional workers can help you explore these important issues.

5. Concentrate on **restructuring** your individual and family structure. In the family structures I mentioned previously in this chapter, you can perhaps see what needs to be changed. Individual and nuclear family boundaries need to be strengthened, as well as boundaries between the family and the outside world. Proper connections need to be cultivated between children and parents and step-parents, between wives and ex-wives, husbands and ex-husbands. And, if new children are born to new partners, room has to be made for them and prop-

er relationships developed between them and their half-siblings and others. Adjustments to grandparents are also important. The list of structure adjustments is almost endless. But the idea is to **stabilize structure** as soon as possible. Why? Because family structure influences individuals within the structure.

6. Decide carefully about **remarriage**. Several questions need to be answered as you decide.

"Do I wish to remarry?" Right after a divorce, many people have no desire at all to remarry. They are not interested and do not believe they will ever be interested in remarriage. They have had enough and do not wish to try again. But some are. If you are one of them, I urge you to take your time and think it through.

"Do I have a scriptural right to remarry?" Many Christians are still asking this important question. Some, however, seem to be saying: "I've got to have a mate. I'm going to remarry, and surely God will go along with it. You don't think God is the kind of God who would make me stay single the rest of my life, do you?" I would be afraid to take God's will too lightly.

Key scriptures you need to study in dealing with these questions are Deuteronomy 24:1-4; Matthew 5:32; 19:1-9; Romans 7:1-4, and I Corinthians 7. Although Paul seems to imply that Jesus did not address a believer married to an unbeliever, people other than his disciples were present when Jesus was speaking in Matthew 5:32 and 19:1-9. Although I have never been able to see the integration of these scriptures as clearly as I would like, I believe that God's law on **marriage** is addressed to all people. Non-Christians who get married are married in the sight of God. God joins them together. And "whatsoever God hath joined together, let no man put asunder."

The following persons clearly have a scriptural right to marry: one who has never been married, one whose mate is dead, and one who put his mate away because of sexual immorality. Beyond this, I feel uncomfortable theologically. I cannot give assurance that I am not sure the Bible gives. I usually help people face the issues, struggle with the relevant scriptures, and decide for themselves. Personal decisions are required in such matters. And some questions may at times be so difficult that only God can unravel them on the judgment day. And he will be the final judge. Remember, the time to think this through is before you remarry.

Another question of importance is: "**Should** I remarry?" This is a slightly different question from the previous one. You may have a scriptural right to remarry but not be a good candidate for marriage for various reasons: personality disorders, emotional conditions, previous experiences, venereal disease, AIDS, specific needs of your children, finances, poor health, immaturity, or other reasons. Jesus recognized the fact that not everyone is suited for marriage. So, don't assume that you should remarry just because you have a right to do so. You as well as others might be better off if you remain single.

Make plans for your future. Look at the past, learn from mistakes, think things through. "Do I begin or continue dating? Get a job? Move to another city?" These and many other questions may be asked and answered, but then proceed on toward a life of usefulness to God, to others, and to yourself. There is no reason why you cannot be a productive person and live a useful and joyful life. The peace that passes understand is not limited to married people (Philippians 4:6-7). Move ahead with your life and press toward the goal of the high calling of God in Christ Jesus (Philippians 3:12-14).

Kaslow in the *Handbook of Family Therapy* lists several requisite actions and tasks for divorced people. His list includes finalizing the divorce, reaching out for new friends, undertaking new activities, stabilizing a new life-style and daily routine, resynthesis of identity, completing psychic divorce, seeking a new love object and making a commitment to some permanency, becoming comfortable with a new life-style and friends, and helping children accept the finality of their parents' divorce and their continuing relationship with both parents. All of these actions and tasks point to many items that you need to discuss. I encourage you to seek God's will to every situation in your life.

If you as a family, friend or counselor are trying to help divorced persons adjust to the crisis brought on by divorce, I offer you these suggestions:

1. Listen and ask questions.
2. Show compassion and understanding.
3. Assign relevant tapes and books for homework.
4. Explore the possibility of reconciliation.
5. Help them make needed psychological adjustments to divorce.
6. Help them work through specific problems.
7. Be trustworthy. Don't ever take advantage of divorced people.
8. Keep confidences. This is essential.
9. Pray together. God promises wisdom (James 1:5).
10. Help them re-establish a healthy family structure.
11. Refer those who need additional help to psychologists, licensed or certified marriage and family therapists, or other professional counselors.
12. Don't leave "singles" out of your "couples'" activities.

DEATH OF A LOVED ONE

The death of a loved one is also very difficult to handle. The pain is indeed intense for close relatives and friends, but healthy families somehow learn to cope with such losses. How? There is no set formula, but I have learned some things from hundreds of grieving persons and from personal experiences and study that I believe can help you grow through grief.

I have learned a great deal about bereavement by studying examples of it in the Old Testament. King David of Israel is a good example, and there are others as well.

The way the Semitic culture handled grief offers help for us today. Their approach was somewhat different from ours in America. They spent a few days alone at first and then began to receive visitors during the latter half of the first seven-day period of grief. Lamentations preceded consolation. Slow to speak, visitors often sat in silence before offering advice. Job's friends provide an example: They wept, then tore their clothes; they also sprinkled dust upon their heads "toward heaven." Then they sat on the ground with him for seven days and seven nights. No one said a word to him, because of how great his suffering was (Job 2:13 NIV). We should empathize, listen, and try to understand before we speak.

During the entire first year of grief, the Semitic culture provided various avenues of working through grief. Friends mourned and then encouraged the griever to turn back toward God in faith, trust, and praise. The grievers attended worship on the Sabbath as a part of the grief process. They were recognized as being in mourning and were supported in their struggle.

Let me give you some specific examples. King David often grieved. Being king did not exempt him from sorrow. One example is the loss of the baby born to Bathsheba and him (II Samuel 12). The baby was very sick, and David prayed to the Lord for the child. He fasted and lay all night upon the earth. This behavior continued for seven days. Then when the baby died, David ". . . got up from the ground. After he had washed, put on lotions and changed his clothes, he went into the house of the Lord and worshipped. Then he went to his own house, and at his request, they served him food, and he ate" (II Samuel 12:20). When his servants were puzzled at his behavior, David explained, ". . . While the child was still alive, I fasted and wept. I thought, 'Who knows? The Lord may be gracious to me and let the child live.' But now he is dead, why should I fast? Can I bring him back again? I will go to him but he will not return to me" (II Samuel 12:22-23). Then David comforted Bathsheba his wife and had sex with her which resulted in her impregnation and the birth of a son, Solomon (II Samuel 12:24). Life must go on. There was a time for sorrow and a time for joy.

One of David's sons, Absalom, conspired against him (II Samuel 15). By deception, he endeared himself to the people and then tried to become king by force. The conspiracy was strong, and the people on Absalom's side increased. As a result, David had to flee to save his own life. War between the two factions resulted (II Samuel 15-18).

Although David's instructions to his military commander, Joab, were to "be gentle with the young man Absalom for my sake," Absalom was killed in battle (II Samuel 18). When a messenger came to tell David of his son's death, David's question was "Is the young man Absalom safe?" (II Samuel 18:29,32). When David heard of his son's death, "The king was shaken. He went up to the room over the gateway and wept. As he went, he said, 'O my son Absalom! My son, my son Absalom! If only I had died instead of you—O Absalom, my son, my son,'" (II Samuel 18:33).

Although Absalom had rebelled against his father and was fighting to win the kingdom from him, David grieved over his death (II Samuel 19). The victory that day was turned into mourning for all of the people, for the king was grieving for his son (II Samuel 19:2). The king covered his face and cried with a loud voice, "O my son Absalom! O Absalom, my son, my son" (II Samuel 19:4)!

Even though David's grief was great, he worked through it toward greater usefulness and recovery. His friend, Joab, encouraged him to go on with his normal activities, to look at what had been saved rather than at what had been lost (II Samuel 19). He especially was encouraging him to remember those who were still alive: "So the king got up and took his seat in the gateway. When the men were told, 'The king is in the gateway,' they all came before him" (II Samuel 19:8). He was grieved, but he went back to work.

Job's grief was cumulative. He lost his property, all ten of his children, his friends, and even his own health (Job 1-2). The three friends came to comfort him: "When they saw him from a distance, they could hardly recognize him; they began to weep aloud, and they tore their robes and sprinkled dust on their heads. Then they sat on the ground with him for seven days and seven nights. No one said a word to him, because they saw how great his suffering was" (Job 2:12-13). He complained and somehow grew through his grief.

Jeremiah lamented for Josiah and ". . . to this day all the men and women singers commemorate Josiah in the laments. These became a tradition in Israel and are written in the Laments" (II Chronicles 35:25). In Jeremiah's prophecy to the people of God concerning the future he says, "Both high and low will die in this land. They will not be buried or mourned, and no one will cut himself or shave his head for them. No one will offer food to comfort those who mourn for the dead—not even for a father or a mother—nor will anyone give them a drink to console them. And do not enter a house where there is feasting and sit down to eat and drink" (Jeremiah 16:6-8). These evidently were some of the common mourning practices of Israel that would no longer be possible because of the extent of the disaster that was coming.

The following message to Ezekial also reflects common mourning customs of the day: "Son of man, with one blow I am about to take away from you the delight of your eyes. Yet do not lament or weep or shed tears. Groan quietly; do not mourn for the dead. Keep your turban fastened and your sandals on your feet; do not cover the lower part of your face or eat the customary food of mourners" (Ezekial 24:16-17).

Psalms 23 has been the most mentioned scripture by our grief therapy groups of widows and widowers. This Psalm will always be especially meaningful to me because it was quoted by my mother while she was in a coma just before she died. It was deeply imprinted upon her mind and upon her heart and is shared by many throughout the world in times of grief: "The Lord is my Shepherd, I shall not want."

Thus far, I have pointed out some Semitic customs of mourning often reflected in the Old Testament and listed and described the grief process that took place in the lives of some of the heroes of the Old Testament. It is apparent from this study that grief was thought of as a process to work through. It is interesting to observe the purpose of the laments. This is the time to protest, to express your feelings of unfairness and anger toward God. But, protest is not the end of the grieving process. Protest turns toward faith and trust in God. By careful study of these Old Testament examples, you can see not only rituals but also stages of working through grief and of resuming one's normal activities. People for ages have worked through grief in stages, have mourned, have cried, have protested and then have eventually returned to normal activities in life. The goal is to work through grief toward increased maturity, to grow through grief.

The New Testament has several examples of people who grieved. Perhaps the most familiar example is Jesus himself.

Centuries before Jesus was born, the prophet Isaiah described him as one despised and rejected by men, a man of sorrows and familiar with suffering, not esteemed. He was to take up our infirmities and carry our sorrows, yet he was to be stricken by God, smitten, and afflicted. He was to be pierced for our transgressions and crushed for our iniquities. His punishment was to bring us peace and his wounds, healing (Isaiah 53:3-5).

Indeed this was the case. Even before Jesus died, he knew what he was to endure. As he faced death, his soul was very sorrowful, "even unto death" as he asked his Father if it were possible to remove the cup from him (Mark 14:34-36). During this time, he prayed so earnestly that his sweat became like great drops of blood falling to the ground (Luke 24:44). Though Jesus had a higher purpose in what he did than helping others in adjusting to his death, some of the things he did probably helped them to do so.

1. Jesus talked. He began to teach his disciples that he must suffer many things, be rejected and killed, and after three days rise again from the dead (Matthew 8:31). He explained to them that some would mock him, spit upon him, scourge him and finally take his life. But after three days, he would rise again (Mark 10:32-35). Jesus talked, and it is very difficult today to adjust to grief without talking.

2. Jesus cried. During his life, Jesus offered up prayers of supplications with loud cries and tears to God who was able to save (Hebrews 5:7). Crying today is thought of as positive behavior for those who are grieving. We are to rejoice with those who rejoice, and weep with those who weep (Romans 12:15).

3. Jesus lamented: "My God, my God, why have you forsaken me?" (Matthew 27:46). He was human; he protested, he questioned.

4. Jesus experienced physical symptoms of grief. As I mentioned before, he was in the Garden of Gethsemane, his sweat became like great drops of blood falling upon the ground (Luke 22:44). Yet, even during this period of anticipatory grief, he expresses his faith unto God. God hear his prayer and sent an angel to strengthen him (Luke 22:43).

5. Jesus surrendered. When he was on the cross, when he

was overwhelmed, when he questioned, he committed his spirit into the hands of his Father (Luke 23:46).

6. Jesus forgave others. Even on the cross, he prayed for God to forgive those who put him there. They did not know what they were doing (Luke 23:34). When people are grieving and feel a sense of guilt, they need to remember that forgiveness is possible. If God could forgive those who took the life of Jesus, he can forgive you.

7. Jesus accepted hostile feelings. When Mary and Martha were upset because Jesus did not come in time to save their brother, Lazarus, he did not get upset with them but responded with gentleness and kindness. He understood their emotional state of mind and was able to comfort them (John 11:21-32). He encouraged them by telling them that their brother would rise again.

8. Jesus continued to work. Even after he knew he was going to die, he continued his activities: praying, teaching, giving hope. When you grieve there is a natural inclination to cease activity. This may be best for awhile, but eventually resumption of work is usually the best therapy for you.

The apostles returned to their normal activities following the death of Jesus. Simon Peter and the others returned to their fishing (John 21:3). This may be a sign of their minds at this point. That was the only thing they knew to do. They could not just continue to grieve over the death of Jesus and remain completely inactive. They went back to their activities. Though this is not biblical advice on how to deal with grief, their work, like that of countless others in grieving situations may have been helpful to them. In light of the death and resurrection, the apostle Paul admonishes us to be steadfast, unmovable, always abounding in the work of the Lord. Such work is never in vain (I Corinthians 15:58).

9. Jesus offered hope. When you are grieving you often go through long periods of despair with little hope. You need hope. Every grief group I have conducted has mentioned something about the resurrection from the dead and life beyond the grave. Jesus knew of this need, and he told Mary and Martha that their brother would rise again (John 11:23). There are many such passages that give hope in the New Testament. Some are

as follows: They that mourn will be blessed and comforted (Matthew 5:4). Jesus said that everyone who drinks of the water he gives will never thirst. Such water will give us eternal life (John 4:13-14). The word of Jesus gives us peace and joy. Jesus has overcome the world (John 16:33).

10. Jesus adjusted to reality. He was willing to accept God' will for his life. He placed his life into the hands of God.

Jesus not only grieved himself, but he also comforted those who were grieving. Perhaps the best illustration of this is his work with Mary and Martha, sisters of Lazarus (John 11). They had called for Jesus because Lazarus was sick. He deliberately waited so that he would arrive after Lazarus died. He could then demonstrate the power of God at work in him. However, the effect upon Mary and Martha was that they were upset with him when he arrived. If he had been there, they believed that their brother would not have died. Why did he take so long? He accepted their apparent anger and cried with them. "Jesus wept" is a very meaningful, though short, verse (John 11:35). We know by this verse that Jesus cares. Jesus saw Mary and Martha weeping and was deeply moved in spirit and troubled (John 11:33-34). He knew their sorrow. He cared. He cried with them.

When we summarize what Jesus did, we see his great concern for us. He tried to minister to the needs to those who grieved. He visited his friends during their grief. He told them that their brother would rise again. Martha understood this in terms of the resurrection of the last day. However, Jesus meant something different. He is the resurrection and the life: if we believe on him, we will live eternally. Jesus responded to their fears by going to the grave of Lazarus. He groaned in himself as he came to the tomb, a cave. He saw a stone lying against the cave and ordered it to be removed. Martha protested because their brother had been dead for four days. But Jesus lifted up his voice and cried for Lazarus to "come forth," and he did (John 11:41-44).

Jesus knows your sorrows. Because he has experienced what you experience, he is in touch with your feelings and understands you. It is comforting for me to know that Jesus understands me even when I do not. He cares. He is with us

219

(Matthew 28:20). This is meaningful even when the pain will not go away.

SUMMARY

Crises are extremely difficult to handle. Whether it's suicide, divorce, death, or some other crisis, it takes its toll on you and your family.

Let me close by giving you some key ideas to help you and your family cope with the crises you may someday have to face:

1. Take charge and do what needs to be done. The more others are out of control, the more you need to be in control. The more you are out of control, the more you need to ask others to take over.

2. Acknowledge loss and allow yourself to grieve through it.

3. Don't pay attention to simple answers that do not help. People usually mean well but sometimes say the wrong thing.

4. Restructure your life and family. Make adjustments for persons no longer there.

5. Don't blame yourself for things you can't help.

6. Do what you can and leave the rest to God.

7. Allow others to help.

8. Work toward a healthy attitude in your home.

9. Keep a list of persons to call in times of crisis.

10. Go to church. God still loves you.

Remember Principle Number 11: Healthy families somehow develop the ability to cope with crises. They hurt, they cry, they stagger, and then they recover and continue on with their lives.

GROWING EXERCISES

For Divorced Persons

1. Read the scriptures I listed on divorced and remarriage and write a summary of what they say.

2. Make a list of reasons why you should or should not remarry.

3. In what stage of grief recovery are you right now? What do you need to do to move on with your life?

4. Draw a diagram of your new individual and family structure. Then make notes on what you need to do to establish a more healthy structure. List changes needed in bonding and boundaries. Then make the changes needed.

For the Extended Family of a Divorced Person

5. List what you need to do to help your loved one adjust to divorce. Include grief needs, financial needs, and structural needs.

For Churches

6. Make a list of what you can do to help.

For People Who Have Lost a Loved One

7. List what you feel guilty about.

8. List what you feel angry about.

9. Discuss memories you have of the deceased with a friend, minister, or a counselor. Good memories as well as sad ones.

10. Make a list of changes you need to make in order to go on with your life, and then make them one at a time.

11. Read my books on *Growing Through Grief* and *From Worry to Happiness*.

12. Read the book I co-authored with several other professional counselors entitled, *Personal Counseling*. There are chapters in it on many topics including grief counseling, counseling suffering people, marital counseling when the woman is already pregnant, and divorce counseling.

Twelve

A Healthy Sense of Humor

Principle Number 12:
Healthy families have a healthy sense of humor.

I grew up in the Union Hill Community of Jackson County, Tennessee, next door to Grab All. In case you don't know where this is, I'll explain. It's about six miles from Nameless, seven miles from Seven Knobs, nine miles from Dudney's Hill, ten miles from Sugar Creek, about a mile north of the "Flatt Holler," and a mile west of the Bullet Hole.

We got electricity when I was 13. Indoor plumbing and city water came after I left home. My experiences make me remember that sometimes you have to laugh to keep from crying.

I'm including this chapter on humor because I value the humor I heard as a child. I've learned to laugh at myself, and many surveys I've seen on essential traits of healthy families include a sense of humor. Also, I've noticed that unhealthy families rarely laugh! They take themselves too seriously!

Some of the stories I'll tell are just a bit amusing; others downright funny. In some, I'll use actual names; in others, change names to avoid possible embarrassment. It's all done **in appreciation and respect** for my rich heritage, to laugh **with** people I love, not at them. I think those who see themselves here will get a kick out of it too! That's my wish.

I don't know much about my great grandparents. I have heard that my great-great-grandfather, John Madison Flatt, fought in the Civil War on the side of the South while my great-grandfather, Thomas Birdwell, fought on the side of the North. They lived a mile or so from each other on Rush Fork Creek and Flynn's Creek in Jackson County. I also heard my grandfather say that the North came through the farm where his family lived, left the barn doors open, and let all the cattle out. When John Madison was discharged in Kentucky, he "hitchhiked" home to make a living on a 40-acre farm.

Ben Flatt, my great-grandfather, was injured by falling off a horse spooked by a wild animal. He was baptized into Christ (Galatians 3:26-27) a few days later and died that night.

I've heard that my great-grandfather, Hiram Farris, was a farmer-gospel preacher, and that he caused quite a stir by divorcing his wife and marrying a much younger woman. Isn't it strange what people remember? That's about all I've heard about him!

I remember a great-uncle who used to preach on three-eye John (III John). He once preached an entire sermon on Ne-co-de-mus from three-eye John (John iii). Made some good points too!

Most of the humor I remember begins with my grandparents and the people of our community. Let's start with Pa Way who lived next door to us. I remember several things about this great man that are amusing. For example, he had a way of offering thanks before a meal that was unique. He'd start in a normal sounding voice and then continually lower his voice until it almost faded away before he'd say, "Amen." Both he and Ma Way called a penny a "copper." The only people I ever heard do that. He also called a tire a "casein."

I remember going with them to preach at Dudney's Hill. While going up the gravel road toward the Bullet Hole, Pa, keeping the 1929 touring car (a Ford Model A convertible) in the ruts of the road with both hands, asked Ma, "How fast am I going, Ollie?" Ma replied, "You're making 37 miles an hour. Better slow down a little."

One story my brother, Leamon, while doing research on Pa Way, dug up had to do with his preaching and farming. He wasn't known as a good farmer but was known as a good preacher and school-teacher. Sometimes he'd get an invitation to hold a meeting in a distant place right in the middle of harvest season. On one such occasion, he left his crops and went to the Bethlehem community in the adjoining Putnam County. Preached for three weeks and baptized 90! But when he got back home his tobacco crop was eaten up by worms. Darmon Huddleston, a neighbor, said that "preacher Way's 'backer' was so eat up that a 'backer' worm crawled out on the road as I passed and bummed me for a 'chaw' of 'backer'!" I discourage the use of tobacco now, but most people raised it in Middle Tennessee back then, and many still do. It's their main money crop.

Pa Flatt used to sit on the porch or around the fireplace and talk for hours, almost in a monologue. He'd talk. We'd listen. I especially remember Christmas time. He'd say, "Mitchell sent me this and Tom sent me that. Mary Lena brought over my supper last night. But the main thing is that we're all well." The first time I ever heard "White Christmas" by Bing Crosby, it was on their little table radio at Christmas time.

Pa was known for his keen sense of humor. He'd get a little gleam in his eyes, tell something amusing, and then laugh a little. He was very witty. Let me share a couple of incidents involving Pa with you.

Pa had a 40 acre farm, mostly very steep hill land. It's hard to understand how we plowed that land. They could not gather corn from the hills with a wagon. Had to use a sled. Pa did have a few acres in bottomland by the two creeks that adjoined his farm. Very rich land which he prized very much. Well, when a gas company surveyed where they wanted to put their gas line through his farm, they decided to run it right up the middle of one of those bottom fields. Pa told the man from the gas company, "You're not going to put that line through the middle of my bottom." The man assured him he was, that he had the authority to do so. Pa ended the conversation by telling him, "You can put it over at the side of my bottom but not up the middle of it. The first man that sets his foot on my bottom will get a load of lead in his hind-end from this shotgun." They backed down and put their gas line up the side of Pa's bottomland.

Once years later, my brother Don heard some people at church in Morehead, Kentucky talking about a certain gas company. Remembering Pa Flatt's episode, Don asked his wife,

Carolyn, "Is that the same company that tried to put a pipe up Pa Flatt's bottom?" A big laugh followed since they didn't know the whole story.

My favorite story about Pa Flatt was told by a game warden at his funeral. He had hear some gunshots over on Pa's place and decided to come over to check it out. "Uncle Henry," he said, "I heard some gunshots over here a few mornings ago and just wanted to see what it was." Pa said, "Yeah, I went up on the fill above the barn to get Deelie a squirrel." Well, the game warden informed him that it wasn't squirrel season and that he couldn't kill squirrels out of season. Pa had never heard of such a thing and kept saying, "Even on my own place?" The warden kept assuring him that he couldn't kill squirrels out of season even on his own place. Exasperated, Pa asked, "How many squirrels does the 'gover-mint' have up here on my place?" The warden had to say that they didn't have any. Pa closed the argument by saying, "That's what I thought, but I was just going to say if they did, for them to come up here and get them so I won't kill none of the 'gover-mint's squirrels the next time I go up there to get Deelie a squirrel." That was Pa Flatt! The game warden said he got tickled, shook his head, and just walked off.

I have always been amused with my uncle J.D.'s unique memory. His son, Ben, told me that he could remember when more than 600 people from Jackson County had died and where they were buried. Why? I don't know. He just does. At any rate, he and Pa Flatt would often get into a disagreement about the exact date someone died. On one such Sunday afternoon discussion (remember we didn't have TV), Uncle J.D. got up, got in his pickup truck, and left. About 30 minutes later, he returned. Didn't say anything for a few minutes. Just went to his chair on the porch looking very satisfied. In a few minutes, not being able to hold it any longer, he said, "I was right about that Pappy." You see, he had gone up to Fox Cemetery and checked the dates on the tombstones. This has become sort of a joke between Louise and me. If I find out that I was right about something we have disagreed about, I may say, "I was right about that, Pappy." Usually, both of us get a chuckle out of it.

Pa and Ma Flatt never wanted to go to a hospital. He never

did until a few days before he died at age 87.

At his funeral, there were hundreds of people who came by the Anderson Funeral Home in Gainesboro to pay their respects. After all, he had 13 children, and I'm not sure how many grandchildren, nephews and nieces. Most people in the county knew him. So, I kept seeing people whom I should know but couldn't call their names. They'd get me confused with my brothers. Sometimes they'd call me Leamon, sometimes Don, and sometimes they would get it right. I corrected them when they missed it for awhile and then decided I'd just let it go from then on. The next cousin I saw said, "Hidee Donald!" I said, "Hi, how are you?" Thought I'd done well. **Then,** he replied, "Saw Billy last night!" Didn't know what to say then, so I just walked off.

I shared this story with Uncle J. D. at the funeral home when his brother, Uncle Mitchell, died. Uncle J. D. replied, "Son, that's nothing. You see that feller right over there in them khaki pants and that red and black flannel shirt? When I come in a while ago he called me Mitchell and said, 'Sorry about your brother.' I didn't let on."

Ebb Wholeacre told me at the funeral home about an amusing incident involving Uncle Mitchell, his longtime neighbor. Uncle Mitchell liked to trade, especially to buy and sell cattle. One day he came down to Ebb's barn and told him that he was in "a trading mood"; wanted to trade **something.** He said to Ebb, "Run that ole cow in that stall out here in the hall and let me get a look at her." Ebb replied, "You don't want to buy that ole cow." Uncle Mitchell kept insisting that he did: "Just run her out here where I can see her. It's too dark in that stable." Ebb replied that she was "kinda wild, hard to get in the stall," and that he didn't want to let her out. Uncle Mitchell didn't give up. "Tradin" was sort of in his blood that day. So, he climbed up and looked in the stall at the cow and finally bought her. They got the cow out, and Uncle Mitchell was looking her over. "Does she have trouble seeing?" he inquired. "Blind as a bat, Mitch," Ebb responded. "Got one on ole Mitch that day!"

Another neighbor sold a crib of corn once to a man who measured the large corn crib to estimate the amount of corn in it.

After the sale, he discovered that there was a large tobacco box turned upside down on the crib floor under the corn. "Why didn't you tell me about the tobacco box?" the buyer asked. "Didn't ask me," came the farmer's reply.

Reminds me of another friend who bought a mule from a neighbor who told him, "Now you don't have to keep that mule if he don't work out!" Well, he didn't work out at all. Wouldn't do **any** work. Just balked! So, back he came with the mule and said, "I've brought your mule back to get my money. He didn't work out, and you said I didn't have to keep him if he didn't work out." "He's not **my** mule," the seller replied, "You **don't** have to keep him. **You can give him away.** You can **shoot him, do anything you want** with him. **He's your mule.**"

Another picture that I still recall from youth is of uncle Joe Way and Aunt Aline. They used to live close to us and farmed Pa Way's Porter Hollow Farm some three miles away. After we'd been in the field for two hours or so, Uncle Joe and Aunt Aline would come around the road ("Hiwassee") going to the Porter Hollow. Uncle Joe would be riding "sidesaddle" (bareback) on the mule and Aunt Aline would be walking behind carrying their dinner (not lunch back then). Daddy, an early bird, would always say something about how you have to get up early to get anything done. If he thought Leamon was not working fast enough, he'd say, "You're as slow as Joe Way." I told Uncle Joe, who has lived a productive life in Detroit, about this recently, and he got a good chuckle out of it. He replied, "Billy, I never would have had anything if I had stayed on the farm."

Once he was driving Pa Way's convertible A-Model and Uncle Leo, his brother, was driving **his** A Model Ford. Well, they got into a race on the way back from church on "Hiwassee," a gravel road. Pa was yelling for Uncle Joe to slow down. Joe kept trying to "outrun" his older brother. Then came devil's elbow, a 90 degree turn in the road. Uncle Leo made it around while Uncle Joe, with Pa still yelling at him, cleaned out a row of fence posts and a fence on Pa Way's farm. Leo kidded him about that for years!

Their younger brother, Uncle Hubert, used to want to borrow his Dad's car to go see his girlfriend. On several occasions when turned down, he would get up at night, put the car in neutral, roll it up the road toward our house, crank it, and proceed. Got by with it at times. Uncle Hubert always had a great sense of humor. He could make a joke out of just about anything you'd say.

Now, back to my immediate family. Pa Way didn't want my Dad to marry his daughter, my Mom. Don't know why. It was sort of a custom back then to object when someone wanted to marry your daughter! Or maybe it was because Dad was a Democrat. So Mom, at age 18, packed her good shoes and another thing or two, sneaked out the window one night, and ran up the road, met Daddy at Uncle Jesse's store nearly one-half mile away, and went and got married. While coming up the road, she lost one of her good shoes she was going to get married in. Got married in her old ones!

Dad was always the dominant one in their relationship. Strong personality! Mom went along usually. Yet, as many other women have done both before and after her, she often found a way to get her own way. It was early in their marriage. They had a few ducks, and Mom wanted to hatch some duck eggs she had gathered from them, whereas Dad wanted to eat them. "Eat the hen eggs," Mom suggested. "No," Dad replied, "They're not as good as duck eggs." So, Mom went to fry the duck eggs. But instead, she fried the hen eggs. As Dad ate them, he remarked, "These duck eggs are great. Taste a lot better than hen eggs!" As I remember it, Mom waited quite a while before getting up enough courage to tell him what she had done. She set her duck eggs and hatched some more ducks.

Our oldest sister, Rose (Rosa Lee), dated Leonard Fox (the man she eventually married when she was 18) primarily at our house. I can remember how Daddy used to call bedtime on Leonard. He'd never say anything to him but would call out to Rose in the next (lower) room, "It's bedtime, Rose." That was Leonard's signal to leave.

Leonard used to come to court Rose on his Dad's mule. I can still hear him riding and singing,

> In the pines,
> In the pines,
> Where the sun never shines,
> And shivers when the cold wind blows.

229

When he would have a spat with Rose, he'd ride away singing something like, "Beautiful, beautiful brown eyes," (Rose's eyes were blue), or,

> I don't want your greenback dollar,
> I don't want your watch and chain,
> All I want is you my darling,
> Won't you take me back again?

Once after a spat with Rose, Leonard left on his mule in a long lope, turned around down the road a piece, and came riding in a long gallop by our house. About the time they got right in front of our house, his mule stumbled and slid down the gravel road for some 20 feet I suppose. Leonard got up, scratched up a bit, and brought his Dad's mule up to our barn, and Daddy helped him pick the gravel out and "doctor" her wounds. His Dad, Burton, would need her to plow the next day.

Daddy sent me once with Leonard and Rose to a movie in Gainesboro. Leonard, wanting some time alone with Rose, kept offering me a dime to go get some popcorn. I, not wanting to be a financial burden on him, kept turning him down, but caught on several years later as we discussed the incident.

My brother, Leamon, was a close friend of our cousin, Lester Flatt, and went on several bluegrass festivals with him. One story Marty Stuart told Leamon about Lester is amusing. Lester, Earl and the Foggy Mountain Boys were in New York to do a bluegrass festival. They were staying in a fancy hotel that had elevator operators in each elevator. When they got into an elevator once, carrying their instruments and wearing their big hats, the elevator operator sort of "looked down his nose" at Lester and asked, "What do you do?" Lester replied, "I'm a bluegrass sanger." Whereupon the operator said, "Well, I'd never want to be a bluegrass singer." Lester responded, "I can't recollect ever wantin' to be an elevator operator either." His band got a big laugh out of Lester's getting even with the "smart alec city boy."

Leamon, Don, Dowell, and I began doing one campaign for Christ a year in 1963. In that first one, there were 46 baptisms, the most we ever had. One night when we were baptizing 12 respondents, one of the elders of the Kingwood Heights

Church of Christ in Murfreesboro, Tennessee where that campaign was held, remarked to me, "I'm glad you boys aren't working on commission."

During these campaigns, we often entertain the young people and others on one night of the meeting. Leamon plays the harmonica, we all sing, and Dowell and I swamp funny stories. Don occasionally shares one with us privately. Don's best one, he told on himself. It's especially funny to me as a psychologist. He and his wife Carolyn were in a small town restaurant somewhere in Kentucky ordering breakfast. Carolyn, who has a keen wit, said it this way, "Our waitress was built like Dolly Parton, if you get my drift." Standing right in front of Don, she asked what he wanted. Don replied, "I'd like to have bacon and two breasts." He quickly tried to correct himself, but both Carolyn and the waitress were laughing too much to accept his explanation. Don said, "I meant two eggs." Carolyn replied, "That's not what you said!"

Dowell always has a good story to share when we get together. Let me relate a few of my favorites from Dowell.

Dowell says he used to have a great squirrel dog. Just had one fault. He was so good that Dowell had to put tape over one nostril before he went hunting with him or he would tree two squirrels at once.

Then there's one he tells about Johnny Majors. Seems he had a star football player who couldn't pass his course work. Johnny offered to give him one more chance. If he could get one answer right out of three questions, he would pass the course and could play football in the big game on Saturday. Here were the three questions:

1. Which two days of the week start with the letter "T?"
2. How many seconds are in a year?
3. And, how many D's are in Dixie?

Johnny gave him a week to prepare for the examination. Upon the student's return, Johnny asked him if he could answer the questions. The athlete replied:

1. "I know the first one about the letter 'T' for sure. It's today and tomorrow."
2. "Number two took me a little longer, but I finally figured how many seconds are in a year. There are 12: January second,

February second, March second and so on throughout the year."

3. "Number three took me even longer," he reported. He figured that there were 117 D's in Dixie. "You know, like D da D. D. D. DD, D D D D . . . (to the tune of Dixie).

Then there was the one he heard in a Flatwoods, Tennessee country store, which was a gathering place for the men of the community to talk and whittle. One day the talk centered around who was the smartest man in the history of our country. Some thought George Washington, others Abraham Lincoln or Franklin D. Roosevelt. One particular farmer with a big dip of snuff in his mouth finally spoke up and said, "Leroy Garrett was nobody's fool!" For you uninformed readers, Leroy Garrett was the man who produced Garrett's Snuff.

Dowell also tells about a neighbor of ours who took his son to a doctor in Gainesboro with a huge gash in his leg. The doctor said that he was going to have to apply a **local** anesthetic in order to sew up the wound. The boy's father said to the doctor, "Now you don't have to just limit yourself to a local anesthetic: Go to Nashville or Chattanooga or wherever you need to and get whatever anesthetic you need. I'm willing to pay for the best they is for **my** boy."

Then there was Dowell's story about a Lincoln and a Rolls Royce at a red light. When the Rolls Royce driver noticed that the Lincoln had a bed in it, he was very jealous and searched for a week before he found a bed and put it in his Rolls Royce. A few days later, he came up beside the Lincoln again, tried to get the attention of the man in the Lincoln and finally did by going over and tapping on his window. He told the man in the Lincoln that he had a bed also in his car. In response, the man in the Lincoln replied, "I can't believe you got me out of the shower just to tell me **that!**"

There's one more from Dowell. It's about a southern boy who got on a Greyhound bus for Detroit. Saw a gorgeous woman in the back of the bus pecking on her portable computer. Wanting to get acquainted, he went back and asked her what she was working on. "I'm writing a book," she replied. It' on 'The Five Best Male Lovers in America,' and I've already finished the first three chapters." When he asked what they were about, she said that the first chapter was on the American male Indian, who could be very wild and exciting at times. Chapter two was on the Jewish male, who could be gentle and affectionate to women. The third chapter was on the Southern Redneck, who could be very macho and exciting for a change of pace. Then, the beautiful woman asked, "What's your name anyhow?" He replied, "My name is Tonto Goldsmith. Down South, they call me Bubba!"

Back to Union Hill. Several fellows in the community provided us with a lot of humor. One whom I'll call Willie was always good for a chuckle. Once during World War II he was asked if either of his brothers had been killed in the war (what a question to ask). He replied, "If they have, they never wrote home and said nothing about it!" At another time, Willie came to church and told me that his sister Ethel Marie had gone to "one of them rubbin' doctors." He added, "He rubbed her in places she had **never** been rubbed before!"

Another friend, Robbie Lee, didn't really have a place to live. Often stayed with a family around on Hiwassee. But, sometimes he refused to go there; said they made him take a **bath!**

Once Robbie was working for a neighbor of ours. It was springtime and had begun to get hot. Robbie kept pulling at the clothing around his neck. It was "binding him around the neck." Well, my neighbor discovered that Robbie had put his longjohns on upside down!

At another time, Robbie was playing "Mumblepeg" with J. Fred, a neighbor. The idea was to take turns throwing a knife and getting as close to the other person's foot as possible without hitting it. Well, J. Fred threw the knife, and it stuck in Robbie's knee. Went right through his overalls into his leg. Robbie looked at the knife and his bleeding leg and said to J. Fred, "Look what you've done gone and done. Ruint my new overhalls!"

One neighbor, Raccoon Haney, had a boy named Crow. Raccoon, who talked through his nose, used to say, "Crow would be a nice looking boy if his nose wudn't crooked."

Two of our neighbors, after a long-standing feud, took their guns one morning and went hunting for each other. The man I'll call D. J. took his shotgun; the other, R. T., his rifle. Well, they finally got a glimpse of one another at about the same time. Both fired and hit their target. Both suffered for months but finally recovered. Years later, my brother Leamon, asked D. J. this heavy question: "D. J., looking back on it now, did you learn any lessons from that shooting incident?" "Yes, I did," came D. J.'s reply. "If I ever go after another man again, I won't go with a single-barrel shotgun! I'll go get at least a double-barreled gun!"

My father-in-law, Paskell W. Dyer, went on to be with the Lord last week. Louise and I just returned from the funeral. It was a beautiful tribute to a good man.

Although he lived to be 89, we still feel the pain involved in giving up someone we love. We're in a transition time I mentioned in Chapter IX. We felt the strain of transition most when with Louise's brothers, Harold and Ernest, we met to divide their Dad's personal property. It was sacred ground! But, he left his mark, and that's what he wanted. He was ready to "go on and be with Ma."

During last weekend, we shed many tears, but there was also the joy of re-connecting with our large extended family. Saw cousins we hadn't seen in years. Our three sons were able to be there too, and it helped them to get a renewed sense of their roots.

We also laughed some while we were together. Remembered funny stories that Pass used to enjoy. Stories connected with our family and community.

Harold Dyer told me of a neighbor named Elmer who once said that things were so bad on his farm that he was going to sell his "taters and go younder Eli," a new expression for me. Harold also told me about a phone call his neighbor, Artie May, made to the fire station to report a fire at her house out in the country. They asked how to get out there. Artie replied, "Ain't younse still got that red truck?"

And then there was the story about two drunks who were walking along a railroad track. One said, "For a little I'd jest **buy** this railroad." His friend replied, "Now, you're talking to a man who'll **sell!**"

Then there was a neighbor who asked $600 for a team of mules. When offered only $150, he replied, "That's a long ways to fall, but here I come!"

Once when I returned to preach at Philadelphia close to home, a local farmer I grew up with said that I had been to school a lot, had several degrees, was highly educated, but "you can't tell it." As one neighbor observed, "It's hard to make a silk purse out of a sow's ear."

The country way of saying some words is funny to me. One friend told that his daughter visited them "yister ening" but that she had gone "summers else this ening." Then, sometimes people used to have long names that were amusing. I knew one woman whose actual name was Mary, Meranda, Martha, Mariar, Frances Cleveland, Fannie Dyer. She was related to Stephen I Kay Woody Smith Dyer.

Harold also tells the story about a preacher who preached strongly against the misuse of alcoholic beverages, as do I. At any rate, this preacher was at a church get-together (they never had parties), and some of the boys spiked his milk. Of course, he kept wanting more "of that milk." Finally, after several glasses of milk and about "half lit," he told the farmer who brought the milk, "If you ever want to sell that cow, I want to buy her."

Let me share three more from Harold. He told me about a workaholic who was always "as busy as a one-eyed man at a burlesque show."

Then there was a smart alec guy who came through a small country town and asked, "Is this town dead or what?" A local man replied, "It musta just died, cause you're the first buzzard I've seed."

My favorite story from Harold is a true story about P. J. who wasn't weaned until he was seven years old. He'd come home from school to nurse. On one such occasion, he said to his Dad, "Give me a chaw of backer (tobacco). Moma's been eating them green onions again." P. J.'s Dad bragged that P. J. had a rail (real) good job. All he had to do was carry brick. They hired an assistant "to lay them for him."

Ernest Dyer told me about a trick Tobie pulled on his dad one time. He put a chicken in the trunk of his new Model T car. Of course, the chicken died and "stunk up the whole car." When Flora, their Mom, found out who did it, she waited one night until Tobie was asleep, chained him to the bed, and beat him with her broom.

He also told me about a neighbor who said she "hadn't sawed me for a long time." Then there was a statement by Gillie Ann that she "didn't have nothing but hard experiences around her husband."

Then, I also visited with cousin J. Fred Pippin who reminded me of several other amusing stories from my past. There was a preacher who came to that tobacco country years ago and preached hard against tobacco. After church, one of the tobacco farmers pulled him aside and said, "Now, if you get paid anything for this meetin', it'll be out of backer money." "Well, in that case," the preacher responded, "I guess it's all right." Reminds me of a preacher who really came down hard against tobacco at a "big meetin'" at Union Hill when I was a boy. What got him in big trouble was an illustration he used. "Why," he said, "You can take yore chaw of backer out before you come into church, lay it out on the steps, and it'll be there when meetin' is over. Even a dog won't bother it!" He had "done stopped preachin' and gone to meddlin'!"

Fred had a neighbor once who went and bought "four 'bran' new sympathic tires" for his car.

There was a farmer, Fred continued, who was learning to play golf. "Take that stick and knock that little ole ball down yonder toward that flag," he was told. He did just that and then asked, "Now what?" When told to take another stick and knock the ball into "that little ole hole over there," he replied, "Why didn't you tell me that back yonder?"

Once as a boy Fred "got into it" with Willie Joe, another boy in our community. Willie Joe threw a rock, cut a gash in Fred's head, and then ran in the house and got under a quilt his mother was quilting. Fred followed him into the house. Willie peeked out at Fred and said, "Fred, you ought to be home in bed."

Then there was that family that was too poor to pay attention. And, a farmer who offerd to pay a man what he was worth only to be told, "I can't live on that!"

I also had a good visit with cousin Lucille who shared some Jackson County humor with me. She told me about a rain that was "like a widow's dance, soon over with." And about Aunt Gillie Ann's problems with her husband, Willard. She tried to get Willard to do some work one time on the fourth of July, only to be told by him that "I don't work on July the fourth." Gillie Ann replied, "Naw, nor on the fifth, sixth, or seventh either!"

Lucille also told me about Dellie Vine and her husband, Will. They got into a spat, Will picked up the "eatin' table" he had made, put it on top of his head and took off up the "Flatt Holler." Just as he left their front-yard, he turned and yelled as he lifted up the table over his head, "See what **you're missing?**" Whereupon, Dellie Vine pulled up her skirt and said, "Yes, and see what you're missing!" They were aware of sex even back then!

Another story that has been told for years by Louise's family is about her great grandfather, Richard Edmonds. He was eating dinner at Mammy Pippin's one day when one of the women spilt some hot coffee in his lap and then asked, "Did it burn you, Dick?" To which Richard responded, "Naw, it jest burnt my leg." Everybody laughed! Isn't that more healthy than getting too uptight about it? Don't take everything so seriously!

I also saw cousin Ava Nell last week-end. She was Uncle Opp's daughter. Uncle Opp always had a great wit about him. Only finished the third grade in school but was very intelligent. He once told me that I must be real dumb because it was taking me so long to get out of school. Only took him three years! Once when his son Thurl was learning to drive, he almost ran off the road coming up Flynn's Creek. Uncle Opp quickly recovered and said, "You'd better hurry up and get your driver's license or you're gonna get us all killed!"

Reminds me of what Jerry Johnson said to a sheriff once who stopped him and was astonished that Jerry had been driving for 30 years and had never had a driver's license. Jerry's response, "Why? I never needed one until now!"

Another saying Uncle Opp had in his prayers at church was for God to be with us "on land or sea or wherever we may be." Had difficulty saying "in the air" when airplane travel became a common possibility. In his dismissal prayers, he would always end with the words, "Go with us to our respective places of abode. Stand by us in death, and in heaven save the faithful." He did have his serious moments. But after church, he would often say to his wife, Aunt Ethel, "Now, don't hang around here too long or somebody'll want to go home with us!" Another saying he had was that he took a bath every year whether he needed it or not.

Daddy told me about an amusing incident involving his grandmother, Elizabeth (Betty) Birdwell. Will Woodall was working for them for a day or so on their farm on Rush Fork. At the dinner table, he stuck his fork right down into the middle of a new bowl of butter Ma had just put on the table. Ma said, "Will, why don't you cut you some butter around the edge of the bowl instead of right in the middle?" "Why, it don't make no difference," Will responded, "We're gonna eat it all anyhow."

Uncle Jesse Flatt once told me a story about P. M. Medley. P. M. had come back from Detroit and was at Uncle Jesse's store. Uncle Jesse said, "P. M., I though you'd be back plowing them mules by now." I can identify with P. M.'s answer as he replied, "The only time I'll ever say 'get up' to a mule again is if one is settin' on top of me!"

I hope you're enjoying these stories. I enjoy telling them. Helps me to keep laughing sometimes when life gets too serious.

Let me share a few more with you. One time our country doctor told my Ma Way that her teeth were poisoning her system and that they needed to be pulled. Ma responded, "Why, Dr. Doe, you pulled all of my teeth four years ago." A good diagnosis, you see, sometimes plays out!

Another community story involved Aunt Elvinie whose husband Bobby Earl always liked to have a good fire in his fireplace at home. When Uncle Bobby died on a cold winter day, she remarked, "I hope he went to a place where they have a good far" (fire).

My wife, Louise, has a twin brother, Ernest. After I share this with friends, I am somtimes asked, "Are they identical?" Finally, I decided on an appropriate response: "No. He's a little taller than she is!"

I also saw my friend, Emmett Tightwad, last week. Once many years ago we were at Odie's Drive-In Restaurant together. I asked him if he wanted a Coke. He responded, "Naw, but I'll take your dime."

Dimes were scarce with us back then. Once I remember being out in Uncle Leo's 1936 Ford with Leamon, cousins Layton and Litton (both now deceased), Harold and Ernest when we ran out of gas as we sometimes did in those days. We took up a collection of all the money we had, and put in 27 cents worth of gas. Told the gas station owner that our tank had a hole in it, wouldn't hold much gas, a common joke in such situations!

One country story I've heard for years involves a mule who was too tall to get into the stall. Her ears would always touch the top of the door opening, and she would immediately back up and refuse to go on in. Well, the farmer got some scissors and started to cut the mule's ears off to enable her to get into her stall. A country cousin came along and asked him what he was doing. He explained, only to hear his cousin suggest that he dig away a few inches of the dirt floor to solve the problem. The farmer replied, "Why, that's the dumbest idea I've ever heard of. It's not his **lags** that are too long. It's his **ears!**"

I heard about a family who only wanted to have two children. Why? They had heard that every third child born in the world was Chinese, and they didn't want to raise a Chinese child!

My barber once told me that he had figured out how old a Christian man had to be before he could become an elder in the church. Forty years old. He continued, "Paul mentioned Crete right before he gave the qualifications of elders. Crete stands for concrete, and everybody knows it takes concrete 40 years to settle. Took me several years to figure that out," he said.

Billy Joe Johnson, a neighbor of keen wit, was always good for a laugh. His more famous stories involved a run-away team of mules pulling a wagon and a sow that habitually got out of the pasture. His son, Donnie Joe, was driving the mules as they got scared and ran like crazy. They tried to jump with the wagon and Billy Joe's family across a high gully. Well, about the time they got about halfway across, Billy Joe could see that they weren't going to make it; so he told Donnie to pull the checklines and turn the mules and wagon around in mid-air. He did, and they came back to the other side of the gully safe and sound!

The sow story was just about as incredible. They finally discovered how she and her pigs were getting out of the pasture. The sow would swing them one at a time across the fence on a grapevine swing!

Incidentally, I fell off one of those grapevine swings once that went all the way across a "holler." It was probably an 80 feet drop. But I was slowed down in my fall by the tree limbs I hit on the way down. I can hear my colleagues saying now, "That explains a lot of things!" No, I didn't hit that hard! Just made me sore for a few weeks. I never told my Dad. Never told him about getting my ribs broken in football either. He was strongly opposed to my playing football (which I can understand better now). He said I might get hurt.

Now, let me take you from Jackson County to a few other places I have lived. I worked for a year in a Detroit factory from age 18 to 19. Left the day I graduated from high school.

Once in Detroit, I was riding to work with my friend Lod Long, from Jackson County's Philadelphia Ridge. Lod got stopped one night by a policeman for driving with one headlight. The policeman gave Lod a warning ticket and told him not to drive anymore at night with one light. Lod promised that he wouldn't and then asked, "Is it all right if I drive in the daytime with one light?" The policeman laughed and assured him that it would be okay. They always thought everybody from Tennessee was stupid and went barefooted anyhow.

Louise and I really enjoyed living for a year in Spencer, Tennessee. They often said that if you lived there a year, you'd never leave—would be too poor to leave. That "ragler (regular) mountain diet of taters, cornbread, and water" would be hard to endure.

One day Loge Flatt was down at Martin's general store, just sitting, whittling, and talking to a group of oldtimers when they began discussing who was saved and who wasn't, "a mighty good way to get into an argument." Well, they wanted to know how Loge could be so sure that he was saved. Loge said that one night when he was in bed "around there in the holler," that an angel of the Lord came and got him "by the hair of the head," flew him through the clouds, and took him to heaven, and introduced him to Jesus, who showed him his

240

name "wrote right there in the Lamb's book of life." Jesus then told him, "Loge, I don't want you to worry nary particle about your soul's salvation anymore." Then, the angel got Loge by the hair of the head, flew him back to his house, and put him back in bed.

Well, after Loge finished, there was silence in the store for the space of some 10 seconds. Then Mr. Curtis, who was hard of hearing, yelled back and said, "Loge, I've only got one thing to say about that. You'd better a stayed while you wuz there. Cause the way you're living, you ain't gonna get back!"

I also heard a couple of backer (tobacco) stories in Spencer. One was about a country preacher who chewed tobacco which greatly displeased one "city slicker" church member who said to him one day, "Just why in the world do you chew that tobacco?" His response right before he spat was, "It's the only way I know to get the ambeer out!"

The other tobacco story also involved chewing tobacco. A certain church member asked his preacher, who chewed tobacco, if he thought it was a sin to smoke. The preacher responded, "Yeah, I do. It's a sin to burn up anything that tastes that good." Then he chewed a couple of times on his "backer chaw" and spat.

We moved from Spencer to Brownsville, Tennessee in 1960. While we lived there, the farmers in Haywood County had hundreds of hogs to die with cholera. So, they had a cholera expert come out from the University of Tennessee to speak to them about the disease. After he finished, he asked for comments. One farmer commented that in his 35 years of experience with hogs and cholera, that hogs that lived for two or three days with cholera had a lot better chance of making it than "hogs that died right off."

One of our wonderful church members, Sadie Jean Talkslow, had divorced her husband. You see, he had tried to kill her twice by burning their houses with her in them. He was about to get out of jail when Sadie came by our house and told me that she wanted me to marry "me and Lonnie" again. She said, "I know you thank I'm crazy, but I still love Lonnie. You can't live with a hog for 20 yere," she continued, "without having some kind of feelings for it." I advised her to get some fire insurance, and I performed the marital ceremony two weeks later. They lived together until he died a few years ago.

Once when I was in a meeting in Morgantown, West Virginia, I stayed with an elder of the church who was also a retired professor of agriculture at West Virginia University. He told me of an incident once that also involved hogs. The University had a feeding program that would speed up growth in hogs and "get them to market **three weeks early.**" Throughout his lectures to farmers he would emphasize **three weeks early.** Once during a question and answer period following his lecture, a certain farmer asked him, "What is time to a hog?"

We moved to Indianapolis in 1963. Saw two Indianapolis 500 races. One funny story I heard there involved A. J. Foyt, famous Indy race car driver. On one of the days A. J. didn't win, he led the race until the last lap only to have a wheel come off his car. "What thoughts do you have right now?" a reporter asked. "Makes me think of a popular song," A. J. responded: "You picked a fine time to leave me, loose wheel!"

It was also in Indianapolis that I had difficulty in answering a question asked me by brother Claude Literal. Brother Literal was upset with me for using filmstrips in my Bible class. He reasoned that "faith comes by hearing and that's seeing. It's sinful!" I tried several approaches: Jeremiah put a yoke around his neck to appeal to the people's sight. "You'll be in bondage if you don't turn back to God," he said. It didn't work! I finally asked Claude if he read the Bible. He said, "Yes, but I read it out loud so that I can hear it."

Since 1965, we've lived in Memphis, and we still love it. Let me close this chapter by sharing some humor I've heard during these years.

First of all, I'd like to tell you about my good friend, Dr. W. B. West, Jr., a great man of God. Also a very unique man who can enjoy humor. He told me once a story about Benjamin Franklin, the subject of study for a third grade class in Boston. The teacher asked her students to write a short biography of Franklin's life. An attempt of one little boy went something like this: "Ben Franklin was born in Boston. He moved to Pennsylvania, got married, and **then** discovered electricity!"

My favorite story from Dr. West was about a couple who fussed constantly throughout their marriage. Not a moment's peace in 50 years. Finally, when he died, everyone wondered what she would put on his tombstone, doubting if she could think of anything nice to say. Here was what she had engraved on his tomb: "Rest in peace. . . . . 'til I come!" Reminds me of an epitaph on a husband's tombstone in Atlanta. It read, "Gone but not forgiven."

Another story somewhat similar is about another fussing, whining couple. Finally the husband died; and after a few weeks, his widow wanted to talk to him. So, she went to a medium, who said she could contact the dead, and asked her to contact her departed husband. After a few seconds, she said she was in contact with him and that the widow could talk to him. "Honey," the widow said, "You always complained about how bad it was to live with me. Is it really better up there than it was living with me?" **"Yes,"** came the reply from her husband (as the story goes), **"much, much better** here than it was living with you; and, incidentally, I'm not **up** there!"

I remember well what Dr. West said to me over the phone right after I was employed by Harding University Graduate School of Religion. He called me in Indianapolis; and, as always, was very encouraging, like they had just hired the best man in the universe for the job. He said, "You've been elected to the faculty, and you're held in such high esteem that they have made you an officer of the faculty. Secretary." I felt great! But, what that really meant was that I was the new man on the block, and the new man **always** has to take minutes of faculty meetings.

My favorite story about my good friend, Dr. West, was told by a temporary secretary of his. She said that Dr. West gave her a letter one day to type with these instructions: "This is a very, very confidential letter. Its contents must not be divulged under any circumstances. I want you to **type** it, but **don't read it."**

People often tell stories about Dr. Jack Lewis, respected professor emeritus at the school. Students used to say that he would stop in mid-sentence if the bell rang. Then, the next week, he would begin his lecture at that same mid-sentence point, and not miss a word. Very organized! Lots of content!

One student also said that he dropped his pencil one day in Dr. Lewis' Advanced Introduction to the Old Testament class and missed 500 years of Old Testament history before he could pick it up and continue his note-taking.

My favorite story about my friend Jack reflects his tough academic standards. When asked once how many **students** we had at the Graduate School, he said, "Oh, about two percent of the enrollment I suppose."

At his retirement dinner, I told a story about Jack that reflected his wish to keep things as they are. I said that Jack had been at the school since 1954, had seen many changes during all of those years, and had been against every one of them.

Dr. Lewis told me one of my favorite stories about psychologists. It involved an Indian Chief who went to a psychologist with an identity problem. Some days he thought he was a teepee; other days a wigwam. Just went back and forth from day to day. "What's wrong with me, Doc?" he asked. "I know exactly what's wrong with you," the psychologist responded, "You're two tents (too tense)!"

Makes me think of another psychologist story I heard in California. This huge woman (or maybe it was a man) went to a psychologist and asked him how she could lose weight. He said, "You need to do three things: (1) Get your id in sync with your super ego, (2) conquer your narcissistic tendency, and (3) stop eating like a pig."

My favorite psychologist story has to do with changing light bulbs. How many psychologists does it take to change a light bulb (not bub)? It takes only one, but the bulb really has to want to change!

I've heard several good stories in the great state of Arkansas. One, told by Dr. Clifton Ganus, Jr., had to do with an unusual way of squirrel hunting. One farmer said he hunted squirrels by uglying them to death. He'd just stare at them and they'd fall out of the tree "dead as a doorknob." Well, his friend had to see it to believe it. Went hunting with him and sure enough, the story continues, the farmer stared at several squirrels in a row and killed every one of them. His friend replied, "I never saw anything like it. Y, I'll bet you're the only person in the world who can do that." "No," the farmer said,

"My wife can do it." "Well, if that's so, why don't you take her huntin with you?" the friend inquired. "No, I tried that once," the farmer replied, "and she tore them all to pieces!"

Then there was the Arkansas story about why a certain man's parents had waited so long to get married. Their son explained, "Well, Daddy drank a lot. Moma wouldn't marry him when he was drunk, and Daddy wouldn't marry her when he was sober."

Once when I was in Little Rock some 20 years ago, a brother Peters told me a true story about a Christian from a country church whom he had invited to one of their services in Little Rock. The man refused in no uncertain terms. "It's an unscriptural church," he said. "What's unscriptural about it?" Brother Peters inquired. "Well, for one thing you count the audience, and they didn't count the audience in Bible times," the Christian said. Brother Peters mentioned the 3,000 persons baptized on the birthday of the church in Acts two only to find out that such a count was an estimate (it said **about** 3,000 souls). What else was wrong? Well, they had a baptistry at the city church, and that was unscriptural. The Bible says they baptized in a certain water (Acts 8), "and they ain't nothing certain about a baptistry. Y, it's liable to bust and run all over the place at any time!"

I heard this story about my friend, Crawford Burris of Arkansas. Burris went on a vacation with three of his friends, one of whom snored something awful. Since they only had two rooms with one bed in each room, they decided to take turns sleeping with Alphis Wooddall, the loud snorer. The other two guys tried it first and didn't sleep a wink. Complained "something terrible" at breakfast. Then, it came Crawford's turn to sleep with Alphis. Next morning at breakfast he looked well-rested and cheerful. How'd he sleep? Slept well! "How in the world did you manage to do **that?**" his two friends asked. "Don't know," Crawford replied, "I just kissed him goodnight, and he stayed up all night and watched me, I think."

Then there was the one about a farmer who bought some medicine at a drugstore for both his wife and his mule. He cautioned the pharmacist by saying, "Be sure to mark which is which. I want my mule to be in shape for spring plowing!"

My good friend, John Simpson, is always good for a humorous story. Here's one he shared with me. A certain man always bought shoes that were too little. They really cramped his feet! Why? He wanted something to look forward to when he went home to his wife. He'd always feel good when he pulled off his shoes!

Ken Jones, another preacher friend of mine, told me about a song leader who always tried to pick songs that would match the preacher's lesson topic. His effort, usually successful, hit a snag one Wednesday night when the minister announced that his lesson topic for the next week would be "sex." He tried all week without success. So, the next Wednesday night, he got up and just told the congregation his dilemma and asked for suggestions. To his surprise, several came. A young man suggested, "Praise God from Whom All Blessings Flow"; an older woman, "O Why Not Tonight?"; an older man, "Precious Memories!"

Dave Maddux, successful Christian businessman of Cookeville, Tennessee told me about two older women friends who were sitting out on the porch "a rockin." One suddenly said to the other, "I'm embarrassed to admit it, but I can't remember your name. What is your name anyhow?" Her friend paused and then responded, "How soon do you need to know?"

Dr. E. Claude Gardner said that he went one Sunday to a church in West Tennessee to preach. Went into the vestibule and introduced himself to an elder gentleman who just looked at him for a while but said nothing. Then, after church, the gentleman came to him and said, "I know I acted strange before church when you introduced yourself to me, but I couldn't remember my name!"

Since I'm a psychologist, my friends continue to share with me humorous stories about psychologists along with some negative remarks about them. Here's one only a psychologist in private practice could **fully** appreciate. A client who was having trouble with his memory went to a psychologist for treatment. "I can't remember anything," he told the psychologist. "Can you treat me?" "Sure," said the psychologist, **"if** you will pay me in **advance!"**

Did you hear about the **paranoid man** who had to quit going to football games? He thought that every time they went into a huddle, they were talking about **him!**

Do you know how a Narcissistic Support Group starts its meetings? They go around the room and introduce themselves by saying, "Hi, I'm _____, and I don't care what your name is!"

Then there was the man who asked his friend if his father had any last words before he died. "No," his friend replied, "Moma was with him up until his very last breath!"

Reminds me of a story G. K. Wallace, well-known preacher, used to tell about a boy who came home and told his father that he got a small part in a school play. He was to play the part of a husband. "Don't get discouraged," said his father, "keep trying, and some day you'll get a **talking** part!"

I heard this pun at a convention. The Indians used to have an unusual custom involving fertility rituals. Before a brave was allowed to marry, he had to go out and kill a wild animal, skin it, and make a bed for his new bride and himself. Three such braves were about to get married and went on a hunt. The first one killed a **deer,** skinned it, and made a bed for his honeymoon. The second one killed a bear, skinned it, and made a bed for his new bride. The third one killed a hippopotamus, skinned it and made a bed.

Nine months later, the first squaw gave birth to a baby boy and the second squaw to a baby girl. The third squaw who slept on the hippopotamus bed gave birth to twins, a boy **and** a girl, which was one of the first proofs of the famous theorem which states that the **squaw** of the **hippopotamus** is **equal to the sum of the other two squaws!**

My good friend John Simpson told me this humorous story about a certain farmer's bull that was not performing well. The vet came and gave the bull some medicine and left some for the farmer to continue giving him. After a few doses, the bull was better, back doing what bulls are supposed to do. When asked by his neighbor "what in the world was in the medicine," the farmer replied, "I don't know. It tastes a little like peppermint!"

John also told me one about a new wig for women. "It is already rolled up in curlers to wear to the supermarket!"

Then there is the one about a farmer who was having real difficulty in telling his two horses apart. He tried all kinds of ways to do this. Once he took all of the hair off one of the horses' tails, but it grew back out. Another time, he put chalk on one of the horses' hooves, but the rain washed it off. Finally, he figured it out. The **black horse** was **four inches taller** than the **white horse!**

I like humorous farmer stories. I grew up on a farm and have tremendous respect for farmers. I never laugh at them or at anyone else but laugh **with** them!

And, since I am a preacher, I especially enjoy preacher humor. Most ministers are witty. Even my dignified close friends Drs. W. B. and Earl West enjoy a good story.

Earl told me once about a woman who wanted to marry four times: First to a banker to get plenty of money; next to an actor who would show her a good time; next to a preacher who would help her be good; and fourth to an undertaker who would give her a nice funeral. "You know," she continued, "Like, one for the money, two for the show, three to get ready, and four to go."

Do you know how many preachers it takes to change a light bulb? It takes only **one.** And all he has to do is hold the bulb. The whole world revolves around him.

Do you know who the shortest man in the Bible was? Some think it was Zaccheus, others Knee High Miah, but they are wrong! It was Bildad the Shuhite!

A preacher is a person who talks in **someone else's sleep.** He also looks at his **watch** when he ought to look at a **calendar!**

One preacher was having difficulty closing a wedding ceremony. He finally couldn't think of anything to say except one verse of scripture which he quoted, "Go and sin no more!"

Another preacher asked a church for a $50,000 salary. When asked why he needed so much money (churches want to get you for the bottom dollar), he replied, "Preaching is hard work when you don't know what you're doing."

Another preacher resigned to take a job in a jail. As is often the case, he had been waiting for years to say something to the elders he wanted to say, so he chose as a text for his final sermon, "I go to prepare a place for you" (John 14:3).

Do you know why some groups bury preachers 20 feet deep? Because, down deep preachers aren't all that bad!

My friend, Tom Holland, tells about a big church wedding in which a friend of his was involved. The groom was so nervous he fainted twice before the ceremony began and then fainted during it. Well, they finally revived him and stood him back up on his wobbly legs beside his bride. At this point, his grandmother on the second row was heard to whisper more loudly than she thought, "He don't look like he's going to be in shape for any honeymoon!"

This reminds me of another wedding between a poor boy and a wealthy girl. When it came to the part about "bestowing **all** of his worldly goods" to his bride, the bride's mother whispered, "There goes his bicycle!"

I might be giving you the idea that I laugh all of the time. Not true. I scored three on a one to ten scale on the sober-serious versus happy-go lucky personality trait on the 16 Personality Factor Test. I don't laugh enough. Take things too seriously at times.

I **do** see the value of laughter and can remember it in our family with Louise, our boys—Steve, Tim, and Danny—and our grandchildren. Let me share a few that are more recent that have to do with David and Kevin, our wonderful grandsons.

David was about two and was staying overnight with us. His bedtime we were told was nine p.m.; so at nine, off to bed he went. But, you know the rest of the story. He already knew his grandparents were not all that tough. So, he talked and jabbered and asked for drinks of water and everything else for the next hour. At 10, I went up to his room, got him out of bed and rocked him until I was about to go to sleep. Then, I told David, **"All** of us have got to go to bed pretty soon!" David's half-asleep response, "We all bedder rock," brought me wide awake laughing.

Once when he was about the same age, he was eating lunch in his highchair beside me. A grape on his "plate" started rolling. Seeing it, David said, "ball?" That's the way they learn. They build on what they know.

Kevin has been equally precious and sometimes amusing to us. Let me share a couple of amusing incidents involving him.

We were riding in the back seat. Me Ma was driving. Kevin was about to go visit Nonnie (grandmother) and Pawpa in Arkansas. As I had done previously, I told Kevin that he'd better not give all of his kisses to them. While before he had made a game of this with me, not this time at age three and a half.

Instead, he thought for a moment and said, "I have plenty of kisses. They always come back. See (while he puckered his lips and threw several kisses out into the air)." Giving them away did not diminish his supply! What an amusing lesson!

Last week, I received the first copy of my new video on *Building Better Homes*. Always curious, Kevin looked at the video and asked what it was. I explained to him that I had made a video for television on *Building Better Homes*. His response, "I like **this** home." Well Kevin, I do too, and you're one of the reason why (right now, Kevin always asks why).

There are some funny statements children make that are related to age level. They just get it wrong. Let me share a few of these with you from our grandsons (unfortunately I've forgotten a lot of what our children said at these young ages). Both David and Kevin are very handsome boys (really), and they have heard a lot of nice comments about how attractive they are, especially their eyes. Once when a clerk at a store was bragging about the beauty of David's different features, he replied in his very pure and innocent little voice, "Did you notice my eyes?"

Several years ago, he and Kevin had a hefty babysitter— very overweight. David took one look at her and asked, "How much do you **weigh?**"

Recently David stayed at home from school with severe tonsillitis. When his concerned teacher called and asked why he wasn't at school, he replied, "I've got arthritis in my throat."

Then there's Kevin. A few days ago we were playing his favorite game of "Where's Kevin?" He hides, and we look. I helped him hide in the closet and then called to Me Ma, "Where's Kevin. Is he with you?" She came looking and talking, "I thought he was with you." When she got right in front of the small closet door where Kevin was hidden, we heard a little innocent voice come from the closet, "Don't open this door!" Next, he hid under a blanket while we pretended we didn't have a clue as to where he was.

Recently, right before they went home, Kevin asked me, "Will you give me some mon-e?" It embarrassed his parents but was funny to us. I had often given him money before as they left; so he thought it was part of the ritual. There is humor that happens all along if you'll watch for it.

A few days ago when the boys got ready to go home, David said, "bag, bag" to me. We then went to our bedroom, as is our custom, and I got my bag of candy down for him. He looked at what I had in the bag and said politely that he didn't want anything he saw. I asked, "Don't you want **anything?**" "Nothing in the **bag**," he responded. I asked, "What do you want?" "It's not polite to ask," David replied. Well, this continued back and forth a few times, and then I noticed my fruit jar full of coins setting on the closet shelf, got it down and asked, "Is **this** what you want?" He smiled and said, "Yes!" So as I had done several times before, I gave both David and Kevin a handful of coins. David was confident enough to hint but too polite to ask.

A few nights ago Kevin and I hid under a blanket. He had our flashlight and turned it on so that we could see. We looked at each other and smiled. It was one of those intimate moments. I asked as we looked at each other, "Did you know you're a sweetie pie?" "Yes," Kevin replied in his sweet, innocent voice. Precious!

Today on Kevin's fourth birthday, as he and his dad were coming to our house, he asked Tim, "Does God have a rope?" Tim asked why God needed a rope, and Kevin replied, "so he can get us up to heaven!" How about that?

Let me share just one more story about David. He came to our house once before I got up. I wasn't feeling well that day and was trying to sleep late. I could hear Me Ma continually telling David to be quiet and not wake Pa Pa up. I could also hear him right next to my bedroom door replying rather loudly, "I won't Me Ma." A few minutes later, I'd hear him again, "Pa Pa bed-der get uuuup." Finally, he quietly came into the bedroom and stood right beside my bed. He then yelled to Me Ma, "Pa Pa's sleepy. It's time for Pa Pa to get uuup!" By that time, laughing under the covers, I turned over, reached and got David, gave him a big bear hug, and let him "sleep" with me for a while. Those moments are precious!

Well, maybe that's enough for now. A sense of humor! I hope you can laugh **with** me and especially that you can laugh at yourself. Don't take yourself so seriously!

One reason I included this chapter in this book is because of what one of our sons said to me a few years ago. It was at a time when things were not going the way I wished at school. I was almost depressed, I think, looking back on it! What our son said was, "Dad, you don't ever laugh anymore about anything. You take yourself too seriously!" He was right. I needed to loosen up a bit and laugh at myself. I needed to learn that I don't always have to get what I want or have my own way. There are usually different legitimate ways of looking at the same situation. Most people who are mentally ill or who are in dysfunctional families do not laugh much.

At any rate, I have learned to laugh again. I often see humor in everyday events, and it lightens my load. I hope you can learn to do this too! Healthy families have a healthy sense of humor.

A GROWING EXERCISE

1. Do you laugh **at** people or with them?
2. What is humorous about what Jesus said in Matthew 7:1-5?
3. Have you stopped laughing?
4. Is "not laughing" an indication of feelings of insecurity or low self-esteem?
5. Are you too dignified to laugh?
6. When is it inappropriate to laugh?
7. Are you afraid to laugh around other family members? If so, talk it over with them.
8. Look for humor in everyday situations.
9. Laugh with your family.

Thirteen

Healthy Self-Esteem

Building self-esteem is a hard and slow process. But it is not an impossible one.

Self-esteem is how you feel about being you, how you feel about being alive. It results from an evaluation of your self-image, how you feel about the way you see yourself. It is influenced by the distance between your self-image and your ideal image. You can, for example, see yourself as being of average intelligence, feel all right about it, and experience high self-esteem. Or you can feel badly about it and experience low self-esteem. You can feel worthy or unworthy, competent or incompetent, significant or insignificant, valuable or worthless, hopeful or hopeless, truthful or deceptive, confident or fearful, withdrawn or sociable, preoccupied or spontaneous. You may be preoccupied with self, feel unloved, overly sensitive to criticism or open to a healthy interaction with others. Self-esteem has an evaluative element: **How do you feel about the way you see yourself?**

Self-esteem has many correlates. Low self-esteem has been correlated with psychological distress, depression, preoccupation with self, fatigue, chronic health problems, negative attitudes toward self and others, being trapped in a self-defeating cycle, a feeling of being a nobody, rigidity, authoritarian families, neurosis, anxiety, defensiveness, drug abuse, alcoholism, interpersonal problems, child abuse, low academic achievᵉ

253

ment, hostility, and even suicide in some cases. High self-esteem is correlated with good health, confidence, accurate perceptions of reality, flexibility, good ability to interact with others, trust, happiness, success, involvement with others, openness, competence, good home life, good decisions, academic success, and self-respect. A person with good self-esteem has a sense of self-worth, yet recognizes his or her limitations. Such a person is not conceited but rather is glad to be himself. "Self actualized" persons tend to have accurate perceptions of reality and adapt well to it. They accept themselves and others but are desirous of correcting their own shortcomings. They are problem-centered, not self-centered: they appreciate the simple things of life, are ethical, able to discriminate between means and ends; they get along in their culture yet resist enculturation and have a genuine desire to help the human race.

Self-esteem may be classified into two divisions: basic self-esteem and functional self-esteem. Basic self-esteem is established in childhood, is hard but not impossible to change; whereas functional self-esteem is derived from daily experiences and changes more readily.

To build self-esteem, you need to know its roots. Parents probably have the greatest influence on self-esteem. A close, healthy relationship between parents and children often leads to high self-esteem in children; indifferent relationships, to low self-esteem. Positive reinforcement and acceptance teaches children to value themselves. They develop attitudes toward themselves similar to those expressed by significant others in their lives. Parents who love, show concern, give attention, direction, and approval to their children teach them to value themselves positively. There is not, however, a direct cause-effect relationship in the building of self-esteem. You are involved yourself and thus help create your own environment. Those who are honest and live with integrity tend to have good self-esteem, whereas dishonest persons do not. It's how you feel about what you have thought, felt, and done that determines your self-esteem.

Healthy self-esteem in **men** is thought to be derived to some extent from vocations, intelligence, wealth, achievements, education, positions of power, and competition. **Female** self-esteem results more from the achievement of goals, self and body image, education, money, everyday concerns, and family relationships. Both sexes are usually affected by their view of how they are evaluated by significant others in their lives.

In summary, there are probably at least seventeen influences on one's self-esteem: self, gender, significant others, social role expectations, family relationships, community influence, psychosocial developmental issues, communication and coping strategies, standards, unrealistic expectations, education, wealth, intelligence, achievements, competition, theology, and thinking. These should be kept in mind as you develop better self-esteem in your family.

SELF-ESTEEM IN CHILDREN

Let me begin by discussing self-esteem in children. They are a heritage of the Lord and his reward (Psalm 127:3). Parents should receive them with love and gratitude. Children should not be provoked or discouraged (Colossians 3:21). Such an approach will help them to have good self-esteem.

Stanley Coopersmith **(The Antecedents of Self-Esteem)** found that many factors influence the development of self-esteem in children: power, effectance, significance, acceptance, affection, virtue, morality, and ethics. Competence, achievement, success, relationships, a sense of belonging, support from others and money are important as well. It has also been demonstrated that physical appearance, intelligence, competition, and the family and community situation also influence self-esteem. Family strengths are so important that they can sometimes overcome social rejection. For this to happen, parents must have definite values, a clear idea of what they perceive as appropriate behavior, and be able and willing to present and enforce their beliefs that self-esteem is highly influenced by personal beliefs about who we are. God made us; therefore, we are worthwhile. If we are worthwhile, then we have good reason to have good self-esteem. Our self-esteem is not a selfish sort of thing but is rooted in faith in our Creator. He made us worthwhile!

As a parent, you may be wanting some specific guidelines for building self-esteem in your children. Although there are n⌐

cookbook approaches that will always be completely adequate, here are some ideas that have proven themselves worthwhile in child rearing:

1. Try to improve your own mental health. It is impossible for you to contribute toward good self-esteem in your child if your self-esteem is extremely low: you can try, but you will probably be unsuccessful unless you start with yourself. In dealing with your children, you teach more by what you are than by what you say. Ask yourself such questions as the following: Since God accepts me, why can't I accept myself? Since God loves me, why can't I love myself? Since God says I am worthwhile, why will I not accept his evaluation? Who am I to question God? Since I forgive others, why can't I forgive myself? Am I easy to be around? Perhaps there is something in me that is worthwhile.

2. If you are married, establish a healthy marriage. If your marriage is unhealthy, you no doubt have unhealthy patterns of interaction in your home which affect your children. The starting place for family health is with individual parents and with the patterns of interaction between them. If you can't work it out yourself, get some help in doing so. It is not a sign of weakness to see your own faults and to try to overcome them. In fact, it is a sign of maturity and strength to do so. Weak people try to avoid such reality.

3. Provide for your family's needs: physical, emotional, psychological, social, and spiritual. When such needs as these are not met, your children will be affected. They need to be loved, fed, clothed, given shelter and safety, given understanding, acceptance, responsibility, a sense of effectance, and spiritual training. If you as parents are relatively healthy yourselves, you can provide the kind of atmosphere your children need to feel good about themselves.

4. Spend time with your children. In these days of two-career families, it is sometimes difficult for either parent to spend much quality time with their children. You as a parent are often not only busy but tired and need rest yourself. However, your children are a priority and must be given some attention. Try to restore the family table to its rightful place. Eat as many meals together as possible. Make such meals a

time of pleasant interaction. No distractions should normally be allowed, such as watching television while you are eating. This is a time for togetherness. It is also good to find other times for mutual participation. I have always had a basketball goal in our yard and have often played basketball with our children as they grew up. I believe this time together helped us to form some bonds that are still strong. You may think of many other situations in which you can find some quality time together. Use your imagination and make this a real priority in your family.

5. Teach them proper values. Children will pick up your values. If they see you living for money and prestige, they will value money and prestige. If they see you laying up treasures in heaven, they will usually value heaven (Matthew 6:19-21). Show them that you value them and that you value spiritual realities. These should have a high priority in your life: God, family, individuals, church, responsibility, and Christian character!

6. Let your children be children. As parents, we sometimes rush our children too rapidly into adulthood. We put them into competitive activities sometimes even before they start to school. They pick up the spirit of competitiveness and create for themselves extreme pressure to achieve beyond what is desirable or possible. Such achievement is often not that important in the overall scheme of things. This is especially true if they get so competitive and so involved in such activities that they miss the opportunity of being a child. Your children need to have some time to just piddle around and do nothing. Let them be creative, try themselves out at different tasks. Encourage them; do not thwart their initiative.

7. Focus upon strengths rather than weaknesses. Be realistic, yet recognize strengths. Get your child to think of what he or she can do rather than what can't be done. If we are unrealistic, we set our children up for defeat. Morris Rosenberg **(Society and the Adolescent Self-Image)** found that high self-esteem children tend to have mothers who are satisfied with average or below average performance. This goes against the grain with most of us because we do not want our children to be average. Yet, if someone pushes his or her child to be

257

above average, about half of them are going to be frustrated and dissatisfied with themselves. I believe the point is to not create unrealistic expectations for them.

Help them to overcome setbacks and to compete. We cannot completely overlook the need for our children to perform. We need to help them to learn, to keep trying when they fail, to overcome setbacks and to compete. Competition is not everything, but self-esteem is related to how well we do in relationship to others. This means doing as well as possible in school, continuing to try when mistakes are made. People with high self-esteem know how to do some things well.

Our son Tim just reminded me that he was cut from his eighth grade basketball team and that I encouraged him to keep trying. He did, and it paid off great dividends: he made All-Memphis and All-State teams in high school and scored 1448 points at Harding University in college.

9. Discipline your children with love. Set certain limits and enforce them but don't over-do it. Overly strict discipline can have a negative effect on self-esteem. Several researchers have found that low self-esteem is highly correlated with permissive parents; high self-esteem with more demanding parents. Discipline pays off. Show your love by your warmth, encouragement, consistency, realistic expectation, and a **balance** between **permissiveness** and **being overly strict.** Use **reward** more often than punishment. When you discipline your children, tell them why you are doing so if they are old enough to understand at all. Discipline with moderation. Discipline according to the age-level of the child.

10. Encourage achievement in school: motivate, help, maximize his or her potential, yet accept them for what they are and not for what you wish them to be. I know of one young man who committed suicide the day after his father forced him to change his educational and career goals. To the son, this meant that the father did not accept him for what he really was. God gave each of us different aptitudes and abilities: we need to maximize them to the fullest.

11. Try to avoid over-protection and dependency. Give your children appropriate responsibilities at different age levels, ask for their input, interact with them, give them responsibili-

ty, and praise them for their achievements. Let them try things out. Give them **wings** as well as **roots.**

12. Explain changes that will occur at puberty. There are still children from good homes who do not know what is going to happen to them at pubescence. They often are embarrassed and scared. We need to teach them that these changes are a part of God's plan and interpret them in terms of becoming mature. They, then, will see them as a positive rather than as a negative factor.

13. Forgive them. Most children are corrected, but many are not forgiven. Children need to hear their parents say, "I forgive you. You did wrong, but you have done what you could to correct it, and I still love you. I forgive you. And, we are going to go on from here."

14. Don't be partial to one child over another. Some believe that this caused Joseph problems with his brothers. Jacob had given him a coat of many colors, indicating some preference for Joseph over his brothers, and this may have caused them to turn against him (Genesis 37-50). It isn't fair to any of the children when we as parents show partiality.

15. Learn to show affection. This is difficult for you if you were reared in a family that did not show much affection. But you can learn to make some kind of appropriate physical contact with your children and show affection. This will help them to feel accepted, valuable, and secure.

16. Help them to belong. God helps us to have a feeling of belonging by saying that we are vital parts in the body of Christ (I Corinthians 12; Romans 12). Each part of the body has its function. Each child has a place of his very own in the family. Giving chores that are appropriate to the child's age level may help him or her have a sense of belonging. Telling them will also help.

17. Help them develop a strong faith in God, the source of our true value. We are worthwhile because God made us, and we are his. His grace is sufficient for us (II Corinthians 12:9). We can therefore glory in our weaknesses because the power of Christ rests upon us.

You may think of other suggestions, but these will perhaps stimulate your thinking and give you some ideas. Don't be afraid to act for fear of doing the wrong thing. We can make mistakes and still do a good job with our children. And, remember that self-esteem is self-perpetuating, either high self-esteem or low self-esteem. Once we get something going in a certain direction, it seems to perpetuate itself. This can be encouraging as we develop self-esteem in our children. With God's help, you can do what he wants you to do.

SELF-ESTEEM IN ADOLESCENCE

Adolescents and adults have many similarities. Teen brain power is almost equivalent to that of adults. Yet, many of the suggestions I made for children also apply to teenagers.

And, there are some special characteristics of adolescents as you perhaps know. One mother of an adolescent fried her 14-year-old son an egg. He wanted it poached. The next morning, she poached it, and he wanted it fried. The next morning, she fried one and poached another, and he said, "You fried the wrong one." It's hard to win sometimes, right? As Aristotle once said, "Adolescents carry everything too far."

Adolescents need attention, and they will find a way to get it. And, it's easier to get negative attention than positive attention. The squeaky wheel gets the grease. Hard rock music, alcohol and other drugs, and sex are opportunities to express **divergence** from the norm for them. And, in music as with drugs, it takes more and more radical statements to be different: satanic lyrics, bizarre ideas . . . . The average age for taking the first drink is now about age eleven. Scary! The extended family and community have broken down, and there are thus fewer and fewer substitute parents for our children. **Television** has become their **substitute parent.** Values taught by many television programs are money, sex, greed, violence, and power. Commercials push chemicals of various sorts to ease our pain.

Adolescent thinking is filled with cognitive distortions. One teenage boy, for example, was carrying a flag to keep the lions and tigers away. When told by his parents that his idea was silly, he responded, "It works. There are no lions or tigers around for miles!"

Teens often ask "Why not?" to get you as a parent to change your mind. They really are not wanting to know. They are wanting you to acquiesce. You as a parent have a right to say no just because you are **uncomfortable saying yes.** Such modeling helps children to say no just because they don't want to do what is being suggested by others: drug dealers, peers, and pimps . . .. They don't have to explain why not. They have a right to live by their own conscience.

Take a stand on drugs, sex, and hard rock music. Most teenagers actually want to know that there are limits and what they are. It lets them know that you care. Remember that young people who **smoke** are more likely to use other drugs such as cocaine. Early **sex** is associated with early drinking and **suicide.** A limit is a guideline. We drive slower when the speed limit is lower, and when we see a patrol car. Car wrecks are associated with alcohol abuse.

I seem to be mixing good parenting practices together with building self-esteem in teenagers. And I think this is appropriate. They go together.

Let me share a few more ideas that are uniquely related to building self-esteem in teenagers:

1. Value them for their innate worth and dignity just as they are.
2. Value them for the things over which they have control, especially their beliefs and values. De-emphasize things they cannot control such as physical features, native intelligence, and athletic ability.
3. Be sensitive to their feelings especially when you are talking about them in front of them.
4. Honor them in your thoughts and in your words.
5. Watch out for loaded words such as big, little, tall, short, pretty, and ugly.
6. Adopt a **no cut-down rule.**
7. Give priority to relationships over performance.
8. Celebrate victories and accomplishments.
9. Show them how to cope.

10. Help them to belong and to be independent.

11. Discipline them. Be creative. Don't go to extremes. Hug, praise, use various rewards, and withdraw privileges. Don't make idle threats. Don't yell. Teach them responsibility. Encourage them (Colossians 3:21).

12. Listen to your teenager, but trust their behavior. Look at what they do and not just what they say.

These ideas are especially relevant to teenagers. Remember, they are not exactly children and not exactly adults. However, suggestions made for adults apply to teenagers as well.

ADULT SELF-ESTEEM

The building of self-esteem begins in childhood and continues throughout adolescence and adulthood. So, begin with your children early and stay with a healthy parenting program as long as they are with you.

Right now, I'm concentrating on you adults who are reading this book. It all starts with you, and you may have low self-esteem. And if you do, you may not be able to help build self-esteem in your children. So, begin by working on your **own** self-esteem. Build it. Learn to like yourself in a healthy way.

How? Here are some suggestions:

1. Accept personal responsibility for your own low self-esteem (Galatians 6:5). The past and the present influence you, but you are a creative factor in the formation of your own thoughts, actions, and feelings. If you do not take such responsibility, you will never change. Your mind does not automatically generate ideas in direct cause-effect fashion similar to the way your heart pumps blood. There is a volitional element involved in your mind's creation of ideas. You are involved. You add a creative part to the production of ideas and self-esteem. You must therefore take responsibility for what you are doing. The same fire that melts the butter hardens the egg. Your locus of control must become internal rather than external (other people, circumstances). You must become less passive and more active. You must realize that it is not outside events which directly cause your feelings but rather your **interpretation** of those events. You need to learn that you **choose** to

think, act, or feel a certain way. You can thus **choose to perceive the past differently** and to see yourself differently. That I was treated badly does not mean that I am worthless any more than a color-blind person's criticism of the color combination of your attire makes it inappropriate. By God's grace, I am of value even if others do not think so. And I feel good about it! These sorts of self statements will start us on the road toward better self-esteem.

2. Restructure your thinking (Philippians 4:8-9). Thinking affects feelings and feelings affect thinking. When you feel worthless, you think negative thoughts which reinforce and perpetuate this feeling. People who are down on themselves tend to make many thinking mistakes such as the following:

a. They **overgeneralize.** From one mistake, they conclude that they can't do anything right.

b. They **eternalize.** From one failure, they conclude that they will never do anything right.

c. They **personalize.** They are too absorbed with themselves. They inappropriately apply comments and criticism from others to themselves: "They are all talking about me." They blame themselves too much: "Others had nothing to do with it, circumstances had nothing to do with it, **I** caused it all. **I'm completely** to blame."

d. They **catastrophize.** What they do is the worst thing that has ever been done: "If you only knew what I did, you would not want me in your church or to be your friend."

e. They **filter.** Many positive things may have happened to them, yet they do not see them. They filter them out. Their whole world is thus negative.

f. They **neutralize.** If they see positive things in their lives, they negate them: "He doesn't really like me. He just needed a date." "My husband doesn't really want me, he just wants a woman. **Any** woman." We can make anyone look bad by filtering out his good points or by concentrating on his bad points.

g. They **absolutize.** Everything becomes a must. "People **must** like me, life **must** be easy, and I **must** be competent. If not, I am worthless and life is not worth living."

Albert Ellis (*Clinical Applications of Rational-Emotive Therapy*) encourages people to make a distinction between desire and demand: It would be **nice** if everyone liked me, but it is not necessary. Persons with low self-esteem often jump to conclusions without adequate evidence.

h. They **dicotomize.** Everything is either black or white: there is no gray. Such persons are often very perfectionistic. **Their** way is always the **right** way about everything. Their **opinions** are always **the truth.**

i. They **self destruct.** They set up negative self-fulfilling prophecies: "No one likes me." So when a person does like them, they are suspicious and uncomfortable, which causes them to send out negative signals, which causes the other person to back off. When they back off, the person says to himself or herself: "I was right. No one likes me." It seems impossible for a person with low self-esteem to feel loved.

Building self-esteem involves several steps such as the following:

(1) Discover thinking mistakes that contribute to your low self-esteem: by looking at your history, by writing down statements about yourself (automatic self-talk) or by keeping a daily journal.

(2) Challenge the validity of each self statement: dispute, challenge, contradict, and reverbalize them one at a time. One idea that is often effective is to try to prove that you are worthless. If you normally tie feelings of worthlessness in with competency, you **can** learn that worth-whileness has little to do with competence. You only **think** that it makes you worthless! If you are alive, you have worth! Learn to test your judgment and validate the relationship between thoughts and feelings. Your belief system can be challenged and changed, and thus your behavior and feelings of self-esteem change also. Beliefs have consequences.

(3) Learn how these misconceptions originated and see that they are inaccurate, unrealistic, and distorted. Learn to view yourself differently and to understand that you are not a victim of thoughts and feelings but rather a participant.

(4) Write a new list of correct beliefs on a card and read the list several times each day. They become your new self talk.

(5) Role-play situations in which you have felt inferior in the past. Learn to perform tasks which you normally avoid.

(6) Practice these new behaviors during the next week, perform needed tasks you previously avoided because of feelings of inferiority, and then properly assess the outcome. Do **not** be **prejudiced against yourself** because of improper assessment of outcomes.

3. Set realistic goals. Paul pressed on toward the mark of the high calling of God (Philippians 3:13-14): that was a realistic goal for him. But it is not realistic for us to think that we can all become the richest, the most attractive, the most effective, the most powerful person in the world. If we set **unrealistic goals,** we set ourselves up for **defeat** and **low self-esteem.**

4. Be fair to yourself. If you would forgive others for doing what you have done, forgive yourself. Don't be prejudiced against yourself. It's not fair!

5. Learn thought stopping. Think inappropriate negative thoughts about yourself, and yell "stop" and slam a book down on your desk. Repeat this practice several times. Next, repeat the process and say "stop" to yourself. Label negative, unproductive thoughts as **garbage!** This helps you to stop thinking such inappropriate thoughts.

6. Substitute positive thoughts for negative thoughts. For example, one might say: "I'll be better off in heaven" instead of "I'm afraid to die," or "I've been successful in many ways" instead of "I'm a failure." Such statements divert one's mind away from negative unhelpful thoughts.

7. Change your **attitude.** People with low self-esteem usually have an attitude of "poor me," "stupid you," and "poor stupid world." They seem to be stuck in their past, their unconscious memories, and in their present situation. Yet, we are not prisoners of these circumstances and can change.

8. Take small steps toward success. Persons who experience success tend to manifest higher self-esteem. Persons with low self-esteem may have known little else but failure. Structure attainable goals or tasks which, when completed, will have a positive effect. One step at a time! Give yourself credit for making small improvements.

9. Institute self-improvement projects. Something as simple as losing excessive weight, an exercise program, physical work, taking a course in school, or just doing some things you believe you ought to do can improve your self-esteem. If you **do** better, you **feel** better (Philippians 4:9).

10. Emphasize and build on strengths rather than weaknesses. One way to do this is to write down positive self-evaluations daily for several weeks. List personal, intellectual, physical, and spiritual assets on cards. Then read these several times a day for a few weeks. Such exercises have been shown to help increase self-esteem. You may compensate for deficiencies by accenting strengths. Think more about what you like about being you and less about what you don't like.

11. Learn coping skills. It has been found that training in progressive relaxation, anxiety management, social skills, and self-reinforcement procedures can help build self-esteem. Learn to avoid argumentative comments, to give encouragement to others, to compliment, and to listen.

The attainment of other skills may also help. If you experience academic failure, learn better study habits and discipline. Learning how to communicate may help you to be less self-absorbed and more aware of others. Additional education may give greater self-confidence.

12. Learn to assert yourself when you need to do so. Contrary to popular opinion, it is not un-Christian to assert yourself in a proper manner under the right circumstances. Jesus often did this himself (Matthew 23). It has been found that assertiveness training can lead to a higher performance

and higher self-esteem. Learn to look people in the eye and say in a calm, factual sort of way, what needs to be said.

13. Build relationships. People with low self-esteem think of themselves as inferior, so they behave that way and expect others to reject them. This blocks the building of relationships. Since the roots of relationship problems are usually in childhood, they need to learn a more mature interaction pattern by making regular contact with each member of their family of origin. A study of their family tree might facilitate interactional patterns in the family and increase understanding. Remembering that we belong to one another in the body of Christ also helps us. Fellowship in Christ and mutual edification help secure our mind and emotions (I Peter 4:7-11; Hebrews 10:19-25).

Group counseling or group discussions may be a good context for relationship building. Anything that encourages us in constructive interaction may help actualize self-esteem. If we feel good about ourselves, we should feel good about interacting with others. If we do not, we won't. Learn to interact and to give to others. Learn to receive and to give.

14. Learn to relax and to visualize yourself with high self-esteem in different situations of life, enjoying being alive and acting with good self-esteem. Be specific in your visualization. **See** yourself becoming what you want to be. We tend to become what we visualize.

15. Reframe experiences. Pictures often look different in different frames. So do experiences, past, present, and future. There is a difference between saying, "I've hit the bottom" and saying, "There is no way for me to go but up." The latter statement leaves you with hope; the former, without hope. Get used to thinking in terms of reframing your negative experiences. It is a powerful tool.

Let me give you a specific example. My uncle, Tom B. Flatt, died about two years ago. He was a well-balanced, fine Christian man. Good mental health. At his funeral, the secretary from the church he attended and helped build, told this story about him. About three days before Uncle Tom B. died, she called him and asked how he was doing. "Just fine," came back his immediate answer. "Getting ready to go to heaven in a few days!" Reframing. Looking at it differently. How powerful!

James asks us to "count it" or to "consider it" pure joy when we face trials of many kinds. This implies that we have the power within us to look at trials in different ways. We can consider it **this** way or **that** way. Trials are terrible persecution or a source of joy, depending upon how we **view** them (James 1:2-4). If we view them as persecution, they are depressing and stressful: as an experience of joy, and they lead to perseverance, completed tasks, and greater maturity. It's **our** choice.

I doubt that James meant to minimize the difficulty of severe trials. They're not easy, but they can lead to personal growth if we view them properly. Reframe them in terms of opportunity rather than merely hardship. Try it! It's a powerful idea. When stuck in the middle of trials and negative thinking, ask yourself: "Is there any other way to look at it?" There usually is. And if you're stuck in your thinking process and can't see it, ask someone else to help you process it. Maybe **they** can offer another view.

16. Learn to build strong spiritual lives. People are of inestimable value in the sight of God. He created us in his own image (Genesis 1:26-27): he endowed us with a measure of himself. We are not a curious accident of change. God loves us (John 3:16): while we were yet sinner, Jesus died for us (Romans 8:6). Christ would not die for worthless individuals. At least in some sense, we are of value to God. God created the world for us (Genesis 1), he listens when we pray (John 15:16), he provides many blessings every day. By his grace, we are significant! We have a high purpose for living. Our labor in him is not vain (I Corinthians 15:58). Self-worth implanted by God is the solid basis of our self-esteem.

We are not totally depraved as some interpret the Bible to say. Such a faulty theology leads to low self-esteem. We are much more than worms. God has given us value. Note the view of mankind reflected in Psalm 8:3-8 NIV:

> When I consider your heavens,
>> the work of your fingers,
> the moon and the stars,
>> which you have set in place,
> what is man that you are mindful of him,
>> the son of man that you care for him?

You made him a little lower than the heavenly beings
    and crowned him with glory and honor.
You made him ruler over the works of your hands;
    you put everything under his feet;
all flocks and herds,
    and the beasts of the field,
the birds of the air,
    and the fish of the sea,
all that swim the paths of the seas.

The value of people was hard for the psalmist to see from his perspective, but such value was implied by creation and assigned position: created a little lower than the heavenly beings, made to be ruler over the work of God's hands.

We are to have sound judgment (Romans 12:3), to mature into the "whole measure of the fulness of Christ" (Ephesians 4:13). We need to be close to God. We find extreme closeness and spiritual life in giving up self (Matthew 10:39) to allow God to make his home with us (John 14:23). We come closer to God by modeling Jesus in our lives.

It is not wrong to love ourselves (Matthew 22:37-39). Love of others and a belief that others love us necessitates such love. God accepts us, he forgives us, he loves us; so we can accept, forgive, and love ourselves. We must value ourselves in order to believe that we can cope in all situations through Christ (Philippians 4:13). To say that we are no good and worthless is to make God a liar, and God cannot lie! To condemn ourselves as faithful Christians is sinful because God justifies us (Romans 8:31-39). To judge ourselves is to judge the servant of another which is wrong since we serve God (Romans 14:4). **He** is our judge. Let us rejoice and be glad! He has delivered us from our sins and given us hope of everlasting life. As we accept these facts and serve others, our minds are less on self and more on other things, and our self-esteem improves. The more we believe in self worth as given by God, the more self-esteem we have. God is able to help us live productive lives.

In conclusion, I offer these comments:

1. Think in terms of what God had in mind for you as a fully functioning person. Choose to become that person. Visualize

269

yourself that way in different situations. Pray for God's help. Then, carry your vision out in action.

2. Live a life of integrity so that by the grace of God you can enjoy being alive.

3. Model Jesus in your life. Accept personal responsibility; practice rational thinking, realistic goal setting, and fairness to yourself. Learn to change your attitude, to take small steps toward success, to initiate self-improvement projects, to learn coping skills, to assert yourself, to build relationships, to visualize yourself with high self-esteem, to reframe destructive experiences, and to build strong spiritual lives. You will grow through these experiences.

SUMMARY

To improve your family, you've got to start with yourself. To build self-esteem in children, you must start with your **own** self-esteem. And remember, self-esteem is not self-centeredness; it's how you feel about yourself. How you feel about being you.

So, start applying principles I've mentioned in this chapter to yourself. Learn who you are. Get in touch with your **total being.** Accept yourself. Then, help build self-esteem in your children by applying good mental health principles in your family. You'll be glad you did. **Healthy families build self-esteem.**

BUILDING EXERCISES

1. On a one (low) to ten (high) scale, how would you rate your self-esteem?

2. Do you still think it's wrong to have high self-esteem? If so, ask someone who seems to be mentally healthy to read this chapter, and talk it over with you.

3. Make a list of family of origin incidents that contributed to your low self-esteem. Ask yourself. Is there any other way of looking at these incidents? Spell it out incident by incident. Maybe it was your parents' problem and not yours. Maybe they gave you all that they were capable of giving. They're human too!

4. List **positive experiences** in your childhood and **maximize** these. **Value** them. **Hold on** to them.

5. Rate the self-esteem level of each of your family members and then ask what you can do to help them build self-esteem.

6. Is the way you feel about yourself your responsibility? Do you still blame others for the way you feel? Does this make sense to you?

7. Keep a record of your **positive self-talk.** Read it several times each day.

8. Write down your negative self-talk, and talk back to each statement. See Appendix C for a worksheet.

9. What would you have to do to feel good about being you?

10. Underline the points I made in this chapter that speak to **your need.** Then, read them over and over again and put them into practice. God bless.

Fourteen

Continuing Efforts to Prevent Divorce

Principle Number 14:
Healthy Families make continuing efforts
to prevent divorce.

I assume that some of you are single, some divorced, and some married. So, what I will say here will apply to you in different ways at different points in the chapter. Just read on, and you'll pick up something that will be helpful to you.

If you are divorced, just remember that God loves you and you can still live a good Christian life. Don't get down on yourself just because your marriage did not work out. Evaluate where you are and proceed from there. And, good luck. I know it must be tough to go through a divorce. I care about you, and wish you well. I know a lot of good people who have gone through divorces. Life doesn't stop there. It must continue. God still has something in mind for you.

If you are single, all of my remaining points may apply to you. If married, all but suggestion one will apply.

The Bible through the prophet Malachi says that "God hates divorce" (Malachi 2:12-16). He hates spiritual adultery; he hates marital adultery.

Yet in America at least 12 percent of all married people get divorced according to a recent Harris Poll. The rate for the 1980's was about 50 percent: We had about as many to divorce as to marry in that decade. Thus, if that rate continues for 60 years or so, the divorce rate in America for all married people will be 50 percent. Eighty percent of those who get divorced get remarried. Some 50 percent of those get divorced. In 50 percent of all marriages in 1989, at least one of the mates had been divorced at least once before. During my lifetime, the divorce rate has escalated rapidly.

We even joke about divorce though it is seldom funny to those involved. I heard this story in Washington, D.C. a couple of years ago. A 94-year-old couple hobbled into court to get a divorce. "Why do you want a divorce at your age?" the judge inquired. "We wanted to wait until the children all died," came the reply.

Right now, I want you to consider what you can do to prevent divorce. Consider these suggestions.

1. Marry the right person. Since the main cause of divorce is marriage, one solution to divorce is to stay single. Yet, this is not a satisfactory solution for most. Marriage serves good purposes and was instituted by God. So, let's proceed with the idea that it's best for most to get married. So, it's vital to pick the right person to marry.

You might want to go back to chapter one at this point and re-read what I said there about beginning your family with a good foundation. Let me just say here that this is extremely important because so many factors are working against the building of stable homes.

People marry people with whom they have little in common: different goals, backgrounds, values, religion, families, communities, and ethnic groups. They may have severe personality conflicts and come from dysfunctional families.

Today, both the husband and the wife usually plan to work outside the home which often makes marriage more difficult. A career gives economic power to the woman, which enables her to divorce more easily. Yes, I can see that marriage should be more than merely a meal ticket for the woman. And, I'll admit that I've seen many cases where I thought it was good for numerous reasons that the wife had a career. Sometimes it is good that she is able to leave. So, I'm not unaware of all that. Right now though, I'm discussing preventing divorce, and sociologists have found that women working outside the home since World War II has contributed to the escalating divorce rate for various reasons.

It throws married people together at work and makes it easier for them to have affairs and to fall in love with someone else. Judith did not intend to have an affair. She just enjoyed talking to a fellow-teacher at school. It was much easier to talk to him than to her husband. He listened to every word she said. Sex was "not the main thing" to Judith. "It just happened" one night. It just seemed to be the thing to do. They were in love. Both Judith and Jerry, her friend, divorced and began living with each other. Five children and two ex-mates were left stranded.

Women who work outside the home still do most of the work at home and resent it. Both mates are tired and more easily irritated: work, scouts, church, Little League, and social obligations all take time and energy. The schedules of most couples in their thirties with whom I counsel are worse than mine. I get tired just listening to them. They often have too many good things to do.

Many today place more emphasis on money and things and less on persons, relationships, and spiritual concerns. Bigger houses, cars, and expensive watches will make people know that they are successful. "I deserve it," many reason. Values that build healthy families are left behind for possessions. It's a bad trade!

Theological and social liberalism make it easier to get divorced. There is little stigma on divorce now (which in itself is not bad) and many questions about what the Bible says about divorced and whether or not it is true. When we really want to divorce it is easy to rationalize away valid objections.

Narcissism is an enemy of healthy marriages: more emphasis on meeting **my** needs and less on giving to the relationship. Most want to be nurtured; few want to nurture.

J. C. was in his fifth affair in seven years of marriage when he and Valerie came for counseling. She wanted the marriage to continue if he would stop his affair and recommit to her. He refused. "How can I know for sure," he asked, "that another woman won't come along sometime in the future who can meet my needs better than she can?" He didn't have any right to think that way! He was married. My point is that he was centered on this own needs, not on his wife's needs. Narcissism works against good marriages!

Extremely high expectations of marriage also prevents happiness and longevity in marriage. Many are saying, "My spouse has to make me happy, meet all of my needs all of the time." That's too much to expect of any marriage. Nobody can make you happy if you don't want to be happy. Nobody can meet all of your needs all of the time. Don't expect too much from your spouse. To do so puts a heavy burden on him or her and a strain on your marriage.

Power struggles can lead to a divorce. Who's in charge? Who gets the last word? Changes in our culture have escalated this problem. I'm seeing it more and more in marital counseling, especially with younger couples.

Ashley and Bill were into a power struggle. My picture of them could be summarized with crossed swords in a fierce battle. They were both armed with shields as well as swords. He was chauvinistic; she, a male-hater. "All of my brothers as well as my father were chauvinists," she said. "I'm not going to serve any man anymore." When she prepared supper, she prepared only enough for herself. "Let him get his own," she said. She refused to have a joint bank account with him: "It's just another male chauvinistic plot to control a woman," she thought. When they went out for a hamburger, he paid for his; she, for hers. A power struggle was the central dynamic of their marriage. Each was afraid of being run over by the other. So, they kept up their guard. They lived in the same house but did not have much togetherness. There was too much individualism to allow that to occur. This was a sad picture indeed!

Promiscuousness and pornography pose a threat to marriage. J. E. got used to masturbating while looking at pornographic materials: girlie magazines, hard pornographic magazines, X-rated movies. This became a fixed pattern before he married Melanie. After the marriage, he supplemented lovemaking with his wife with pornographic material which really upset her. "Why does he have to have another woman to look at?" she wondered. "It's like he is not excited about me," she continued. She felt cheated and turned off. She then pulled away from him which made the problem worse. Sex was rather impersonal to him; very personal to her. He finally learned to be intimate and to enjoy exciting times with his wife: she learned to "enjoy sex" as well as to "make love."

Marriages are threatened by all kinds of conflict because many couples do not know how to handle conflict well. As we grew up, many of us were conditioned to see conflict as something bad. We thus get uptight, defensive, and sometimes explode when in conflict. We don't think of it as an opportunity to solve problems, to work things out, to develop closeness. So, conflict is often divisive though inevitable. Females pursue, males withdraw. Arguments escalate. Negative interpretations are made as couples try to read each other's minds. They invalidate each other when they expect validation. They do not discuss feelings but rather suppress them or let them explode. Then, they are controlled by issues and driven by their feelings.

We need to learn that we have sore spots emotionally. Our button can be pushed. Old angers, rage, disappointments, and hurts can be triggered, and we can be controlled by emotions which may hurt our relationships.

I have found these ideas to be helpful to keep old hurts from causing relationship problems.

a. Notice how you are feeling. Get in touch with bodily sensations and feelings when you are in conflict situations. Or, if this is impossible, do it in privacy after the conflict. Get in an easychair or on a bed. Close your eyes, breathe deeply, and relax. Then, visualize the conflict you just experienced. Make it as real as possible in order to reproduce the feelings. Notice bodily sensations, emotional feelings, and self-talk. Then, take a trip backward in your mind to previous times when you had similar feelings. Jot these down after you open your eyes.

b. Examine these episodes and think them through. Notice what was happening, who did what, how you saw it then, and how you see it now.

c. Write down destructive negative self-talk that you experienced in each episode. Then, talk back to it. "No, it wasn't that I was no good, I just made a mistake," might be an example of such talk back. Or as Catherine expressed it, "That's the way I felt when my first husband bullied me, but my boss is not my first husband. Why let him push those panic buttons now. He's just trying to do his job." What this does is to allow present cognitions to regulate emotions that result from suppressed pain and anger as it surfaces in new situations.

d. I have also found it helpful to work on being open with myself and with God as much as I am able to do. This allows him to come in and heal the old wounds. If he can make something out of nothing, he can make something out of my hurt ego if I will let him do so. Pardon, peace, and joy come from his grace in which we stand (Romans 5:1-5). In this I rejoice!

I have counseled numerous couples whose marriages were threatened by alcohol and other drugs. A. T. used drugs as a "cop-out," reported Annie, his wife. Instead of making love, he smokes marijuana. Instead of doing chores, he gets high. To Annie, it was like "he was not there."

What I am saying is that there are many factors that can destroy your marriage. And all of it starts with your marital choice. After you make your choice, you've got to make every effort to prevent divorce in order to build a healthy marriage.

2. Do premarital counseling and study. Go to your minister and ask him if he does premarital counseling. If he doesn't think he is competent to provide this service, ask him to refer you to someone who is. It's worth the money it will cost you to do such counseling with a competent professional counselor who shares your values. He or she will assist you in many ways: helpful books to read, tapes to hear, significant questions to discuss, and possibly some dysfunctional patterns to overcome. I counseled with one couple for 12 sessions to help them overcome some dysfunctional patterns before they got married. Most couples can explore such questions as those listed at the end of chapter one in three sessions with a counselor. I believe such exploration can be very helpful before marriage when the couple is in a good frame of mind with each other.

I also recommend classes and seminars for such couples. Churches sometimes sponsor such activities which often include books to read, videos to see, brief lectures, and discussions.

You might check public and church libraries to see what is available there. I know that many people think they know all about the opposite sex before they get married, but they don't. I read James Dobson's book on **What Wives Wish Their Husbands Knew About Women** after I had been married 20 years and learned some things which I didn't know. Why not give it a try?

3. Remember that divorce is sinful. Adam and Eve were to **cleave** to one another (Genesis 2:24). God hates divorce (Malachi 2:16). We are not to put our mate away except for fornication (Matthew 5:32; 19:1-9). The Bible does not authorize the Christian to divorce the non-Christian (I Corinthians 7:15). Paul does not authorize the non-Christian to leave the Christian. He merely speaks to the situation in which the unbeliever leaves. The Bible teaches that divorce was never God's will (Deuteronomy 24:1-4; Genesis 2:24). He just allowed it because of the hardness of their hearts, their rebellious nature (Matthew 19:1-9; Mark 10:2-12; Luke 16:18).

I emphasize this biblical teaching because I believe it is right and because I have seen it keep hundreds of couples together. This allowed them to work out their problems and build and healthy home.

4. Keep telling yourself that divorce hurts people: the marital partners who divorce, grandparents, the church, friends, and especially children. No one escapes divorce unscathed.

What evidence is there for such a conclusions? Much from many sources. I have spoken to some five retreats for divorced Christians with an average attendance of more than 100 at each retreat. We never got to bed by midnight. There is always so much pain that leads to much discussion in small informal groups as well as in formal program situations. Even those who initiated the divorces often express deep sorrow over the loss of what could have been. Divorced persons who were put away by their spouses are almost always more devastated than were their mates by the divorce. And this was often true years after the divorce: anger, guilt, panic, depression, fatigue, confusion, low self-esteem, feelings of rejection, shame, and a sense of failure are still present. Some are still preoccupied with such grief years after the divorce.

These seminar experiences have been reinforced by my counseling experiences as a psychologist, marriage and family therapist, minister, and elder for many years. Divorce hurts people, not only spouses, but children, and others. They often feel rejected by the church and sometimes stay in therapy for several years working through their grief, pain, and disappointment, as they try to readjust in their single and/or blended family situations following the divorce. Their family structure is broken—a new structure must emerge. Everyone feels the chaos. There are conflicts over roles, anarchy, and confusion over new boundaries around and within the nuclear and extended family. And when children are involved, in one sense, there is no divorce. Parenting issues, visitation rights, and family rituals (graduations, weddings, funerals, socials. . . .) keep the divided family in some degree of contact over the years.

The pain continues. Even when the divorce is carried out in a relatively friendly way, when parents do not triangle their children into their adult problems, and when children are not used as weapons against one's ex-spouse, pain is still there. Ex-spouses and children of divorce are often insecure, lonely, and empty. One child of divorce described it as "a hole in my heart." Such a hole is hard to fill. Such pain continues for years.

To put it into a more personal perspective, let me give you a few examples. John Doe, age 40, was divorced by his wife who "ran off" with another man. The whole community noticed that "he never smiled again." A twenty-eight-year-old woman, Jane Doe, was divorced because her husband "didn't want to be married any more." She became despondent, cried for years, blamed herself, attempted suicide, lost her job and continued to punish herself for twelve years after the divorce. Many children are shuttled back and forth, sometimes on airplanes, between parents. They lose a sense of having a home, a real base of operation. The look on their faces as their parents leave them tells the whole story.

Jim Doe, a client of mine, age thirty-five, brought a tape recording of a telephone conversation between himself and his three-year-old son to a counseling session. The boy's mother had taken the boy and run off, not leaving a forwarding address. The boy told his dad over the phone, "I **miss** you. I want to see you." His dad replied, "I want to **see** you too, but I don't know where you are." The boy replied, "But, I want to **see** you. I **miss** you." Something like this sequence was repeated several times, and by that time, I felt the pain of both of them and had to get out my handkerchief. How sad! And this scene is multiplied thousands of times each year throughout our country.

A book, published in 1989, which emphasizes the effects of divorce, has shocked the world of psychologists and marriage and family therapists. Entitled *Second Chances*, it is authored by two psychologists, Judith Wallerstein and Sandra Blakeslee. It is the most extensive longitudinal study of the consequences of divorce ever published. Its impact has been powerful!

The authors of this extensive study began with a commonly-held assumption of mental health professionals that the effects of divorce were relatively minor and of short duration. They thought that everyone would be relieved of a bad situation, feel better, and be well-adjusted by the one-year follow-up time. False! They secured more research money, and followed up the sixty divorced couples and their 131 children after five years. They would surely be fully recovered by then! False! More research money and five more years brought similar results! The researchers had difficulty believing what they found. But they reported it, and their book is wet with tears—although several stories of good adjustment are a part of the report.

Marital partners suffer from divorce. Research indicates that there are still painful scars from divorce five and ten years after the break-up—wounds that will not heal. Someone said that obtaining a divorce is like being hit by a big truck. Remarried persons and single again persons often suffer because of the same problems they had in their marriages: depression, irritations with people, passive-aggressive or narcissistic tendencies, low self-esteem, and other problems. Women and children are usually drastically poorer after divorce and men are better off financially.

Wallerstein and Blakeslee found that:

a. Recovery is not guaranteed. Feelings such as anger, hurt, and humiliation often remain for many years after divorce.

b. Women with young children are especially at risk: single parenting, financial problems, career pressures, and other concerns take their toll. Many feel dead inside.

c. Older men and women feel alone and unhappy. Opportunities for work, play and marriage decline rapidly with age, especially for women.

d. Younger men are often adrift, arrested in their normal development into adult roles as husbands and fathers.

e. Those who remarry often are divorced again and such failure the second time around is often more devastating because it powerfully reinforced their first failure.

Wallerstein and Blakeslee also found that there were serious consequences for parents and children of divorced families. "Evidently," they said, "the relationship between parents and children grows best in the rich soil of a happy, intact family" (*Second Chances*, p. 301). Without this nurturing family situation, parent-child relationships can become very fragile and may be easily broken. Specifically, they found that:

a. Continued parenting is necessary but much more difficult following divorce. Fathers often become more distant and about half of them disappear after one year.

b. Most divorced parents experience a diminished capacity to parent: less time, less will to discipline, less sensitivity to children, and more preoccupation with personal issues of divorce and its aftermath.

c. Some children of divorced parents who did well were helped by the example of parents who were able to rebuild their lives after divorce while others were able to turn away from bad examples set by their parents. Those who seemed to do best had parents who were able to cooperate in the task of childrearing. Cooperating grandparents and step-parents also made important contributions.

d. Almost half of these children of divorce entered adulthood worried, underachieving, self-deprecating, deprived, troubled, depleted, neglected, and sometimes angry.

e. Boys had difficulties in school achievements, peer relationships, in handling aggression, and in maturing.

f. Girls struggled with anxiety and guilt in efforts to seek commitment with young men, which led to multiple relationships, impulsive marriages, and early divorced.

g. Adolescents reported a strong need for family structure, family protection, clear guidelines, and more encouragement from parents. They felt abandoned and were haunted by inner doubts and uncertainties.

h. The divorce experience affected the way children of divorce viewed themselves and society. Their negative experiences in families in conflict were **not erased** by divorce. Divorce does **not rescue** the children.

i. Half of these children saw their mother or father obtain a second divorce in the ten-year period after the divorce.

j. Half saw their parents remain angry at each other.

k. Sixty percent felt rejected by at least one of their parents.

l. Very few were helped financially with their college educations, even though they stayed in contact with their fathers who could afford to provide such help.

m. Many turned out well: compassionate, courageous, and competent young adults.

n. Divorce is more devastating for children than for their parents.

o. It is very difficult for fathers who move out of the home to sustain a close, meaningful, loving relationship with their children, especially if one or both parents remarry.

p. Some children of divorce are overburdened by the parentification of children or by serving as a pawn in continued parental battles.

q. All children suffer from divorce (*Second Chances,* pp. 297-303). Wallerstein and Blakeslee concluded (*Second Chances,* p. 305), all families are not alike in the protection they extend children. Moreover, the voices of our children are not represented in the political arena. Although men and women talk **about** children it is hard for me to believe that they are necessarily talking **for** children.

Children of divorce often grow up thinking that love can be transient and commitment temporary. Most children today live with the fear that their families may come apart as have so many others.

The only conclusion we can make with all of this data is that DIVORCE HURTS—spouses, children, and others. Divorce is NOT THE ANSWER! Most couples with whom I have counseled were not divorced for physical abuse or adultery, although some were. Most list such problems as lack of communication and intimacy, a lack of affection, financial problems, sexual adjustment problems, family of origin intrusion, religious differences, problems with parenting, personality differences, incompatibility, "power struggles," and unhealthy family patterns. Such problems are difficult but not impossible to solve. Most marriages are worth saving. Most divorced spouses with whom I have counseled have told me that they wished they had tried harder to preserve their marriage, feeling they moved too fast to get their divorce.

Remember the consequences of divorce. Divorce hurts. Try hard to prevent it.

5. Look for solutions, not just problems; look for strengths, not just weaknesses; look for possibilities, not just impossibilities. Most couples can work out their difficulties. But we must emphasize **strengths** rather than **weaknesses** for we tend to find what we are looking for, and the couple tends to be influenced in their thinking by the questions we ask. I encourage you as a couple to look at the good years you have had together and try for more good years. Look at the hundreds of problems you have solved and seek to solve others. Look at what is different about the times when you are getting along well and repeat your actions. Emphasize what you have going for you and what you like about each other, and continue to try. Look for healthy patterns of interaction and repeat them over and over again. A good snow-ball effect can be self-perpetuating.

Quit thinking of divorce as a solution. Usually, it is not. It becomes a part of the problem. Look for alternatives. Seek help. A well-trained professional can sometimes see things more clearly than you can. You are often too emotionally involved to be objective.

6. Be loyal to your mate. Faithful. Do not commit adultery (Exodus 5:14; I Corinthians 6:9-11). Keep your vows even when it hurts (Psalm 15:1-4). Do what you said you would (Numbers 30:2). Think in terms of a permanent covenant of love, grace, intimacy, and empowerment. It is very difficult to sustain a marriage while having affairs. If you do not want a divorce, be faithful to your mate. Flee youthful lusts (II Timothy 2:22). Nip it in the bud before it goes too far. Limit the amount of conversation time you have with persons to whom you are attracted. Avoid inappropriate touching and compromising situations.

7. Take **all** of the Bible seriously, not just the sections on divorce and remarriage. Just to stay married is not enough. Build a good marriage! One Christian man refrained from having affairs but "did not speak to his wife for a whole year." How cruel! John Doe desperately encouraged me to prove to his wife that she could not divorce him after he had hit her in the stomach area and caused her to have a miscarriage. He had not taken the total biblical message seriously and had neglected the weightier matters of the Bible: love, kindness, and consideration. Jesus reminds us to do unto others as we would have them do unto us (Matthew 7:12). Paul says to follow after righteousness, faith, love, peace, and purity (II Timothy 2:22). Walking the walk of Jesus will help you to be a good spouse and help prevent divorce. It will not always stop divorce, but it will usually help. Real conversion to Christ (Matthew 18:3)—letting Jesus live in you (Galatians 2:20)—will make a difference.

8. Love your mate. Love needs to be singled out as a biblical principle in marriage. Husbands are to love (and sacrificially care for) their wives (Ephesians 5:25). Older women are to teach younger women to love their husbands (Titus 2:2-5). They are to be friends, partners, companions. They are to be romantic, passionate, one flesh (Genesis 2:24, Proverbs 5:18-19). Paul recognized that both husbands and wives have sexual needs. The husband's body belongs to his wife and her body

belongs to him (I Corinthians 7:1-5). The idea that women have no sexual needs was a Victorian idea and is not biblical.

As God loves us, love your spouse even when they do not deserve it. God loves us that way.

9. Encourage one another. So many people in troubled marriages are in dysfunctional patterns of criticism. We need to break such patterns and encourage one another. Pat one another on the back. Show appreciation. One day faithful Christians will hear Jesus say "Well done" (Matthew 25:21). Paul often complimented people to whom he wrote such as Phoebe and others (Romans 16). One man told me that his wife had never expressed any appreciation for him and what he did in their twenty years of marriage. Many wives have expressed similar sentiments about their husbands. How sad! Encouragement is justified and is a practical marital builder: it reinforces behavior that we wish to recur. Encourage one another.

10. Realize that divorce will not solve all of your problems: personality disorders, a bad temper, moodiness, low self-esteem, depression, a lack of interpersonal skills, and other problems. If you have such problems, you would probably have them if you were married to someone else. So, divorce will not solve them. **They** will remain, and divorce will create additional problems such as loneliness, guilt, a sense of failure, financial problems, damage to children, and others. Let marriage reveal personal weaknesses you need to grow through and proceed toward such confrontation and growth. Otherwise you may be running from your own problems for the rest of your life. Problems tend to repeat themselves.

11. Try to become a better marital partner yourself. Be more responsive, cooperative, committed, loving, submissive, sharing, complimentary, and fun to be with. It will be harder for your mate to leave in such cases. And if he does leave, he will know what he is missing. Jane Doe serves as a example. Her husband complained of her coldness and dominance for twenty-five years of marriage. She concentrated on the children and was always too tired for him. Finally, in desperation, he decided to divorce her. She then realized that the marriage was extremely important to her and changed her attitude toward him immediately. She began to cook his favorite food, massage

his back, and be very passionate. He pushed her back at first but then was gradually won over. I have also seen it work the other way around. Neglectful, abusive, and aloof husbands became responsive and attentive and recultivated their wives. It will not always work, but it is worth a try.

There are many causes and consequences of divorce. Divorce is painful. It is wrong. It can always be stopped if both partners will work constructively at the marriage. It can often be stopped by one partner's initiative. The key is submission to the reign of God and to the Lordship of Jesus Christ in every aspect of our lives—the husband **and** the wife—each equally concerned. Preventing divorce will not be easy even then, but it will be possible and rewarding.

I realize that many good people get divorced. Some try hard to prevent divorce but are not successful.

If you are divorced already, please remember that God still loves you and that you can live a good, productive life as a single person. I don't know of anyone who teaches that you have to be married to go to heaven.

Press on toward the goal. Live a good life. Ask what God wants you to do with your life now that you are single again. Look at the advantages you have in your situation and live an abundant life.

If you are single, concentrate on picking a good mate and then on being a good mate. Marriage can be fun and very fulfilling.

If you are married, try a little harder to build a healthy marriage. Remember that there are many ways to make love (to express love).

God bless!

BUILDING QUESTIONS TO CONSIDER

For Singles
1. What kind of person do you wish to marry?
2. What do you need to do to meet and cultivate such a person?
3. What do you need to change about yourself to be a good mate?

For Married Couples

4. How can staying married be a growth opportunity?

5. What problems do you have that are common in your relationships with several people? An example might be keeping people at a distance or latching on too much.

6. What are you doing to become a better marital partner?

7. What are some possible strengths in your mate? Share these with him or her.

8. Are you willing to go for professional counseling if you need to do so?

9. What would it be like to live with you?

10. What problems would you still have if divorced?

11. How would divorce affect you and your children (if you have children)?

12. Can you visualize how divorce might look to you at age 80?

13. Are you getting too close to someone of the opposite sex who is not your mate?

14. List some passage of the Bible you ignore? Why?

For Divorced People

15. What did you learn from your previous marriage?

16. What baggage are you carrying from it that may affect other relationships?

17. Do you think a few counseling sessions might help you get back with you former mate or disengage from your former marriage.

18. What do you believe God's will is for your life right now?

19. Do you need to do anything to make things right with God and the church?

20. Do you think of your future as well as your past?

Fifteen

Other Healthy Traits

Principle Number 15:
Healthy families have realistic expectations

Principle Number 16:
Healthy families spend a significant amount
of quality time with each other

Principle Number 17:
Healthy families learn to work and to assume
appropriate responsibilities

Principle Number 18:
Healthy families seek help when they need it.

Thus far, I've discussed 14 healthy family traits. Now, I want to conclude by giving you four more.

First, I want to emphasize realistic expectations. And every family member needs to get involved in this.

Ellen was very lonely, depressed, and panicky. She blamed it all on her husband. If he would just be there for her, everything would be all right. Yet, she had "always" had a negative view of herself. People who knew her in grade school said that she was easy to crush back then. I was the same story in high school and during her dating years with several boys including Edgar, her husband. But, she had always thought that it was "their fault." If her husband were what he ought to be, she would be okay.

I doubt it. Perhaps a perfect husband would make life easier for Ellen; but, in such a case, everything wouldn't be okay.

Ellen is expecting too much of Edgar. No man can live up to those expectations: "Make me happy. Cure me of all of my illnesses. Ease all of my discomfort. Remove all of my stressors!" Such expectations are unrealistic and will lead to grave disappointment. Be more realistic. Take responsibility for your own feelings, thoughts, and actions. Life is sometimes hard, but it can be meaningful.

Destin had received numerous toys and other valuable gifts for Christmas. Yet, the look on his face was a look of sadness. "Is that all?" he inquired of his parents and grandparents. You see, he had seen some other toys on television that he did not have and thought that "they ought to get them for me. They are supposed to get me anything I want," he thought.

John was disappointed with his wife. She did not anticipate his needs as effectively as did his mother. Why, she had to ask him what he wanted for Christmas or for his birthday; whereas, his mother "always knew." Problems mounted!

Betty's problem was that Frank, her husband, did not know how to make her feel sexy. He didn't know where to touch or how. He had no idea of how long it took her to get ready for intercourse. But, "he should know all of that if he is a real man," she thought. High expectations!

Michelle came from an upper-middle-class family. After she married Ron, they started out on a meager budget while he finished college. It was not what she expected. They had to live "like poor folks," she stated. Their problems multiplied.

In all of these cases, serious problems arose out of unrealistic expectations. I see it every week! Husbands and wives expect their mates to be perfect lovers without much information or assistance from them. They just should! Children are somehow led to believe that they deserve everything they want. We all can be so self-centered, narcissistic! An example I see more often is the expectation that "my mate ought to make me happy. If I'm not happy, it's his fault." That's too much of a burden to place on a marriage. The way it comes out sometimes is that "my marriage is a five on a one to 10 scale, and it ought to be a 10. Sex is good most of the time, but I don't hear bells ringing!"

Let me say that most of us want to hear bells ringing, but it's too much to expect that they ring constantly! We all want a 10 marriage, but most of us realize that a five or a seven is better than a zero! It's like always expecting an A but sometimes getting a B or a C. That's still better than an F! And often we need to put more effort into it ourselves. In my work at Harding University, students who are most completely crushed are usually students who expect to get all A's but sometimes get B's. Such students need to change their expectations and to change their image of themselves. They need to see themselves as people who at times can make a B and then see that as okay.

Healthy homes have realistic expectations of each other. They accept what **is** while trying to improve. They don't have to have everything they want. They can accept other family members, including parents and grandparents, as being imperfect, yet valuable, decent human beings. That's what I want for you and your family.

SIGNIFICANT QUALITY TIME TOGETHER

"My wife and I don't eat over three meals a week together. She gets up before I do, doesn't eat breakfast, and goes to work. I get up later and fix my own breakfast. We both eat out at lunch with friends. She gets home before I do and usually eats something she picked up on the way home. I grab a chicken leg somewhere and eat in the car. That's just the way it is," a preacher friend of mine recently told me.

His story is similar to many others I have heard. "We just don't have time to be together," they say. As a teen-age girl said to her busy father recently, "But life goes on all of the time Dad, and you're never here." He didn't have time. It took 16 hours a day to be successful in his business, at least to be as successful as he wanted to be.

Family priorities are lost in the shuffle of many things to do. I grew up in the depression of the 1930s and feel insecure when our funds get low. So, I work to get ahead a little, to provide a cushion for unforeseen setbacks.

That philosophy, though not all bad, can get out of hand. How much is enough for a cushion? It's getting bigger all of the time. Money won't buy what it used to buy.

Ministers have a special challenge with a proper distribution of their time. Their work is "for God, and God comes first." So, where does that leave their family? As one 12-year-old son of a preacher recently said to his parents and me, "Why do I always come last? Dad has time for every other person who calls but not for me." This caused his dad, a good father and minister, to reassess his priorities and do some special activities with his son.

I was especially conscious of family time when our boys were teenagers. I was away a lot. I drove out on Sundays to preach. What I did was to agree to preach out of town on Sunday mornings, not on Sunday nights. I came home to be with my family, and I'm glad I did.

I remember having driven 170 miles one Sunday to return for a concert in which Tim was playing saxophone. In all of my studies toward a doctorate, I never "closed the door of my study" if my family wanted to come in to see me about something. I often played basketball and football with them out in our yard. We took vacations in state parks that had plenty of room for us to run and play together.

Louise and I often go out together and eat. We go occasionally to a movie as well as to other entertaining events. We often walk or swing in our back yard together.

I'm saying all of this not to boast, but to say that it is time well spent. I wish I could have spent more quality time with all of my family.

The other side of the coin is that I was in a position where I could earn a living and did so. That required a lot of my time. We all worked hard to support ourselves, to send our boys to college and to help launch them into good careers which hard work and God's grace made possible.

Hard work takes time. Both parents can't stay with the children all of the time. At least one often needs to be at work. That's the way it is, and healthy families can adjust to that. The parent left with the children can assure the children that their other parent is at work "so that we can have the things we need and because he or she loves us." The whole family should show appreciation to the parent who has to be at work as well as to the parent who stays home. In two-career families, each parent needs to teach appreciation of hard work to the children.

I just had to say all of this because many bread-winners feel underloved and not appreciated. In their heart, they are often doing it for their family. They want them to have more than they had.

Another reason I mentioned my family's activities together is to say that it can be done. I've been extremely busy but have found at least some time for my family.

Israel was told to not assign any official government duties to a newly married man for a year that he might stay at home and "cheer his wife" (Deuteronomy 24:5). There is a time for every purpose under heaven (Ecclesiastes 3:1-8). It takes time for bonding with babies. It takes time to build relationships in a family. "Redeem the time," Paul says (Colossians 4:5). Make it count!

Before I leave this point, I want to tell you spouses what I sometimes do to guard my time for Louise. Though I probably don't do this enough, I do it every week: I write her name down on my schedule book to preserve some special time for her which we both enjoy very much. Why do I do this? If anyone asks me if I have anything scheduled for that particular time, I can truthfully say, "Yes. I already have something scheduled." Obviously, I have to break such a schedule at times, but scheduling her still helps me to save more time for her.

I'm glad I spent as much time as I did with my family. It was time well spent. I plan to continue to do so. It was and is healthy! I hope you'll take another look at your calendar. You'll be glad you did.

WORK AND RESPONSIBILITY

A certain rather shiftless man was sued by his wife for divorce. Although they had three children, the man had never learned to work and take responsibility. It sort of ran in the family.

The judge finally told him, "I'm giving your wife a divorce and $300 a month child support." The man, looking rather pleased, replied, "I appreciate that your honor, and I'll throw in a dollar or two myself." He just didn't get it!

This reminds me of a man who stopped to help a stranded woman change a tire on her car. After the spare tire was bolted on snugly to the car and the man began letting the car down, the woman cautioned him, "Let it down easy. My husband is asleep in the back seat, and I don't want to wake him up."

Though I'm being rather hard on men, sometimes it's women who refuse to work and take responsibility. As I mentioned previously, I've seen homes crumble because of such women as well as such men.

No wonder the Bible admonishes us to work! The apostle Paul gives this rule, "If a man will not work, he shall not eat (II Thessalonians 3:10 NIV). Some were idle. Some were busybodies, not busy. At the same time, Paul worked night and day, laboring and toiling so as not to be a burden to anyone (II Thessalonians 3:6-13). What a good example!

To the young evangelist, the same apostle wrote, "If anyone does not provide for his relatives, and especially for his immediate family, he has denied the faith and is worse than an unbeliever" (I Timothy 5:8). Work! Take responsibility!

Our Korean students have taught me a valuable lesson in this regard. I have observed some of them not only support themselves and sometimes their husbands in school, but also at the same time send money back home to support their aging parents! I conversed with a Japanese woman last week who is doing the same noble deed. I'm worried about how they can get by on what they are earning, and they are sharing it with their relatives back home! What a lesson!

Men have traditionally assumed the role of breadwinner in American culture. Women have cooked, cleaned house, canned food, managed the household, and done many other necessary chores. Since my grandmothers, my mother, and Louise, were all full-time homemakers, I never ask a husband, "Does your wife work?" If I inquire, I would ask instead, "Does your wife work outside the home?" Full-time homemakers work hard if they do their jobs well! This is especially true if they have children or grandchildren, and if they manage their husbands and their households as well as does Louise. We've always been a team. Louise has worked with me in everything I've done. She has gone with me to visit the sick and others in church work, she has made appointments for me, kept books, mailed bills, ordered and shipped books, paid bills, typed manuscripts, and managed our household. We work together. This is not the only way to do it, but it has worked well for us.

The apostle Paul wrote to Titus, "Likewise, teach the older women to be reverent in the way they live, not to be slanderers or addicted to much wine, but to teach what is good. They can train the younger women to love their husbands and children, to be self-controlled and pure, to be busy at home, to be kind, and to be subject to their husbands, so that no one will malign the word of God" (Titus 2:2-5 NIV). The home was the center of their work.

Solomon spreads the woman's work beyond the home. Such a noble woman is worth more than rubies. She works with wool and flax, brings her food from afar, buys a field and plants a vineyard. She works vigorously. She trades, grasps the spindle with her fingers, helps the needy, clothes her household in scarlet, and makes coverings for her bed. She makes fine linen garments and sells them, supplies the merchants with sashes, gives faithful instruction, and watches over the affairs of her household. She fears the Lord: Her children and husband rise up and call her blessed (Proverbs 31).

One woman at church told me once to never read Proverbs 31 again publicly. It made her tired!

I can see her point. I doubt if anyone can perform that well continually. And there is more to life than work.

Yet, to build a healthy family, parents have to take appropriate responsibility and to teach their children to do likewise. It takes time and patience, but it's a necessary part of a successful building strategy.

To do this, we must begin early. Give them appropriate jobs for their age level. Have them put toys in their storage space, make the bed, set and help clear the table, and do whatever is appropriate. As a parent, pick something your child can do. Show him or her. Then follow up with praise.

I always thought I had to work too hard as I grew up on a small farm in Tennessee. Our day started with feeding the mules, cows, and hogs. We then milked the cows, ate breakfast, geared the mules, got our hoes and mattocks and went to the field. Or we might take an ax, a saw, and a team of mules and go to the woods. I "snaked" wood out of a hollow when I was a small boy. I "grubbed sprouts," chopped out corn, plowed the mules, and gathered corn. I set out tobacco, hoed it, suckered it, cut and sticked it, hauled it to the barn and hung it on poles, stripped it and helped take it to the market. I helped sow hay, cut and haul it to the barn. If you have never pitched dry lespedeza hay back into a barn loft under a hot tin roof, you haven't missed a thing!

Our day usually ended by doing chores at the barn again and carrying in wood. Daddy couldn't understand how we still had enough energy to sometimes run and play after supper. His philosophy of success was somewhat like that of Kemmons Wilson: Work only half a day—and it doesn't make any difference which half, the first 12 hours or the last 12 hours.

I wouldn't expect you to have all of those jobs I did for your children, but you have trash cans to take out, beds to make, and dishes to wash. It might be easier to do such jobs yourself rather than teach your children to do them, but they need to learn how to do things with their hands and to take appropriate responsibility. Remember, you're raising children, not just getting chores done. Show them. Teach them. Praise them.

My workload as a child was heavy, but I and my siblings were able to handle it. Leamon was my usual work partner: sawing with a cross-cut saw, and working in the fields. The point is that we learned responsibility by being given responsibility. You can teach your children likewise. Good luck. It isn't easy, but it's worthwhile! Healthy families learn to work and accept responsibility.

ASKING FOR HELP

Healthy families also ask for and accept help when they need it. It's a sign of strength, not weakness. Most of us would accept help if our house were destroyed, just as my friend Burton Fox did. Everybody would understand.

But what if we were severely depressed? Panicky? What if our marriage were coming apart? What if our children were rebellious? What if they were into drugs or in trouble with the law? What if we couldn't get a job?

We'd be too embarrassed to ask for help, right? Many would. But, what's the difference? Burton couldn't help it, right? Right! But neither can we help it when we are ill mentally, or when we are stuck in dysfunctional family patterns that are beyond our control. The family and community systems are much larger and stronger than we are. Many try for years to get a job but can't! When drugs take over, somebody is out of control and needs help. When someone is suicidal, they need someone to listen and to intervene. And, if we **could** have helped it, we still need help. We are human and humans make mistakes and sometimes need help.

In my experience, some families need little help, others much. Most of us need help from someone, at some time. Sometimes it's informal, sometimes formal.

I have seen families grow through many difficulties as a result of seeking professional help. I've seen drug addictions conquered and persons strengthened. I've seen hundreds of depressed people revert back to normal and panicky people overcome their fears. I've seen dysfunctional families become functional. I've seen divorced marriages torn by coldness, dysfunctional patterns and affairs become more intimate and stable. Both partners were willing to seek help, to change their attitudes and their actions. They learned to focus on the needs of each other, to do things differently.

Cary and Donna are an example. Married for 10 years, they had grown apart. Cary went his way; Donna went her way. Cary was "sex crazy," and Donna soon tired of it. She let herself go, gained a great deal of weight, and had lots of headaches at night. "That's all he wants is sex," she often said. He hardly ever touched her without sexualizing the touch. He pursued; she turned him down. He got his feelings hurt and questioned his manhood until he met a woman at church who was on his wavelength. They talked, they touched, they hugged, they kissed, and finally they had intercourse. Donna got mad at his attention to the other woman of course and got colder!

Finally, after some 30 affairs, they sought help and found it. She admitted that she was "at fault, and just didn't realize that men need sex that much." He apologized many times over for what he had done and took responsibility for his actions. "No matter what she did, I did not have a right to have affairs," he stated.

You can imagine the rest. She altered her eating and exercising habits and lost weight. He saw her as attractive again. He broke off from his latest affair and didn't leave even a small crack in the door. He began to spend more time with his wife, to be affectionate at times other than on certain nights, and to be considerate of her needs. He learned that he wouldn't die if he didn't get sex every time he wanted it; whereas Donna learned to enjoy sex for the first time in her life. He was romantic, patient during foreplay, and was very attentive to her feelings. They talked, took daily walks, and went out at least once a week.

They had been in a destructive pattern. They sought help, accepted suggestions, and changed their actions. Both "came back to the church" and changed as persons and as a couple. Both they and their three children are greatly blessed because they were courageous enough to seek and accept appropriate help.

Healthy families seek help. I have seen it over and over again. You can do likewise.

BUILDING PRINCIPLES

I want to conclude by giving you my list of BUILDING PRINCIPLES:

1. Healthy families build on a solid foundation.
2. Healthy families are committed.
3. Healthy families are emotionally mature.
4. Healthy families develop spiritually.
5. Healthy families build on love and affection.
6. Healthy families build around a healthy family structure.
7. Healthy families are led by effective parents.
8. Healthy families communicate effectively and grow through difficulties.
9. Healthy families are able to grow and change from one stage of development to another.

10. Healthy families are able to cope successfully with anger and manage conflict well.

11. Healthy families somehow develop the ability to cope with crises.

12. Healthy families have a sense of humor.

13. Healthy families build self-esteem.

14. Healthy families make continuing efforts to prevent divorce.

15. Healthy families have realistic expectations.

16. Healthy families spend a significant amount of quality time with each other.

17. Healthy families learn to work and to assume appropriate responsibilities.

18. Healthy families seek help when they need it.

May God bless you as you build a better home. I'm interested in you and in your family. Thanks for the journey through this book with me. I hope the experience has been a blessing to you.

Re-read. Underline. Do exercises. Apply principles. You'll be glad you did. You can build a better home!

BUILDING EXERCISES

1. What expectations did you have of your spouse before you got married?
2. How has that changed?
3. What are you willing to do to meet your spouses' needs?
4. How much quality time do you spend with your family each week?
5. How many hours do you watch TV?
6. What can you do to restore family meals together?
7. Do you accept responsibility for your thoughts, feelings, and actions?
8. Do you do your work well?
9. Do you teach your children to work and accept appropriate responsibility?
10. Do you seek help when you need it?

References

Balswick, Jack O., and Judith K. Balswick. *The Family*. Grand Rapids, Mich.: Baker Book House, 1989.

Beach, Stephen R. H., Evelyn Sanden, and Kay Daniel O'Leary. *Depression in Marriage*. New York: Guilford Press, 1990.

Beavers, W. Robert. *Successful Marriage*. New York: W. W. Norton and Company, 1985.

Beck, Aaron T. *Cognitive Therapy and the Emotional Disorders*. New York: International University Press, 1976.

Beck, Aaron T. et al. *Cognitive Therapy of Depression*. New York: Gilford Press, 1979.

Beck, Aaron T. *Love is Never Enough*. New York: Harper & Row, 1988.

Bowen, Murray. *Family Therapy in Clinical Practice*. New York: Jason Aronson, 1978.

Carlson, David E. *Counseling and Self Esteem*. Waco, Texas: Word Books, 1988.

Carson, Donald. *The Interpreter's Bible*, Vol. 8. Nashville: Abingdon Press, 1951.

Chapman, Gary. *Toward a Growing Marriage*. Chicago: Moody Press, 1979.

Collins, Gary. "What Makes a Healthy Family?" *Christian Counseling Today* I (October 1992): 8-12.

Conway, Jim and Sally. *Traits of a Lasting Marriage*. Downers Grove, Illinois: InterVarsity Press, 1991.

Coopersmith, Stanley. *The Antecedents of Self-Esteem*. San Francisco: W. H. Freeman & Co., 1967.

DeAngelis, Barbara. *How to Make Love All the Time*. New York: Raveson Associates, 1987.

Diagnostic and Statistical Manual of Mental Disorders (DSM-III-R). Washington, D.C.: American Psychiatric Association, 1986.

Dobson, James. *What Wives Wish Their Husbands Knew About Women*. Wheaton, Illinois: Tyndale House, 1975.

Ellis, Albert and Michael Bernard, eds. *Clinical Applications of Rational-Emotive Therapy*. New York: Plenum Press, 1985.

Figley, Charles R. *Helping Traumatized Families*. San Francisco: Jossey-Bass, 1989.

Flatt, Bill. *Building Better Homes*. A video cassette. Jackson, Tennessee: The Way of Life Television Studio, 1992.

Flatt, Bill, Jack Lewis, and Dowell Flatt. *Counseling Homosexuals*. Jonesboro, Arkansas: National Christian Press, 1985.

_____. *Growing Through Grief*. Nashville: Gospel Advocate Company, 1987.

_____, and others. *Personal Counseling*. Searcy, Arkansas: Resource Publications, 1991.

Glasser, William. Reality *Therapy, A New Approach*. New York: Harper & Row, 1965.

Gottman, John, Cliff Notarius, Jonni Gonso, and Howard Markman. *A Couple's Guide to Communication*. Champaign, Illinois: Research Press, 1976.

Gross, Jerry and Becky Gross, eds. *Growing Through Conflict*. Abilene, Texas: Quality Publications, 1984.

Grunlan, Stephen A. *Marriage and the Family*. Grand Rapids, Michigan: Zondervan Publishing House, 1984.

Guernsey, Lucy and Dennis. *Real Life Marriage*. Waco, Texas: Word Books, 1987.

Hailey, Homer. *The Divorced and Remarried Who Would Come to God*. Las Vegas: Nevada Publications, 1990.

Harley, Willard F., Jr. *His Needs, Her Needs*. New York: Fleming Revell Company, 1978.

Harrell, Pat. *Divorce and Remarriage in the Early Church*. Austin, Texas: R. B. Sweet Co., 1967.

Hart, Archibald D. *Counseling the Depressed*. Waco, Texas: Word Books, 1987.

Hazelip, Harold. *Happiness in the Home*. Grand Rapids, Michigan: Baker Book House, 1985.

Heth, William and Gordon J. Wenham. *Jesus and Divorce*. Nashville: Thomas Nelson Publishers, 1984.

Kerr, Michael and Murray Bowen. *Family Evaluation*. New York: Norton, 1988.

Luck, William. *Divorce and Remarriage*. San Francisco: Harper & Row, 1960.

Masters, William and Virginia Johnson. *The Pleasure Bond*. Boston: Little, Brown, and Company, 1970.

Millon, Theodore. *Disorders of Personality: DSM-III, Axis II*. New York: Wiley, 1981.

Minuchin, Salvador. *Families and Family Therapy*. Cambridge, Massachusetts: Harvard University Press, 1974.

Money, Royce. *Building Stronger Families*. Wheaton, Illinois: Victor Books, 1978.

Murray, John. *Divorce*. Philadelphia: Presbyterian and Reformed Publishing House, 1961.

Osburn, Carroll. "The Present Indicative of Matthew 19:9." *Restoration Quarterly* 24 (1981): 193-203.

Payne, Reed, Allen Bergen, Kimberly Bieloina and Paul Jenkins. *Psychologists Interested in Religious NEWSLETTER* XVI (Summer 1991): 3-14.

Piper, John and Wayne Grudem. *Recovering Biblical Manhood and Womanhood*. Wheaton, Illinois: Crossway Books, 1991.

Quick Reference to the Diagnostic Criteria from DSM-III. 3d ed. Washington, D.C.: APA, 1980.

Rosenberg, Morris. *Society and the Adolescent Self-Image*. Princeton, New Jersey: Princeton University Press, 1965.

Ruben, Harvey L. Super Marriage. New York: Bantam Books, 1986.

Snyder, Chuck and Barb. *Incompatibility: Grounds for a Great Marriage*. Sisters, Oregon: Questar Publishers, Inc., 1988.

Stinnett, Nick, Barbara Chesser, and John DeFrain. *Building Family Strengths: Blueprint for Action*. Lincoln: University of Nebraska Press, 1979.

Stinnett, Nick and John DeFrain. *Secrets of Strong Families*. Boston: Little, Brown, 1985.

Wallerstein, Judith S., and Sandra Blakeslee. *Second Chances: Men, Women, and Children a Decade after Divorce*. New York: Ticknow and Fields, 1989.

Warren, Thomas B., ed. *Your Marriage Can Be Great*. Jonesboro, Arkansas: National Christian Press, 1978.

Weiner-Davis, Michele. *Divorce Busting*. New York: Summit Books, 1992.

Appendices

Appendix A

Some Guidelines to Effective Communication

SOME DON'TS

1. Do not mind read, attribute mistakes or assume the intentions of others.

2. Do not jump to conclusions. Check it out to see if your thinking is correct.

3. Do not act on false assumptions.

4. Do not develop a negative mind set or put on negative glasses.

5. Do not develop excessive, rigid expectations, or unreasonable rules.

6. Do not overgeneralize, "awfulize," or "eternalize."

7. Do not engage in all or nothing thinking: that everyone is either good or bad, honest or dishonest, straight forward or manipulative; there are no gray areas in such a mindset.

8. Do not develop negative self-fulfilling prophecies. You tend to confirm your mental constructs.

9. Do not expect others to read your mind.

10. Do not interrupt when others are talking.

11. Do not ask many "why" questions. They tend to bog-down conversation. Do not probe too much.

12. Do not use "should" and "ought" very often in talking to other adults.

13. Do not always be totally frank. Use diplomacy.

14. Do not be defensive, counteract negatively, or become "historical."

15. Do not engage in fault-finding or concentrate on blaming.

16. Do not label people by such words as sloppy, a liar, or a manipulator. No one label is completely adequate to describe most people.

17. Do not put others down.

18. Do not be biased against yourself (low self-esteem) or others (wear negative glasses).

19. Do not be so self-centered, so preoccupied with your own issues that you have no energy left for the concerns of others.

20. Do not change wishes into rules: "You must satisfy me at all times."

21. Do not negate the positive. Accept it as real and build on it!

22. Do not hog the conversation.

23. Do not nag.

SOME DO's

1. Be the kind of person you ought to be. A salt spring cannot produce fresh water (James 3:9-12).

2. Practice the golden rule: Do unto others as you would have them do unto you (Matthew 7:12).

3. Realize that misunderstandings can cause big problems. They can come from personality differences or one's present mind-set.

4. Learn that behavior or words do not always mean the same thing to different people.

5. Be specific: "When you do X, I feel Y. Instead, I'd like you to do Z."

6. Send I messages, not you messages. "I feel that you are keeping me at a distance" is better than "You never let me get close to you."

7. Form tentative conclusions. Clarify. Be humble.

8. Empathize. Try to understand the impact you are having on others. See it through their glasses.

9. Focus on changing yourself instead of changing others.

10. Develop positive self-fulfilling prophecies. Expect the best.

11. Build relationships. Your relationships determine how you "frame" others.

12. Express your desires clearly. Be direct. It is sometimes hard to read hints.

13. Try to understand what others are saying. Actively listen and give "listening signals." Tune in to others. Be quick to listen, slow to speak, slow to wrath (James 1:19).

14. Understand that there are important differences between men and women in conversational styles and their meanings. Talking can be viewed as evidence of trouble or as a means toward a solution, for example.

15. Talk. Initiate conversation. Answer. Say something in addition to your answer. Share thoughts and feelings.

16. Ask questions skillfully.

17. Be tactful. Let your conversation be always seasoned with grace (Colossians 4:6).

18. Compromise. It's better to lose a battle than to lose a war.

19. Solve problems. Go to the person with whom you have conflict and work it out (Matthew 18:15; 5:23-24).

20. Be brief. Long speeches hinder give and take.

21. Avoid absolutes when dealing with opinions.

22. State what you would like rather than complain.

23. Find points of agreement.

24. Apologize. It sometimes takes a mature person to do so.

25. Overlook the rough spots in others. Give them the benefit of the doubt.

26. Forgive until "seventy times seven."

27. Remember that if you are looking for a quarrel, you'll find it.

28. Show restraint in what you say. Guard your tongue (Proverbs 21:23).

29. Learn to give in. It's often a sign of strength.

30. Edit what you say. If you guard your mouth, you'll keep yourself out of trouble (Proverbs 21:23).

31. Examine your attitude.

32. Respond all over, not just with words. Stoic faces are hard to read.

33. Control your anger (Ephesians 4:26).

34. Be kind (Ephesians 4:32).

35. Draw others out. Ask questions. Listen. Respond.

36. Listen to advice and try to avoid strife (Proverbs 19:20; 20:3).

Appendix B
Commitment - Marriage Vows
Vows Taken "Before God and Witnesses"

"I _____ take you _____ to be my wedded _____. To have and to hold from this day forward, for better for worse, for richer for poorer, in sickness and in health, to love and to cherish 'til death us do part."

Genesis 2:24: "For this reason a man will leave his father and mother and be united to his wife, and they will become one flesh" (NIV).

Numbers 30:2: "When a man makes a vow to the Lord or takes an oath to obligate himself by a pledge, he must not break his word but must do everything he said."

Psalm 15:1-4: "Lord, who may dwell in your sanctuary? Who may live on your holy hill? He whose walk is blameless and who does what is righteous, who speaks the truth from his heart and has no slander on his tongue, who does his neighbor no wrong and casts no slur on his fellowman, who despises a vile man but honors those who fear the Lord, who keeps his oath even when it hurts."

Proverbs 20:25: "It is a trap for a man to dedicate something rashly and only later to consider his vows."

Ecclesiastes 5:4-7: "When you make a vow to God, do not delay in fulfilling it. He has no pleasure in fools; fulfill you vow. It is better not to vow than to make a vow and not fulfill it. Do not let your mouth lead you into sin. And do not protest to the temple messenger, 'My vow was a mistake.' Why should God be angry at what you say and destroy the work of your hands? Much dreaming and many words are meaningless. Therefore stand in awe of God."

Jonah 2:9: "But I, with a song of thanksgiving, will sacrifice to you. What I have vowed I will make good. Salvation comes from the Lord."

Malachi 2:16: "'I hate divorce,' says the Lord God of Israel, 'and I hate a man's covering himself with violence as well as with his garment,' says the Lord Almighty."

Matthew 19:9: "I tell you that anyone who divorces his wife, except for marital unfaithfulness, and marries another woman commits adultery."

Appendix C

SITUATION	NEGATIVE SELF-TALK	TALK BACK

Appendix D

A Problem-Solving Worksheet

1. What is your problem as you see it?

2. How does your spouse see it?

3. Theoretically, what are some possible solutions?

4. Discuss this with your spouse.

5. What is a solution that is fair and that both of you can live with?

Appendix E

12 Ways Husbands Can Say, "I Love You"

1. Treat her as an equal. She is, you know.
2. Respect her as a person in her own right.
3. Take her out to eat on a regular basis. She may also enjoy movies or other appropriate entertainment.
4. Remember her birthday and other special occasions.
5. Be sensitive to her feelings. Talk to her.
6. Express appreciation for what she does and for what she is.
7. Don't make big issues out of small problems. "Love covers a multitude of sins."
8. Be a pleasant partner.
9. Don't say negative things about her in front of others.
10. Give her some nice surprises such as special cards or flowers at times other than special occasions.
11. Respect her family as well as your own.
12. Be as generous with her as you are with yourself. If she is a full-time homemaker, the money you bring home is "ours" rather than "yours."

Appendix F

12 Ways Wives Can Say "I Love You"

1. Let him know how much you appreciate his hard work.
2. Support his leadership in the family.
3. Do things that will bring him pleasure.
4. Do not put him down in front of others.
5. Give him some time alone when he is tired.
6. Help make a good home for him.
7. Show interest in things that are important to him.
8. Be easy to live with.
9. Help him to be successful in his work.
10. Help him live a good Christian life and go to heaven.
11. Do little things for him.
12. Agree and support his ideas as much as possible.

Appendix G

Many Ways of Loving You
by Bill Flatt

There are many ways
    to cruise the town.
There are many ways
    to roam around.
There are many ways
    to sing the blues.
There are many ways
    of loving you.

I can take you out,
    We can stay at home.
I can settle down,
    Never more to roam.
I can give you space,
    I can be there too.
There are many ways
    of loving you.

We can swing and talk,
    We can take a ride.
We can dine at home,
    by candlelight.
We can hug and kiss
    'til we get through.
There are many ways
    of loving you.

So come up close
    and stay around.
I'm ready now,
    to settle down.
I need you so,
    Why don't you see?
I'm steady now,
    Depend on me.

Appendix H

A Budget Worksheet

1. Take home pay   _____

2. Contributions, 10 percent   _____

3. Housing, 25 percent   _____

4. Cars, 14 percent   _____

5. Food, 14 percent   _____

6. Insurance, 5 percent   _____

7. Entertainment, 4 percent   _____

8. Clothing, 6 percent   _____

9. Medical, 9 percent   _____

10. Indebtedness, 4 percent   _____

11. Savings, 5 percent   _____

12. Miscellaneous, 4 percent   _____

Some guiding principles: Don't buy it if you don't need it or can't afford it. Learn to do without if possible. **Things** don't make life **worthwhile**. Make a budget, and stick with it. Wait 30 days before you buy major purchases. Be unselfish. Put off unnecessary spending if money is tight. Shop for better prices. Wait for legitimate sales. Late July and January are usually good months for such sales.

Appendix I

Promise Yourself

To be so strong that nothing can disturb your peace of mind.

To talk health, happiness and prosperity to every person you meet.

To make all of your friends feel that there is something in them.

To look at the sunny side of everything and make your optimism come true.

To think only of the best, to work only for the best, and expect only the best.

To be just as enthusiastic about the success of others as you are about your own.

To forget the mistakes of the past and press on to greater achievements of the future.

To wear a cheerful countenance at all times and give every living creature you meet a smile.

To give so much time to the improvement of yourself that you have no time to criticize others.

To be too large for worry, too noble for anger, too strong for fear, and too happy to permit the presence of trouble.

— Author unknown.

Appendix J

A Challenging Poem

When you get what you want
    in your struggle for self
And the world makes you a
    king for a day,
Just go to the mirror and look at yourself
    and see what THAT man has to say.
For it isn't your father or mother or wife
    Who judgment upon you must pass,
The fellow whose verdict counts most in your life
    Is the one staring back from the glass.
Some people may think you a straight-shootin' chum
    And call you a wonderful guy,
But the man in the glass says you're only a bum
    If you can't look him straight in the eye.
He's the fellow to please, never mind all the rest,
    for he's with you clear up to the end,
And you've passed your most dangerous, difficult test,
    If the man in the glass is your friend.
You may fool the whole world down the pathway of years
    And get pats on the back as you pass,
But your final reward will be heartaches and tears
    If you've cheated THE MAN IN THE GLASS.
        — Author unknown.

Appendix K

A Commendable Motto

Take time to work.
It is the price of success.
Take time to play.
It is the secret of perpetual youth.
Take time to think.
It is the source of power.
Take time to read.
It is the fountain of wisdom.
Take time to pray.
It is conversation with God.
Take time to laugh.
It is the music of the soul.
Take time to listen.
It is the pathway to understanding.
Take time to dream.
It is hitching your wagon to a star.
Take time to worship.
It is the highway of reverence.
Take time to love and to be loved.
It is the gift of God.

— Author unknown.

65403

Building a healthy family
248.4 F586b   65403

Flatt, Bill W.
Overton Memorial Library